The Cokesbury
Party Book

The Cokesbury
Party Book

Revised Edition

ARTHUR M. DEPEW

ABINGDON PRESS
New York • Nashville

THE COKESBURY PARTY BOOK

Library of Congress Catalog Card Number: 59-10358

SET UP, PRINTED, AND BOUND BY THE
PARTHENON PRESS, AT NASHVILLE,
TENNESSEE, UNITED STATES OF AMERICA

Dedicated to My Son

Arthur M. Dayton, Jr.

who although his years had lived such a life
that his parents even had many reasons
for pride and happiness
because of him

Preface

THIS BOOK IS INTENDED TO MEET A NEED IN THE SOCIAL LIFE AND recreation field for an entertainment guidebook that actually plans the party. Most books of this type are merely a collection of games and stunts. One must search through them to find the games desired for any particular occasion. They require much work in the selection of material, or one must be content with a miscellaneous collection of games and stunts that are in no way related.

The parties in this book are planned around a central theme or idea, and this idea is carried throughout the evening. Most of the parties are so full that many of the games and stunts will have to be eliminated. This is done so that the social leader will have a large number of events from which to choose and may pass over those he does not wish to use. The writer is willing to guarantee that if all plans are carried out as suggested, any party in this book will furnish entertainment for two full hours. The games and stunts are arranged so that an active game is followed by a mental or quiet game. Guests at a party soon become bored with too many consecutive mental or active games. By alternating them this can be overcome.

The parties are planned so that they will fit into the different seasons and months of the year. Beginning at the first of the book, the first four parties are thought to be suitable for January, the next four for February, and so on throughout the book. Outdoor parties are planned for the summer months.

Many of the parties are planned for large groups and are suitable for young people's conferences, united Christian youth groups, summer retreats, and any other gathering of from one to two hundred persons. Parties recommended for such occasions are: Calendar Party, Mother Goose Party, World-Tour Party, Newspaper Party, Bible Party, College Field Day, Stunt Night, Gypsy Party, and Kid Party. All of these have been used successfully.

One will find many ideas for Pay parties and games. Among these are: Selling the Calendar, the Circulating Pig, King Neptune's Carnival, Measuring Party, Cootie Party, Fifty Party, Heart Dice, Box Supper and Cakewalk, Street Carnival, and Vanishing Party.

Many of the games used in this book are quite well-known. Very likely you will find most of your favorites, with variations or in a different setting. The many new games and entertainment ideas have come from the actual experience of the author in teaching young people's conferences and other work among church and civic groups. All new material has been thoroughly tested.

The fact that this is a book of *planned* parties does not prevent its being used like any other book of games and stunts. The Alphabetical Index and Classified Index take care of this. If one desires to find active, writing, or quiet games, it is only necessary to look in the Index. This enables one to find any particular game or stunt readily and renders the book usable for all purposes.

The ideas in this volume are passed on to the reader with the hope that the parties described will be the means of developing the social nature of many, and that the social gatherings in which they are used will result in many lasting friendships.

ARTHUR M. DEPEW.

The years since 1932, when *The Cokesbury Party Book* was originally published, have seen many changes—in the ways we entertain and in the language we use every day, to name only two. The time has come for a new edition of this collection of parties, to bring it up to date and make it even more useful to a new generation. A completely new party has been added, bringing the total to fifty-two—a party for every week in the year.

A.M.D.

Introduction

THIS VOLUME IS NOT A TREATISE ON THE PSYCHOLOGY OF PLAY AND recreation, nor does it contain a detailed discussion of the principles of program building. In this field there are books without number. It does contain fifty-two full evening parties, meeting in a splendid way the demand for parties with which to entertain smaller and larger groups.

The Cokesbury Party Book is distinctive in that it contains four or five complete and carefully planned parties for each month in the year. The instructions for the games and events in each party are given in full so that there can be no failures, providing the leader and social life committee thoroughly acquaint themselves with the plan of each party and prepare, in advance, any and all materials suggested for games and events.

Jane Addams says that "vice is the love of pleasure gone wrong." That it is "the illicit expression of what might otherwise be a normal, recreational amusement." If this statement is true, and I believe all leaders of youth of wide experience will concur in it, one of the most important contributions which any leader of youth can make is in the field of helping young people to plan their social life programs in such a rich and varied way as to produce character development as one, at least, of the real values of parties and good times of all sorts and kinds.

The author of this book, Mr. Arthur M. Depew, has been a successful pastor, Y.M.C.A. Recreational Director, U.S.O. Director, and missionary. He has been very successful in planning social programs with and for his own church people. He has also had wide experience in planning good times for civic organizations. For several years he taught social life and recreation in summer young people's conferences in a number of states, including Florida, Georgia, South

Carolina, Alabama, Louisiana, and Missouri. In this capacity he
has had unique opportunity to enlist the active co-operation of a
host of young people, and to evaluate their reactions to the program
materials contained in this volume, as well as to appraise their skill
in the leadership of these social life activities.

As one who has on two or three different occasions served as
dean of the Florida Young People's Conference, I have had opportunity to witness the use of the social life programs which Mr.
Depew has included in this volume, as well as to observe and
evaluate the type of leadership he gives to youth in the field of social
life and recreation.

It is not the intention of the author of this book to cripple the
initiative of young people, but rather to guide them in planning
worth-while and stimulating parties for the entertainment of groups
of young people. This book will serve as a continual source of information and guidance to leaders of young people and adults, if
they will follow the suggestions of the author, in enlisting the co-
operation of others in building social life programs, and in using
young people in the largest possible way in the direction and leadership of the various games and activities suggested for each party.

It gives me real pleasure to add my word of commendation to the
splendid contribution which Mr. Arthur M. Depew has made in
the field of social life entertainment and amusement for adult and
young people's groups.

CYNTHIA PEARL MAUS,
*Pioneer Young People's Superintendent, United Christian Missionary Society,
Disciples of Christ* and author of *Christ and the Fine Arts, The Old Testament
and the Fine Arts,* and *The World's Great Madonnas.*

Contents

11

Contents

chapter 1

Watch Party

WATCH NIGHT, OR NEW YEAR'S EVE, IS THE ONE NIGHT OF THE YEAR when almost everyone expects to go to a party that will last until twelve o'clock and enable them with their friends to watch the old year go out and the new year come in. It would be well to have the guests come late, for it is hardly possible to keep everyone enjoying themselves together for more than two and a half hours. Invite the guests to come at nine or nine-thirty. The following is a suggested invitation.

1. *Invitation*

> The watch—it is a funny thing,
> To never wash its face;
> It doesn't even scrub its hands.
> What a shame and a disgrace!
> And more about the watch you'll know
> When our Watch Party's ended.
> You'll see the years come and go,
> And may meet your intended.

2. *Decorations.*—Green, red, and white will make a good color scheme for this time of the year. Crepe paper could be used with bells of red and green. Also use holly and cedar and other evergreens. Cotton makes a good imitation of snow. Artificial snow and icicles may be used.

3. *Dividing into Groups.*—The company should be first divided into groups. If the number is large enough, there should be four divisions, which should be named Spring, Summer, Autumn, and Winter. If it is thought better to have only two groups, name them

15

Summer and Winter. These groups may be selected by having those born in their seasons form the groups. This may divide them unevenly however. The best way to divide them equally is to number 1, 2, 3, and 4.

4. *Reminiscences.*—Number ones, or those in the Spring group, are asked to tell all the other members of that group, one at a time, how he spent the Fourth of July, or what he did on Thanksgiving, what he wore on Easter Sunday, or how he spent the last Watch Night. Let each group do this simultaneously. Another interesting topic for conversation would be a trip that had been taken during the year.

5. *Spelling.*—Letters should be printed with crayons on cardboards six inches square. These can be used for numerous other games in this book. If you have four groups, you will need four sets of the following letters: J, A, N, U, A, R, Y, F, E, B, M, C, H, P, I, L, R, G, U, S, T, E, E, O, O, V, D. All these letters with the duplications are needed to spell all the months of the year.

The groups are assembled on the longest side of the room and each given a letter. If there are too many letters, give some two or three. The leader pronounces the names of the months, of course out of their regular order, and when the word is pronounced, those holding the letters in it run to the opposite side of the room and arrange themselves in the proper formation to spell the name of the month pronounced. The group spelling the word the quickest may be given a score of ten points, and the group making the largest score may be given a prize.

6. *Resolutions: For Yourself.*—Each one is asked to write a New Year's resolution for himself, but of course not to sign his name to it. These are collected and read, and the group tries to guess the author of the resolution. If the crowd fails to guess, the writer is expected to confess. It would be well to suggest that these resolutions be humorous.

7. *Resolutions: For Someone Else.*—Each one is asked to write a resolution for someone else. Perhaps it would be better to have those in the Spring group write resolutions for persons in the

Summer group and *vice versa*. Also those in the Autumn group write resolutions for those in the Winter group and *vice versa*. These are then read, and all try to guess for whom the resolution was written. If no one guesses, the writer is asked to confess.

8. *Watch Conversation.*—Give each guest a card on which has been drawn the dial of a watch and on which has been placed the numbers on a watch face. Hang up a large cardboard on which has been drawn the face of a watch with moveable hands. Below the dial of the watch has been written topics for conversation numbered from 1 to 12.

Before the conversation starts each man secures a partner for each of the twelve hours, writing her name on the number of the hour. She also writes his name on her card for the same hour.

When the leader's whistle blows and the conversation begins, each man finds the girl with whom he is supposed to converse during the Hour No. 1. In about one minute, or not more than two minutes, the leader's whistle blows, and all find partners for the second hour. The conversation during these hours is on the topics suggested for the hour on the large card. As the game proceeds the time for conversation should be shortened, not allowing more than a minute or half a minute for some of the topics. The entire game should not last for more than ten minutes.

9. *Watch Trick.*—The leader may do the following trick with a watch or with the clock on the mantle. He asks someone in the group to decide on a number on the face of the clock. This may be done by groups, each group being asked to select a number, any number between one and twelve. The leader then tells the group to start counting with the next number after the one selected and count to twenty and stop. They are to count one number every time the leader touches the face of the watch or clock with a pencil or pointer. When they reach the number twenty, the leader's pointer will be on the number selected by the group. It is important that the group understands that they are to start counting with the next number following the one selected. For example if the number selected is seven, the group must count (silently of course) 8, 9, 10,

17

11, 12, 13, 14, 15, 16, 17, 18, 19, 20. When they reach 20, they tell the leader to stop, and the pointer will be on 7, the number which was chosen, on the face of the clock or watch.

How is that done? The leader starts counting, too, and may move the pencil or pointer to any part of the watch or clock dial he chooses until he counts seven. Beginning with eight, however, the leader must start with 12 and follow the figures of the clock in the reverse order, placing his pointer on 12, 11, 10, 9, 8, and so on, until he is told to stop. Try this to convince yourself it works, and practice some before the party.

10. *Watch Contest.*—Slips of paper with the following writing game on them must be prepared in advance. It is little work to prepare these with a typewriter and carbon paper. At least three copies can be made with one typing.

SOME THINGS WE FIND ON A WATCH

(1) Breadwinners. Hands.
(2) Seen at a circus. Ring.
(3) Something you should not take in vain. Maker's name.
(4) Something used before. Second hand.
(5) Between heaven and earth. Space.
(6) What we give at the fifteenth wedding anniversary. Crystal.
(7) Caesar, Mark Anthony, and Brutus. Roman characters.
(8) What we extend to our friends. Our (hour) hand.
(9) Something women love to wear. Jewels.
(10) What a policeman should do. Watch.
(11) Places where water bubbles up. Springs.
(12) Something read by the secretary. Minutes.
(13) Opposite of front. Back.
(14) Supports a flower. Stem.
(15) Something of which every pretty woman is proud. Face.
(16) Something a lawyer tries. Case.
(17) Something to ride on. Wheel.
(18) A book in the Bible. Numbers.

11. *Current Events.*—Each person is given a paper and pencil and asked to write the important things that have happened dur-

ing the year. The one writing the largest number will receive a prize. It will be of interest to read some of the lists other than the prize-winning one.

12. *Gossip.*—The leader announces: "We are going to play Gossip. When the whistle blows we are going to ask you to start talking on the subject we give you. You are to talk on that subject to anyone you choose. There will be special recognition for the best talker." The leader then announces the subject on which they are to talk. This should be the outstanding event of the year, for example, "The drought in the Middle West," the latest moon rocket, or some other important event of the year. When the whistle blows, the judges should pick the best talkers and the most reticent. They should be selected by couples. The best talkers are asked to discuss the question, "Which got here first, the hen or the egg?" or "Should Uncle Sam provide chairs for the standing army?" The reticent couple may be asked to imitate a recently married couple having their first breakfast.

13. *Make-Up Contest.*—A couple is selected from each group. The man is given a box containing a red cord, rouge, lipstick, eyebrow pencil, and powder. The leader tells the man that he is to take the cord and tie the girl's hands behind her, and then he is to take the make-up material and make her up as he imagines the girls of 1975 will make up. A prize should be given for the best in the estimation of the judges.

14. *Jumping the Candles.*—Provide twelve candles, light them, and place them in a row. Each person is required to jump the candles, one at a time. The candle that is first extinguished indicates the month in which that person will get married. If no candle is extinguished, it indicates that he will not get married during the year.

15. *Donating White Elephant.*—The leader will call attention to the fact that the New Year is approaching and ask each guest to write the name of some object that he will not need in the coming year which he wishes to give away. These are read, and the guests try to guess the writer. Some of these might be: "A tendency to lose

19

my temper," "An inclination to fall in love with every pretty girl I meet," "A disposition to worry," and so forth.

16. *Watching the New Year Come In.*—As the New Year approaches, different groups will want to do different things. Church groups will want to have a worship service. Others will want to make a noise and shoot off fireworks. If the Watch Night chances to be on a leap year, the girls are privileged to propose to their lovers at the hour of midnight.

17. *Properties*

(1) Four sets of letters on cardboards as required for game number 5.
(2) Pencils for all in the groups.
(3) Four slips of paper for each person.
(4) Cards prepared for Watch Conversation, number 8.
(5) Watch or clock in the room.
(6) Papers prepared for Watch Contest, number 10.
(7) Make-up for number 13.
(8) Twelve candles.

18. *Refreshments.*—Hot oyster stew and saltines would make splendid refreshments. Another suggestion would be hot chocolate with whipped cream and sandwiches.

chapter 2

Calendar Party

(*COSTUME*)

THIS PARTY IS PLANNED FOR A LARGE GROUP AND IS VERY SUITABLE for Young People's Conferences. It is suitable for any other large group of from one hundred to two hundred persons, but it is nevertheless just as suitable for smaller groups.

ONE

1. *Invitation and Costumes*

> Young people, young people, listen here,
> There are just twelve months in a year,
> And on this coming Friday night
> We'll find the best in each all right.
> At our Calendar Party be sure to appear,
> It'll be an evening remembered all the year.
> Place ....

Dress to represent the month in which you were born.

The invitation should suggest the following costumes:

January—Men, Father Time; ladies, Snow Girl.
February—Men, Abraham Lincoln; ladies, Martha Washington.
March—Men, Irish boys with clay pipe and shamrock; ladies, Irish ladies.
April—Men, fools with caps and bells; ladies, Easter angels.
May—Men, baseball suits; ladies, May queen.
June—Men, cap and gown (graduation) ; ladies, brides.
July—Men, Uncle Sam; ladies, Liberty.
August—Men, summer clothes (white) and tennis racquets; ladies, summer clothes with tennis racquets.
September—Men, overalls; ladies, schoolgirls with books.
October—Men, dressed as ghosts; ladies, dressed as witches.

November—Men, football players; ladies, Puritan girls.
December—Men, Kings of the Orient; ladies, Mary.

2. *Decorations.*—Use a green and white color scheme. This can be done with crepe paper and evergreen plants. Cotton snow and artificial snow and icicles can also be used.

3. *Games Representing Each Month.*—Before starting these games, the guests should be divided into three groups. Have all those born in the first four months of the year form one group, those in the second four months the second group, and those in the last four months in the third group. If there is a great deal of difference in the numbers in these groups, changes should be made to make them number approximately the same.

January. The leader will have cotton snowballs, which will be given to each group. A barrel hoop has been arranged to represent a holly wreath, and a bell has been suspended in it. Every time a player throws the cotton snowball through the holly wreath without ringing the bell, it will count five points for his group.

February. Valentine Heart Hunt. A large number of red and white hearts have been hidden all over the room. At a signal from the leader, all start hunting for the hearts, the girls for white hearts, and the boys for red hearts. Every heart found counts one point for the group finding it.

March. For March have a grand march.

Figure A. Grand march formation. In the grand march it is assumed that the group is composed of men and women. Two separate lines face the director in march formation, men in one line, women in the other at opposite sides of the room. Tune, "Turkey in the Straw." At a signal, both groups move forward and form circles, ladies on the outside, men on the inside. Repeat. Meet at opposite end of the room, the ladies taking outside and the men the inside. Come up the center in pairs, hand in hand. Form circle in pairs.

Figure B. Down center in fours. This figure is a continuation of the preceding formation. Come down the center in pairs; separate, one to the right and one to the left. They should continue marching until they meet again, then come up the center in fours. Repeat.

Figure C. Down center in eights. Continue the preceding formation, two couples go left, the next two couples go right. These
couples meet at the opposite ends of the room and come down in
eights.

Figure D. Get them back to couples. Have two couples go to the
left and two couples to the right. When they meet at the opposite
end of the room, they sandwich in, two couples behind two couples,
and come down in fours. One couple is then sent to the left and one
couple to the right, and on the opposite end of the room they
sandwich in and come down in pairs.

Figure E. London Bridge. Continuing the preceding formation,
all couples are sent to the left, and when they reach opposite end of
the room the first couple forms an arch, the second couple passes
through and forms an arch, and so on until all the couples have
passed through.

Figure F. Forward, march! March toward each other and return
to places, four steps forward and four steps back to line. (Repeat.)

Figure G. Crossing through. Ladies and gentlemen march toward
each other and pass through, face front, and return to former position.

Figure H. Single grand right and left. Come up center in twos,
separate right and left, ladies to the left and gentlemen to the right.
When the two lines meet at the opposite end of the room, form the
grand right and left. The leaders of each line grasp each other by
the right hand, the second person by the left, the third by the right,
and continue with right and left in this manner, interlacing throughout the entire line.

Figure I. Double grand right and left. Up the center in twos, first
two to the right, second two to the left. Meet at the far end of the
room and grand right and left in doubles.

Figure J. Countermarch. Come up the center in twos; separate
in single files, the leader turning sharply to the right and counter-
marching up and down the room three times so that on the third
time each line will be on the outer edge of the room. At the far
corner of the room the leaders angle their lines so that they inter-

sect at the center. Leaders continue to opposite corners of the room, turn sharply, and each continue to corner of the room opposite to that from which he started.

Figure K. Spiral. Come down the center of the room in single file, ladies stepping before gentlemen, the entire column forming a circle on the outer edge of the room, and the leader gradually narrowing the circle until a large spiral is formed. At the signal, all face about, the end man thus becoming the leader and unwinding the spiral.

April. The leader will announce that somewhere hidden in the room is a five-pound bag of peanuts, and that a handsome prize will be given to the one who finds it. After they have searched for a few moments, the leader then blows the whistle and says, "April Fool."

Play Whistle. Have a small whistle attached to a string about eighteen inches long. On the end of the string a hook has been made out of a pin. A player is blindfolded, and the whistle is hooked to his clothing on his back. He is told that if he tags the person with the whistle, that person so tagged has to take his place. It would be well to have the party separated and bring in the players one at a time from an adjoining room. When the player has discovered the ruse, or has failed for some minutes to discover it, another is brought in, and the one who has been "It" takes his place in the circle to laugh at the others.

May. Play the game Looby Loo. All join hands, forming a circle. They sing "Looby Loo" and go through with the actions of the song. The song and music follows:

24

Calendar Party

Introduction and Refrain

Here we go looby loo,
Here we go looby light,
Here we go looby loo,
All on a Saturday night.

Verses

1. Put your right hand in,
   Put your right out,
   Give your right hand a shake, shake, shake,
   And turn yourself about.
2. Put your left hand in, *etc.*
3. Put your right foot in, *etc.*
4. Put your left foot in, *etc.*
5. Put your head 'way in, *etc.*
6. Put your whole self in, *etc.*

As the group marches and sings, each player acts out the words of the verse, putting his right hand in the circle, then turning and putting it out of the circle, then shaking it, and then turning about. As the chorus, which in this case will be the first verse, is sung, all march around.

Others actions are as follows: I put my left hand in; I put my right hand in; I put my left elbow in; I put my right elbow in; I put my left foot in; I put my right foot in; I put my little head in; I put my whole self in (jump in and out of the line of the circle).

This is the best singing game we know.

June. Have a Rose Relay. Each of the three groups forms a circle by joining hands. The leader of each group is given a rose. He must hold the rose in his hand and weave in and out through the circle of players until he has made the entire circle. He then gives the rose to the one who was on his right at the start, and this one must weave in and out around the circle until he reaches his original position. This continues until each one in each of the circles has made the circuit. The object is to see which group can complete the race first.

July. Have a blindfold test. Select one person from each group.

Blindfold these who have been selected, and have them identify different articles by the sense of smell. Use cloves, potato, ammonia, limburger cheese, castor oil, and so forth.

August. Apple relay. Select four from each group, either men or women. Give the first one in each group a paring knife and an apple. The first one to peel the apple, the second must quarter it, the third cut out the core, and the fourth eat the apple. Make a rule that number four cannot start eating until number three has finished cutting the core from all four quarters.

September. Spelling lesson. Each group has been supplied with an alphabet on cards six inches square. A captain is selected by each group. The leader appoints a scorer for each group. The object is to see which group can think of and spell by arranging their players in the proper formation the largest number of words in a given time, say five or ten minutes. At the end of the allotted time the whistle blows, and the scorer reports the number spelled by his group. Any word may be allowed, or there may be a rule that they must be words of two syllables.

October. Each group may select a representative to tell a Halloween story. Give a prize for the best.

Meeting the Queen of Halloween. Have the Queen of Halloween dressed up as a ghost. On her right hand the Queen has a glove that has an egg concealed inside. When she shakes hands with a guest, the guest gets egg on his hand and will draw back in surprise.

Shake Hands with the Mummy. A glove has been filled with ice cold sawdust or sand. Persons are blindfolded and asked to shake hands with the mummy. This hand is operated by the leader.

(Any of the above suggestions may be used.)

November. Football Game. Have Indian clubs or pop bottles on the bottom or base of which the plays have been pasted. Have football field with ten-yard lines marked out on floor with chalk. Eleven players are selected from each group. A smaller number may be selected if the groups are small. Use a basketball or indoor baseball to roll at the clubs or bottles to knock them over. One team comes up, each member rolls, and the score is kept. Then another team tries. As many rounds are played as desired, the final score announced at the end.

On the base of the clubs or bottles should be pasted the following: (1) Forward pass, 10 yards; (2) penalty for holding, 15 yards; (3) end run, 30 yards; (4) penalty for off side, 5 yards; (5) line plunge, 15 yards; (6) penalty for slugging, 15 yards; (7) safety, score 2; (8) touchdown, score 6; (9) field goal, score 3.

December. Decorate Christmas Tree. Have three small Christmas trees to be decorated. These might be stuck into pots of dirt. Provide each group with materials with which to decorate them. Select one person or a couple from each group. They are allowed five minutes to decorate the tree. The person or couple doing the best job in the estimation of the judges wins.

4. *Selling the Calendar.* If it is desirable to turn this party into a money-making plan, it may be done in the following manner:

A Sunday-school class or young people's society might try the plan of selling the calendar. At this calendar party would be a good time to start such a plan, but of course it would be better to let it run over several months. Perhaps a group of young people may use it to raise money to send some of its members to Summer Conference.

Have someone who draws and prints well to reproduce the calendar on a large piece of Beaverboard, four by six feet. The entire calendar for the year should be drawn on this board. Have it done in an attractive manner. Leave space under the year for the printing of one or two names in large letters. Those who buy the year should be required to pay five dollars for it. It may be sold two or three times. Then under the name of each month leave space to print in large letters the names of the person buying the month, which should sell for two dollars. Then sell each week for one dollar and have the person's name who buys it printed in the week. Then sell the days for twenty-five cents each, and write the names of the purchasers out on a typewriter and paste them in the space drawn off for that day.

This was done by a Sunday-school class in a church and was

posted in a conspicuous place. Members of the church were asked to buy their birthday. In this way throughout the year they sold out the entire calendar. Many times visitors would buy a day when they would drop in. They sold out the calendar for about two hundred dollars in all. The above suggestion of selling the year for five dollars, the months for two dollars, the weeks for one dollar, and the days for twenty-five cents, will bring in when completed one hundred seventy-two dollars and twenty-five cents.

5. *Properties*

(1) Barrel hoop made to represent holly wreath and about six cotton snowballs. Bell in wreath.

(2) Large number of red and white hearts cut from cardboard.

(3) Whistle on string about eighteen inches long, with pin hook on end. Blindfold.

(4) Three roses.

(5) Blindfolds for three persons. Cloves, potatoes, ammonia, limburger cheese, castor oil (or substitutes for these).

(6) Three apples and three paring knives.

(7) Three complete alphabets on cards six inches square.

(8) Egg in glove for Queen of Halloween.

(9) Glove filled with cold sawdust or sand.

(10) Nine Indian clubs or bottles, basketball or indoor baseball, with writing on bottles or clubs.

(11) Three Christmas trees and decorations.

(12) Calendar on Beaverboard for Selling Calendar.

6. *Refreshments.*—Hot chocolate with marshmallows and sandwiches. Hot tea or coffee with cake or sandwiches.

chapter 3

Automobile Party

THE AUTOMOBILE PARTY IS SO ARRANGED THAT IT CAN BE USED FOR either a large or small group. As many as two hundred could be entertained by leaving off writing game and others that require too much time or equipment. Divide guests into four groups— Ford, Dodge, Buick, and Chevrolet.

1. *Invitation and Decorations*—The following is a suggested invitation:

> On next Thursday night come to our blow-out;
> Let's all be there and make it a knock-out.
> It's an Auto Party—and won't we joy ride!
> So bring your husband, sweetheart, or bride.
> We believe this is all U auto know;
> If we told you more, you couldn't wait to go.
> Time and Place ....

Signs should be posted in several places. On an easy-chair or a nook on the porch such as "Five-Minute Parking Limit" might be placed. In front of the house a sign saying, "For Unloading Passengers," might be placed. You might have a "No Parking" sign and a "Safety Zone," and for the door of the kitchen or place where the refreshments are to be served, "Filling Station." Auto license numbers might be placed about the room, and favors of toy automobiles may be used.

2. *Auto Advertisements.*—Have cars cut from magazines pinned on the curtains or other places about the room. Give each guest paper and pencil. As the names have been cut from the advertisement, he is to guess the make of the car. Give a prize for the one guessing the largest number.

3. *Auto Assembling.*—Give an envelope to each guest in which has been placed an auto picture cut from a magazine and cut up into a puzzle. He is told to take the pieces and assemble the car. Give a prize for the one doing this in the quickest time.

4. *Auto Fruit Basket.*—The names of makes of cars are given to the guests. "It" is the chauffeur. He calls the names of two makes of cars, and they have to exchange places. While the change is being made the chauffer tries to get one of the places. If he succeeds, the one left standing becomes the chauffeur. When the chauffeur says, "Auto turns over," all must change places, and the one who fails to get a seat becomes the chauffeur.

5. *Auto Relay Race.*—The four groups form parallel lines facing the leader. The first one in each group is given a toy automobile, which should be about four inches long and preferably of wood with wheels that turn easily. A string about three or four feet long is attached to the toy auto. The four front players must race to a goal, or rather four goals which have been marked on the floor about twenty-five to fifty feet in front of each line, and they must pull the toy car with the string. The rule is that if the car turns over the one who is pulling it must stop and replace it on its wheels before he continues the race. It is best for the leader to urge everyone to play fair, for after the game starts it is almost impossible to stop it to enforce the rules. When the first player has completed his run, he gives the string to the next one on the front and takes his place at the back of the line. The object is to see which group can finish first.

6. *Filling the Gas Tank.*—Keep the same formation as in the preceding relay. Each of the four groups face the leader. A peanut is given to each player and a vegetable dish placed about eight feet from the front of each line. Each player has one throw for the bowl with a peanut. Allow five points for each peanut that remains in the bowl. If the crowd is not large, two or three peanuts may be given to each.

7. *Filling the Radiator.*—A couple is selected from each group. The girl is given a glass of water and a teaspoon. Each one of the

girls must feed the water to the boys with the spoon. The couple first emptying their glass wins for their group.

8. *Unlocking the Car Door*—Secure from an automobile dealer four large pictures of cars. Fasten these on the wall or draperies. Select four groups of three contestants each. Blindfold each contestant, taking one group at a time. Give each one a piece of cardboard cut into the shape of a key, with a pin in it. The person in each group who gets the key pinned nearest the handle of the front door of the car is the winner. The winner in each group may have a contest with the winners in the other groups. Give a small token prize to the final winner.

9. *Sounding the Horn.*—Select one from each group. The leader might say he wanted someone who could sing. They are then asked to try one at a time to imitate an automobile horn. The one making the best imitation of a horn sound, in the estimation of the judges, wins a prize. A toy horn might be used for this prize.

10. *Blow-Out Race.*—The group assembles as for previous relays, facing the leader in parallel lines. About thirty-five feet in front of each group a sufficient number of paper bags, about five- or six-pound size, has been placed so that each one may have a bag. At the sound of the leader's whistle, the one on the front races to the chair, picks up a bag, inflates it, pops it, and races back, touching off the next one in front and taking place in the rear of the line. The group finishing first wins.

11. *Changing Attire.*—Select a boy from each group, each one wearing a coat. These contestants are told that at the sound of the whistle they are to take off their coats, turn them wrong side out, replace them, take them off again, turn them right side out, and replace them. The one doing this first wins.

12. *Lost Tool.*—Something to represent a lost tool is placed on the floor. This might be a book or block of wood or a toy automobile. One is selected from each group and shown the tool on the floor. That one is then blindfolded, or rather all are blindfolded

at the same time and sent to look for the tool in the dark. The one first finding a tool wins for his group.

13. *Hunt for Hidden Cars.*—A large number of cars cut out of paper or cardboard have been hidden about the room. These cars might have numbers on them, 5, 10, 15, 20. The leader tells the guests about the cars, and they hunt for them. The numbers are added on the backs of the cars found to get the score for each group.

14. *Rhyming Auto Parts.*—Each group is given words with which to end each line of a four-line poem. Prizes will be given to the group making the cleverest poem. Prizes may also be given to the group making the largest number of poems. Allow five minutes for this, and give the groups the following words: (1) Gear, dear, brake, cake. (2) Door, bore, hood, good. (3) Seat, neat, wheel, eel, (4) Switch, ditch, clutch, Dutch.

15. *Grandpa's Motor Romance.*[1]—Use the following as a writing game, leaving the words in parentheses blank to be filled in. Another method of using this game is to have the leader to read the story and the players, one at a time, are asked to supply the missing word with an auto part. The story follows:

> Alice and her beau one day
> Went riding in his (Chevrolet).
> Her beau was fat, his name was Frank,
> And he was somewhat of a (crank).
> It was too bad he wasn't smarter,
> But he couldn't work the (starter).
> She showed him how, the little dear,
> And also how to shift the (gear).
> Away they went, but something broke;
> 'Twas just a measly little (spoke).
> He fixed it with a piece of wire;
> Then something popped—it was a (tire).
> 'Twas mended soon, but next, ker-flop,
> They struck a branch and smashed the (top).

[1] Adapted from *Phunolgoy,* by E. O. Harbin (Abingdon Press). Used by permission.

32

Automobile Party

"Dear me," cried Alice, "that's too much!"
Then something happened to the (clutch).
And next poor Frank, unlucky dub,
Just grazed a rock and smashed a (hub).
They crossed a brook but missed the ford,
And sank down to the (running board).
"Oh, Frank," cried Alice with a squeal,
"I think we're going to lose a (wheel)!"
They climbed a hill and then 'twas seen
The tank contained no (gasoline).
They coasted downward toward the lake,
But Frankie couldn't work the (brake).
They struck a post a moment later
That almost wrecked the (radiator).
So both climbed out, and poor old Frank
Bought gasoline and filled the (tank),
And gathered up from road and field
The fragments of the broken (shield).
They fixed the engine tight and snug
And had to use a new (spark plug).
Just then he slapped at a mosquito
And dropped a wrench on the (magneto).
'Twas useless then to sweat and toil,
Nothing would run, except the (oil).
They journeyed home with Frankie pushin'
While Alice sobbed upon a (cushion).
So poor Frankie's hopes were doomed to blight,
And Alice married (Willy-S Knight).

16. *U Auto Know.*—Answer with names of automobile makes.

(1) The crossing of a stream. Ford
(2) The colony of the Pilgrims. Plymouth
(3) A chief of the Ottawa Indians. Pontiac
(4) A tramp. Rambler
(5) What is put in a thermometer. Mercury
(6) A martyred president. Lincoln
(7) To avoid. Dodge
(8) Discoverer of the Mississippi. De Soto
(9) His father made the Flivver. Edsel

(10) A mythical bird causing lightning and thunder. Thunderbird
(11) French explorer, founder of Detroit. Cadillac
(12) Pertaining to an empire. Imperial

17. *Auto Race.*—Each one of the four groups divide and form two lines facing each other. At one end of the line a toy automobile is started and passed across zigzag fashion from one side to the other. The car must make four laps down and back, and the group finishing first wins.

18. *Motor Romance.*—Cut from magazines pictures of persons in automobiles. It will be better if pictures are selected which show only a young man and a young woman. Use a folder and paste the picture on the outside cover. Have the guests to write a motor romance around the characters in the picture. Have a committee of three to decide the best story, and have the five best ones read. Give a prize to the guest with the most vivid imagination. This game should not be allowed to consume more than ten or fifteen minutes.

19. *Automobile Spelling Match.*—The four groups assemble on the longest side of the hall. Each one in the group is given a lettered card six inches square. Letters sufficient to spell all the names of cars pronounced should be given out. If there are too many letters to give one to each, give some two. The leader pronounces the names of cars, and each group tries to get its members in formation on the other side of the hall with the letters that spell the word pronounced. The leader pronounces the names of the following cars: Buick, Chevrolet, Lincoln, Ford, Dodge, Cadillac, Plymouth, Oldsmobile, Pontiac, De Soto, Studebaker, Mercury, Rambler, Corvette, Thunderbird, and Edsel. Each group should have a complete alphabet, printed with colored crayons on 6 x 6 inch cards, with the exception of the letters J, Q, W, X, and Z. In addition each should have duplicates in A, C, D, E, L, N, O, R, and T.

20. *Blow-Out.*—The leader has copied on a card a list of the following auto parts:

Fan	Cylinder	Axle
Steering wheel	Differential	Door
Seat	Gas tank	Radiator
Pump	Clutch	Horn
Glove compartment	Horn	Mirror
Tires	Headlight	Valve
Fan belt	License	Key
Wheel	Brake	Carburetor
Nut	Radio	Spring
Inner tube	Ventilator	Speedometer
Bumper	Cap	Air conditioner
Tail light	Spark plug	Cigarette lighter
Windshield	Fender	Windshield wiper

Players are seated in a circle, and all chairs are filled. The mechanic has the names of the auto parts written on a card, and he has given each player in the circle the name of an auto part. The mechanic walks around the circle, calling at random the names of auto parts. Those who have the names of these parts must get up and follow him around the circle. When he calls, "Blow-out," all dash for a seat, and the one who fails to get a seat becomes the mechanic, the new mechanic taking the list on the card, and the game continues. Don't play this game too long.

21. *To Find Partners.*—Cut out of magazines the pictures of cars, and cut also the name of the car, and keep the picture of the car and the name of it separate. Give the women the picture of a car and the men the name of a car, and let them match in this way. For a large group there may be several of the same kinds of cars.

22. *Properties*

(1) Advertisements of cars cut out of magazines with the names removed to pin up on curtains and other places in room.

(2) Pictures of automobiles cut up into picture puzzles and placed in envelopes.

(3) Four toy autos, preferably of wood with wheels that will turn easily, and strings to pull them with.

(4) Enough peanuts to give one to each guest. Four vegetable dishes the same size and shape.

(5) Four glasses of water and four teaspoons.

(6) Large pictures of cars. It is better to have four of these although one would do. Four pieces of cardboard cut in the shape of a key with a pin in each piece.

(7) Enough five- or six-pound paper bags to furnish one to each guest.

(8) Block of wood or toy automobile. Four blindfolds.

(9) A large number of cars cut out of cardboard with numbers on them, such as 5, 10, 15, 20.

(10) Pencils and paper for each one present.

(11) Typewritten copies of "Grandpa's Motor Romance" for each guest. These may be made with carbons three or four at a time.

(12) Toy automobiles for number 17.

(13) Magazine pictures of a man and woman sitting in a car.

(14) Complete alphabet on six inch by six inch cards, with exception of J, Q, W, X, Z, and the following letters in duplicate: A, C, D, E, L, N, O, R.

(15) Card with names of auto parts written on it to be used in number 20.

(16) Cars cut out of magazines with name removed.

(17) Folder, magazine pictures, and paste.

23. *Refreshments.*—Serve no-nox gas (fruit punch colored with grape juice) and auto tires (doughnuts).

NOTE.—All of the games suggested in this chapter could not be used in one evening. The social committee or the host should select those desired and plan the games so that they will not last longer than one and one-half hours.

chapter 4

Mother Goose Party

(COSTUME)

A NOVEL IDEA FOR A PARTY FOR A LARGE GROUP IS A MOTHER GOOSE Party. This party has been successfully used in young people's conferences with a group from one hundred to two hundred. It would be a good idea to secure a Mother Goose rhyme book that could be torn up and given in advance to the guests, so that they could use the pictures and rhymes in getting ready their costumes and preparing to act the part of the character they represent.

1. *Some of the Most Familiar Characters*

(1) Simple Simon.
(2) The Pieman.
(3) Old King Cole.
(4) Fiddlers Three. (This part may be taken by three persons who play the violin, and this may be a part of the entertainment.)
(5) Tom the Piper's Son.
(6) Little Jack Horner.
(7) The Old Woman Who Rode on a Broom.
(8) The Queen of Hearts.
(9) The Knave of Hearts.
(10) Little Miss Muffet.
(11) The Spider.
(12) The Old Woman Who Lived under the Hill.

(13) Mary, who had a little lamb.
(14) Mary, Mary, Quite Contrary.
(15) Diddle, Diddle Dumpling, My Son John.
(16) Little Bopeep.
(17) Little Polly Flinders.
(18) Polly Flinders' Mother.
(19) Humpty Dumpty.
(20) The Little Man with the little gun.
(21) Old Mother Hubbard.
(22) Curylocks.
(23) Bessie Bell.
(24) Mary Gray.
(25) Little Boy Blue.
(26) Goosey, Goosey, Gander (one that will require a lot of imagination).

(27) The Old Woman Who Lived in a Shoe.
(28) Jack Sprat.
(29) Jack Sprat's wife.
(30) Little Tommy Tittlemouse.
(31) Jack.
(32) Jill.
(33) Mother Goose.

(34) The Bachelor Who Lived by Himself.
(35) Georgy Porgey.
(36) Wise Men of Gotham (may be taken by three young men).
(37) Fat Man of Bombay.
(38) Jack Be Nimble.
(39) Tommy Tucker.

Almost any public library will have a book of Mother Goose rhymes and illustrations of the characters. Announcement should be made of this fact so that those who are going to come may work up some kind of clever costume.

2. *Invitations.*—The following is a suggestion for an invitation to this party:

Old Mother Goose, when
    She wants to wander,
Rides through the air
    On her very fine gander.

She'll stop any place where
    Her children will meet her;
She likes jolly crowds
    To come out to greet her.

She'll meet all young people, who'll
    Dress up just right,
And come to the Smiths,
    On next Friday night.

3. *Grand March.*—At all costume parties there should be a grand march. This gives everyone a chance to display his costume. See Chapter 2, page 22, for the figures of the march. End up with the Foolish Grand March. (See Index.)

4. *Judging Costumes.*—A prize should be given for the best costume for the girls and one for the best cosutme for the boys. In case of large groups like conference, where for the purpose of

stimulating rivalry the group has already been divided into three or four groups, there should be prize winners in each group, and then the best one selected from all of the groups.

5. *Acting Out the Mother Goose Rhyme.*—The following are some suggestions for the acting out of the Mother Goose rhyme. In the first place, the character should memorize the rhyme and be able to repeat it. Simple Simon should have a fishing line and pretend to be fishing. Jack Be Nimble should jump over his candlestick. Old King Cole should call for his pipe and bowl and fiddlers three. The fiddlers should render a musical number on their instruments. Of Tom, Tom, the piper's son, it is said:

> Tom, Tom, the piper's son,
> He learned to play when he was young;
> But all the tune that he could play
> Was "Over the hill and far away."

So Tom might also render this or some other number on a horn of some nature. Little Jack Horner might sit down in the corner and start eating pie. The Old Woman can ride her broom. The Queen of Hearts can display some tarts she has made. These are stolen by the Knave of Hearts. Mary ought to improvise some kind of a lamb which she drags around. The other Mary ought to be quite contrary. Humpty Dumpty ought to fall off the wall. Old Mother Hubbard ought to have a toy dog and look for a bone for him. Little Boy Blue ought to blow his horn. Jack and Jill ought to have a pail and fall down. The old woman who lived in a shoe ought to spank her children and put them to bed. Georgy Porgey should go through the motion of trying to kiss the girls, and so on. Others are Tommy Tucker, who might sing for his supper; the Bachelor Who Lived by Himself, who might ride his bride in on a wheelbarrow.

Have the characters around the room in a circle seated. Call on them one at a time in turn.

6. *Finding the Magic Couple.*—The leader picks out one couple and tells them secretly that they are to be the Magic Couple. They are to be separated a great deal of the time, but occasionally they

will be together. If anyone asks them while they are together, "Are you the Magic Couple?" they are to answer yes. As soon as anyone finds the Magic Couple he is to retire from the group and take a place at the other end of the room. If anyone asks the girl or the boy of the Magic Couple the question while they are separated, they are to answer no. They of course are not the Magic Couple while they are separated. If the game is getting too long, it would be well for the couple to stay together all the time.

7. *Blackboard Relay.*—Secure a large blackboard and place it in one end of the room. The players line up in two or more columns facing the blackboard. At a signal from the leader, the first one runs to the blackboard and writes a word and runs back, giving the chalk to the one in the front of the line. This one writes another word and one that will follow the first one written and make a sentence. So both lines continue to build a paragraph. A prize may be given to the side that finishes first and also to the side that writes the best paragraph. The prizes should be something that can be divided, like a box of candy or a bag of peanuts.

8. *Gossip.*—The players are standing around the room in a circle. The leader says: "We are going to play Gossip. We are going to give you a subject on which to talk, and you must talk to someone on that subject until the whistle blows." The leader then should announce the subject to talk on, such as "The Weather," or "Mosquitoes." When the whistle blows, the leader should pick out about two couples of the best talkers and tell them that they have been picked as the champion talkers but that they must decide in a contest which couple is the best of the two. The leader then tells the first couple the following story: "A man is out squirrel hunting. He sees a squirrel on a large tree. The squirrel sees the hunter, and so gets on the opposite side of the tree. The man walks around the tree, the squirrel keeping on the opposite side of the tree." The leader should then say: "The question is, Did the man go around the squirrel?" The boy should be told to take the negative and the girl the affirmative and argue the question. The next couple might

be asked to imitate a newly married couple in the group having their first breakfast together.

9. *Make-Up Contest.*—Choose two or more couples. The boys are given a box which contains a red cord, with which he is to tie the girl's hands behind her. The box also contains make-up materials—rouge, lipstick, eyebrow pencil, powder, and so forth. The boys are told to make up the girls like their favorite actress of movie, stage, or television. Judges pick the winner.

10. *Heel and Toe Relay.*—Players line up in two or more equal groups, one behind the other, and all facing a goal about twenty to thirty feet away. At a signal from the leader, they start walking toward the goal, but must place the heel of one foot against the toe of the other as they step. They walk this way both to the goal and back. The first one returns and touches off the second one, then the first one takes his place at the back of the line. The first group to finish wins.

11. *Mixed Quartet.*—The leader has prepared a number of popular songs or old familiar songs by copying them on a typewriter and cutting them into four parts. These parts are given out, one part to each guest. At the signal from the leader the quartet that possesses different parts of the same song tries to get together. When they have assembled, some of them may be asked to sing their song. The quartet that renders the number best may be given a prize that can be divided among them.

12. *Do You Know Your Physiology?*—For the following game slips of paper should be prepared in advance with the question on it, as follows:

Of what part of the body is the egotist most fond? Eye—I.
What part of the body is the tree? Palm.
What part of the body is a part of a tree? Limb.
What parts of the body are two animals only spelled differently? Hair—Hare, Heart—Hart.
What the doctor does to the body? Heels—heals.
What the slave gets? Lashes.
Part of a shoe, something to eat, and a language? Tongue.

What part of the body tells which way the wind blows? Vanes—Veins.
Something we fill with treasures? Chest.
Sold by the pound in the hardware store? Nails.
Baby cows? Calves.
Something we chew and do not swallow? Gum.
Seat of a man's affection? Stomach.
A shellfish? Muscles.
Front part of a clock? Face.
Third part of a yard? Foot.
Little white things in the head that bite? Teeth.

13. *Poison Penny.*—This game will cause a lot of excitement and hilarity. A penny is given to one player in the circle and passed around among the players as long as music is played. The player who has the penny when the music stops must drop out of the game. No player must hesitate to take the penny when offered to him, but must take it and pass it on quickly. If the group is large, more than one penny should be used.

14. *A Mother Goose Romance.*—Following may be used as a writing game, furnishing each guest with a copy made on a typewriter with carbon copies, or it may be mimeographed, and they may be asked to write the word represented by the initial letter. Or it may be read by the leader, and let the guests see who can supply the word represented by the initial letter.

Old M. G., riding on her G., went on a visit to all of her subjects. She met S. S. with his fishing rod, and she met the P. as he journeyed to the fair. She visited the palace of O. K. C. and heard him call for his P. and his B. and his F. three. After leaving the palace of O. K. C., she saw a boy running with all his might. It was T. the P. S. He had a P. under his arm. Her attention was next attracted by a very peculiar traveler. It was the O. W. W. R. O. a B. She next passed the kitchen as the Q. of H. was finishing making her T., and was just in time to see the K. of H. steal one of them. She then passed by the tuffet where L. M. M. was sitting and saw the S. come up and frighten her away. She next went to the home of the O. W. W. L. U. a H., but she was not at home. She then passed the G. of M. M. Q. C., and asked her how her G. G. She saw little B. returning with her S. She saw H. D. sitting on a W. She also saw H. D. get a G. F. She passed the home of O. M. H. just as she went to the C. to get her

P. D. a B. She saw her turn away in despair as she found the C. B. She saw the S. in the M. and the C. in the C. and heard a call for L. B. B. to come and B. his H. She passed the home of the O. W. W. L. I. a S., who H. S. M. C. S. D. K. W. T. D., and went in to dine with J. S. She was amused that J. S. could eat no F., and that his wife could eat no L., but between them both they licked the P. C. She then passed the house of L. T. T. and the lonesome place of the B. who L. B. H. She saw J. and J. go up the H. to fetch a P. of W. She saw J. fall down and break his C. and J. come tumbling after. She saw some more children at play, and among them was G. P. P. and P., who K. the girls and made them C. Her tour of inspection ended. Old M. G. said to her G., "Home, James."

The following is the key to the story:

Old Mother Goose, riding on her gander, went on a visit to all of her subjects. She met Simple Simon with his fishing rod, and she met the Pieman as he journeyed to the fair. She visited the palace of Old King Cole and heard him call for his pipe and his bowl and his fiddlers three. After leaving the palace of Old King Cole, she saw a boy running with all his might. It was Tom the Piper's Son. He had a pig under his arm. Her attention was next attracted by a very peculiar traveler. It was the Old Woman Who Rode on a Broom. She next passed the kitchen as the Queen of Hearts was finishing making her tarts, and was just in time to see the Knave of Hearts steal one of them. She then passed by the tuffet where Little Miss Muffett was sitting and saw the Spider come up and frighten her away. She next went to the home of the Old Woman Who Lived under a Hill, but she was not at home. She then passed the Garden of Mary, Mary, Quite Contrary, and asked her how her graden grew. She saw little Bopeep returning with her Sheep. She saw Humpty Dumpty sitting on a wall. She also saw Humpty Dumpty get a great fall. She passed the home of Old Mother Hubbard, just as she went to the cupboard to get her poor dog a bone. She saw her turn away in despair as she found the cupboard bare. She saw the sheep in the meadows and the cows in the corn and heard a call for Little Boy Blue to come and blow his horn. She passed the home of the Old Woman Who Lived in a Shoe, who had so many children she didn't know what to do, and went in to dine with Jack Sprat. She was amused that Jack Sprat could eat no fat, and that his wife could eat no lean, but between them both they licked the platter clean. She then passed the house of Little Tom Tinker, and the lonesome place of the Bachelor who Lived by Himself. She saw Jack and Jill go up the hill to fetch a pail of water. She saw Jack fall down and break his crown and Jill come tumbling after. She saw more children at play, and among them was Georgy Porgey Puddin' and Pie, who kissed the girls and made them cry. Her tour of inspection ended, Old Mother Goose said to her gander, "Home, James."

15. *Refreshments.*—Punch and cake, or hot tea and cake would be suitable. As this party is not connected with any particular season, any refreshments that are convenient and within the means of the one entertaining may be served.

16. *Decorations.*—Use bright colored crepe paper and hand streamers over the room in which the party is to be held.

17. *Properties*

(1) Blackboard and chalk for relay.
(2) Make-up materials in boxes for Make-Up Contest.
(3) Songs written out on typewriter and cut into four parts.
(4) Papers with physiology writing game written on them.
(5) One or more pennies.
(6) Mimeographed or carbon copies of A Mother Goose Romance.

chapter 5

Valentine Party

VALENTINE'S DAY COMES ON FEBRUARY 14. IT IS THE DAY OF THE month of February that is most conducive to having a good time. This is the time you are supposed to lose your own heart and win another. Up until the close of the nineteenth century the custom of sending anonymous love notes and tokens on this day was fairly general. Valentine's Day marks the beginning of the coming of spring.

1. *Invitation.*—A suggestion for an invitation follows:

> Come to our house on Valentine night
> At eight o'clock or so.
> Dan Cupid will be there all right
> With his arrows and his bow.
> There'll be many lads and lasses here,
> So watch for Cupid's dart.
> The only thing you have to fear
> Is losing your fond heart.

2. *Decorations.*—Pink and white streamers or red and white streamers. Red cardboard hearts could be used in various ways for decorations. These could be suspended from the ceiling or pinned on curtains around the room. Cut-out cupids would also make a good decoration. An attractive centerpiece for a table would be a miniature cupid with bow and arrow drawn ready to shoot.

3. *Mixer: Heart Going to Jerusalem.*—This game is played somewhat like Going to Jerusalem. Pin hearts on the window curtains or put them up with thumb tacks. There should be one less hearts than guests. While the music plays all march around the room. When the music stops, they all put one hand on a heart, and there must be

only one hand on each heart. The person who does not have a heart to put his hand on must retire from the game and take his place in the center of the room. When the music starts again, the leader takes down one of the remaining hearts, and so on, until only one heart remains. If the game is continuing too long, the leader may take down more than one heart each time.

4. *Heart Hunt.*—A large number of hearts have been hidden around the room before the party starts. Among these there should be a gold-colored heart and a silver-colored one. Give three prizes, one to the person finding the largest number of hearts, one to the person finding the gold heart, and one to the one who finds the silver heart. Candy hearts or candy in heart-shaped boxes would be appropriate for a prize.

5. *Pulling the Heartstrings.*—Hang from the doorway between two rooms a large heart made of red cardboard through which is a hole. Through this hole hang red cords, having half as many cords as guests. Care should be taken that these cords are large enough that they will not tangle easily. Girls go into one room and the boys into the other. The girls take hold of one end of a cord and the boys the other, taking care not to pull until the leader signals. When the whistle is blown, all pull at the same time, and those who have opposite ends of a cord are partners and will work together in the following games.

6. *Heart Puzzle.*—Give each couple an envelope containing a large cardboard heart cut into eight or ten odd-shaped pieces. When the whistle blows, all try to assemble the heart by putting the pieces together. The first couple to finish wins the prize.

7. *Lovers' Vocabulary.*—Guests are to write the words represented by the jumbled letters:

(1) Teeth ears w. Sweetheart.
(2) Yenho. Honey.
(3) Reda. Dear.
(4) Ringlad. Darling.
(5) Voel. Love.
(6) Guh. Hug.

(7) Skis. Kiss.
(8) Missrope. Promises.
(9) Palsrospo. Proposals.
(10) Widnged Singr. Wedding Rings.
(11) Korenb Ratshe. Broken Hearts.
(12) Elvo L street. Love Letters
(13) Gag men neet Ginrs. Engagement Rings.
(14) Ageirram Ratla. Marriage Altar.
(15) Noonmoyeh. Honeymoon.
(16) Direb. Bride.
(17) Gorean Mossobls. Orange Blossoms.
(18) Rovesl Squarrel. Lovers' Quarrels.

8. *The King and Queen of Valentine.*—A girl and boy are chosen to act as King and Queen of Valentine. They are seated on an improvised throne, while the other guests sit in a circle. The King and Queen each have a large red heart in their hands. The Queen calls the boys to her one at a time, and the King calls the girls one at a time. The Queen instructs the boy to take the heart to the prettiest girl in the room. The King instructs the girl to take the heart to the handsomest boy. These next appear before the King and Queen and are told what to do with the heart, and so on until each one of the guests in the room has had a chance to come up and have the heart. Each must remember the instructions given by the King or Queen, and to whom the heart was given, but is to tell no one until told to do so by the King and Queen. Each one has had the heart at least once; the King orders all players to tell to whom they gave the heart and for what reason, beginning with the first player to report to the throne, and so on to the last. Some suggestions for the King are: The boy with the largest ears, the best athlete, most courteous boy, youngest boy, handsomest, biggest feet, noisiest, quietest, most learned, laziest. Suggestions to be given to the boys by the Queen: Prettiest, best cook, most beautiful eyes, sweetest, neatest, best musician, most ideal for wife, best athlete, and so on.

9. *Valentine Relay Race.*—Divide into two or more groups. About twelve to fifteen on a side is a good number for this relay. Each group

stands one behind the other, facing three circles eighteen inches in diameter which have been drawn with chalk on the floor. Three Indian clubs or pop bottles for each circle have been dressed up with crepe paper to represent valentines or cupids. They are standing in the circles. When the whistle is blown, the one on the front of the line runs to the circle and sets the bottles out of the circle. He must leave them all standing up. He runs back and touches off the next one in front of the line and takes his place at the back of the line. The next one must place the clubs or bottles back into the circle. This continues until all have had a chance. The group that finishes first may give a yell and perhaps win a prize.

10. *Making Valentines.*—Find again your former partner for this game. Each couple is provided with some magazines, a tube of paste, a pair of scissors, and a cardboard or blank sheet of paper. Each couple is to make a valentine, using pictures and words cut from magazines. A good prize should be given for the best one and another for the most comic one.

11. *Drawing Hearts.*—On a chart of white paper hung on the wall, or a writing board with black sheets of paper on it, have each guest draw the picture of a heart and write his name in it while blindfolded. The best effort will receive a prize.

12. *Living Pictures.*—Make a large frame about eight feet square. Decorate with valentine colors. Have lights in the frame so that other lights may be turned out except those about the frame. Have some good soloist or a quartet sing some of the old love songs while others represent the characters and stand behind the picture frame. There should be a curtain over the frame, and the curtain should be drawn after each song is finished. Some suggestions would be: "In the Good Old Summer Time," "Love's Old Sweet Song," "Put on Your Old Gray Bonnet," "I Want a Girl Like the Girl That Married Dear Old Dad," "When You I Were Young, Maggie," "Let Me Call You Sweetheart," "School Days," "When Your Hair Has Turned to Silver."

13. *Flour Heart Hunt.*—The group has already been divided for the relay race, so choose one boy from each group for the Flour

Heart Hunt. Perhaps it would be better not to tell the name of the stunt until all is ready. When the boys have been chosen, bring in saucers of flour in which are hidden cardboard hearts. They are to dig these out without the use of the hands, and are to use only the teeth and tongue.

14. *Heart Archery.*—Draw a large heart on a piece of cardboard about thirty inches square. Draw circles on the heart, one within the other as an archery target is made. In the inner circle write "Ideal Lover." The ring next to center should be labeled "Lovers." The next circle should be marked "Somewhat Affectionate." The next circle should be marked "Indifferent to Love," and the outside circle "Girl Hater, Boy Hater." Bows and arrows can be purchased at any toy or novelty store. If arrows with rubber tips are used, they may be touched to a rubber stamp or lampblack so that they will make a mark on the target. Burnt cork will also do. Fortunes are determined by the circle which the player hits.

15. *Making the Most of Valentine.*—Give blank slips of paper and pencil to each guest. Tell them that they are to see who can make the most of Valentine. They are to see how many words they can make out of the letters in the word Valentine. Give a prize to the one who has the largest number.

16. *Cupid Is Coming.*—Guests sit in a circle around the room. The leader says, "Cupid is coming." The first one indicated by the leader repeats this and adds an adverb, as, "Cupid is coming affectionately." The next one on this player's right continues, using the next letter of the alphabet, as follows: "Cupid is coming affectionately, bountifully." The next one must add an adverb beginning with "c" and repeat all the preceding ones, as, "Cupid is coming affectionately, bountifully, charmingly." This continues around the circle until each player repeats the list and adds an adverb. If any player makes a mistake on any word, he must drop out of the circle.

17. *Refreshments.*—At this season of the year ice-cream companies and bakeries are making their products in heart molds. Serve ice cream in heart mold and heart-shaped cookies or cakes. Another suggestion would be cherry Jello with whipped cream and cookies

with white frosting and heart-haped candies and this served with coffee. An attractive plate could be arranged with sandwiches cut in heart shape and a basket of candies served with hot chocolate with marshmallows or whipped cream. Kisses or taffy could be served with any of these and would be appropriate.

18. *Properties*

(1) Cardboard hearts for mixer. Pin or thumbtack for each heart.

(2) Small hearts for heart hunt, among them a gold heart and a silver-colored heart.

(3) Large red cardboard heart and half as many cords as guests.

(4) Envelopes containing heart puzzle, one for each couple.

(5) Papers for Lovers' Vocabulary.

(6) Large red heart for King and Queen of Valentine.

(7) Six or more Indian clubs or bottles dressed in crepe paper to represent valentines or cupids for relay race. Chalk.

(8) Making valentines. You will need to provide magazines, cardboard or blank sheet of paper, and paste.

(9) Chart of white paper or writing board with paper for drawing hearts blindfolded. Blindfolds for each guest.

(10) Large frame eight feet square with light around frame for Living Pictures.

(11) Saucers of flour for Flour Heart Hunt. Hearts in them. Also put saucers on a newspaper.

(12) Large cardboard prepared for Archery Contest and bow and arrow. Ink pad.

(13) Blank paper and pencils for Making Most of Valentine.

chapter 6

Famous Lovers' Party

THIS PARTY IS PLANNED AROUND THE IDEA OF WELL-KNOWN LOVERS OF sacred and secular history. It might well be used for Valentine, but would be appropriate for any time of the year.

1. *Invitations.*—Write invitations on heart-shaped cards or paper or draw a picture of a heart on a correspondence card around the following or similar invitation:

> Have you ever met Miss Juliet,
>   Or the charming Romeo?
> Do you know Rowena,
>   Or the brave knight Ivanhoe?
> Then come to Smith's on Friday night
>   To our famous Lovers' Party;
> You'll meet them every one all right,
>   And receive a welcome hearty.

2. *Decorations.*—Use large hearts and suspend them from the ceiling, or hang them on pink and white streamers, or pin them on the curtains and draperies.

3. *Opening Mixer: Color Eyes and Hair.*—Give each guest a piece of paper and pencil. They are, at a signal from the leader, to go to every other guest and write each name, the color of the hair, and the color of the eyes. When this game has been in progress long enough for the fastest ones to be through, the leader should blow the whistle and give a prize to the one having the longest list. One or two of these lists may be read, and it will probably be found to have some mistakes in it.

4. *Famous Lovers Jumbled.*—Give each one a slip of paper on which to write the names of the following famous lovers which are

51

given them on the paper with the letters jumbled. The couple finishing first wins a prize. Let each boy choose a partner for this game.

 (1) Beg Liar, Even I angel. Gabriel, Evangeline.
 (2) Ozba, Hurt. Boaz, Ruth.
 (3) Natyonh, Artapocle. Anthony, Cleopatra.
 (4) Cunhp, Yudj. Punch, Judy.
 (5) Onapenol, Pejiheson. Napoleon, Josephine.
 (6) Acais, Bcreeac. Isaac, Rebecca.
 (7) Emoro, Letuij. Romeo, Juliet.
 (8) Nojh Endla, Capsirill. John Alden, Priscilla.
 (9) Nlatolce, Aeienl. Lancelot, Elaine.
 (10) Iprsa, Nlehe. Paris, Helen.
 (11) Dmaa, Vee. Adam, Eve.
 (12) Boacj, Elhrac. Jacob, Rachel.
 (13) Lhatme, Lohiepa. Hamlet, Ophelia.
 (14) Rabhmaa, Hasar. Abraham, Sarah.
 (15) Tenda, Tribecea. Dante, Beatrice.
 (16) Cjka, Llij. Jack, Jill.
 (17) Whiataha, Nahmiahen. Hiawatha, Minehaha.
 (18) Hivneao, Norawe. Ivanhoe, Rowena.

5. *Continuous Love Story.*—As the crowd sits in a circle they are given paper and pencil. About every sixth one should get the paper and pencil, and this one should write the first line of a love story. He passes it to the next one on the right, who looks at what he has written and writes another line. These are folded each time so that only the last line can be seen, and so each one reads the last line, folds it over, and writes another line. Let each one of the stories go all around the room so that each one will have to write a number of times. When all have been around the circle, collect them and read some of them.

6. *Progressive Proposals.*—Give each boy a number of paper hands and a number of paper mittens. There should be as many or more of these given to each boy as there are girls in the party. Give the boy also a fan behind which to hide when he blushes. The

girls go around the circle, kneeling before each boy and pleading their cause. When this is completed, they are given either a hand which means acceptance, or a mitten which means refusal. The girl who has the largest number of hands receives a prize and is crowned the most popular girl at the party.

7. *Needle and Thread Relay.*—The leader should explain that every man who will make a good husband should be able to sew. The boys line up in groups of equal number as for relay race, the groups facing two tables on which have been placed needles and thread. Each boy must run to the table, pick up a needle, break off a thread, thread the needle, and lay it back on the table. He then runs back and touches off the next one in front and takes his place at the back of the line. The group that finishes first wins. Let them give a yell.

8. *I Love My Love.*—Players seat themselves in a circle about the room. The leader should start off by saying: "I love my love with an A because she is attractive. Her name is Ann. She lives in Albany, and I gave her an apple. The first one indicated starts off with B: "I love my love with a B because he is broke. His name is Ben. He lives in Birmingham, and I gave him a button." Let this go all around the circle.

9. *Affinities.*—Give a prize to the couple that can write the largest list of affinities—i.e., things that are usually thought of together. The leader should suggest three or four of these to start out the guests well. Some affinities are:

Oil and Gas.	Hand and Glove.
Bigger and Better.	To and Fro.
High and Dry.	Ball and Chain.
Hide and Seek.	Hit and Run.
Thick and Thin.	Tried and True.
Soap and Water.	Nip and Tuck.
Collar and Tie.	Ever and Anon.
Horse and Buggy.	Due and Payable
Watch and Chain.	Far and Near.
Black and Blue.	Needle and Thread.

See additional affinities in "Bride and Groom Party," page 135.

10. *Elopement.*—This is a relay race for the girls. Have a dress and hat in a suitcase, and other garments if desired, perhaps a coat, all to be put on over other clothing, and large enough so this is possible. The two lines of girls face tables or chairs on which have been placed the suitcases. They must run to it and open it and put on the clothing and take it off and close the suitcase and run back and touch the next girl in line, taking their place at the rear of the line. The group that finishes first wins. This will cause much merriment if executed properly.

11. *A Love Story in Flowers.*—Have the following questions written on slips of paper. Use a mimeograph or typewriter with carbon copies. The questions are to be answered with the names of flowers:

(1) Her name and the color of her hair. Marigold.
(2) The color of her eyes. Violet.
(3) The color of her cheeks. Pink.
(4) What did she wear on her hair? Bridal wreath.
(5) Her brother's name and what he wrote it with? Jonquil.
(6) Her brother's favorite musical instrument? Trumpet.
(7) With what did his father punish him when he made too much noise with it? Goldenrod.
(8) At what time did his father awaken him? Four-o'clock.
(9) What did he say to him? Johnny-jump-up.
(10) What did she call her love? Sweet William.
(11) What did he do when he popped the question? Aster.
(12) What did he lay at her feet? Bleeding heart.
(13) What did she give him in return? Heartsease.
(14) What flower did he cultivate? Tulip.
(15) To whom did she refer him? Poppy.
(16) Who married them? Jack-in-the-pupit.
(17) What were the names of the bridesmaids? Rose-Mary.
(18) When he went away what did she say to him? Forget-me-not.
(19) With what did she punish her children? Lady's-slipper.
(20) What hallowed their last days? Sweet peas (peace).

12. *Catching a Lover.*—The lover is a rolling pin with one handle

cut off, or a bottle dressed up with crepe paper or cloth. It is placed in the center of the floor, and the party stands in two lines on either side of the room, half on one side and half on the other. They number, beginning at opposite ends. Then the leader calls out a number. Suppose this number is 1, then the numbers 1 from opposite ends of the two lines would run and try to catch the lover. The one who gets the lover tries to get back to his place in his line before he is tagged by the one who failed to catch the lover. If he succeeds, his line gets a point. The line which has the most points wins. This is a game in which care must be taken not to be too rough, for someone is likely to get a bruised knee or elbow unless care is exercised.

13. *Making the Most of Matrimony.*—Guests are provided with pencils and paper, and all try to see who can make the largest number of words from the word "matrimony."

14. *Impromptu Wedding.*—Write on slips of paper the names of the principals of a wedding party. Give out to some of the male guests the male parts, as, preacher, groom, best man, bride's father, rejected suitor, and ring bearer. Give to some of the ladies the names of the feminine participants, as, bride, maid of honor, two flower girls, bridesmaid, bride's mother.

Let the wedding party retire and arrange for the ceremony. There should be a processional, as follows: The preacher, bridesmaid, maid of honor, ring bearer (holds large ring or bracelet on large pillow), flower girls (scatter some kind of leaves or torn-up paper). Bride and father enter at the same time as groom and best man, the groom meeting the bride at the improvised altar. The rejected suitor and the bride's mother follow the bride. (Both should be weeping.) The bride's father stands between the bride and groom until the bride is given away.

As the procession enters the wedding march may be played, or some battle song may be sung.

The preacher may use the alphabet as a ceremony, merely repeating the letters of the alphabet in an oratorical manner. First the preacher should address the audience and repeat the letters of the alphabet. He should next address the bride and groom, repeating some of the letters of the alphabet. Next the bride's father should be addressed and should give away the bride, and in doing so should himself repeat some of the letters of the alphabet. Next should come the ring ceremony, in which the preacher addresses the groom and requires him to repeat some of the letters of the alphabet after him. Next they join right hands, and the preacher addresses first the groom and then the bride, and they respond by repeating some of the letters of the alphabet when he has finished with each of them. The preacher should again address the audience, repeating in an impressive manner some of the letters of the alphabet. His conclusion should be: W, X, Y, Z, &, $3.95.

The rejected suitor and the bride's mother should then weep, and the preacher should kiss the groom, and any other exaggerated actions that may be thought of may be introduced.

15. *Heart Hunt.*—A number of hearts have been hidden about the room before the guests arrive. Before the hunt starts the company should be divided into groups with five or six in each group. Each group has a leader and is assigned a song to sing or whistle, as "Let Me Call You Sweetheart," "Always," "When Your Hair Has Turned to Silver," "Love's Old Sweet Song," "I Love You Truly," "Silver Threads Among the Gold," and so on. When the whistle blows, the hunt starts. While everyone may find hearts, only the leader can pick them up. When one finds a heart, he must sing his song until the leader comes to pick up the heart. This is both a noisy and an active game and full of plenty of fun.

16. *Refreshments.*—Lemonade and heart-shaped cookies. Heart-mold ice cream. Frosted cake with hearts of candy stuck in the frosting. Fruit punch and heart-shaped sandwiches.

17. *Properties*

(1) Paper and pencils.
(2) Jumbled lovers' names prepared for each guest, written on typewriter.

(3) Paper hands and paper mittens.
(4) Needles and thread for each boy.
(5) Two suitcases with girls' clothing in them.
(6) Papers prepared with typewriter for Love Story in Flowers.
(7) Rolling pin or bottle dressed in crepe paper or cloth dress.
(8) Cardboard hearts for the Heart Hunt.

chapter 7

Washington's Birthday Party

(COSTUME)

WASHINGTON'S BIRTHDAY IS CELEBRATED IN ALL PARTS OF THE NATION. In many places it marks the height of the social season. Why not make it the occasion for an enjoyable party in your class, club, or society? The things that are suggested center around the things that are generally associated with Washington and colonial times.

1. *Invitations.*—Get from a novelty store or from the bookstore small cards in the shape of a hatchet. These can be cut from colored cardboard. Write the invitation on these, stating the time and place, and by all means that it will be a costume party.

2. *Decorations.*—American flags could be used about the room; also blue and white bunting would make a splendid decoration. If this is not desired, use red, white, and blue paper, with hatchets and cherries in evidence.

3. *Costumes.*—The ladies should try to imitate a Martha Washington costume. The ladies will wear kerchiefs and dresses made with tight bodice and full skirts. The skirts should be to the ankles. Hair should be powdered, and the face decorated with black court-plaster patches. Find a picture of a Martha Washington costume and copy it.

The men should wear knee breeches, hose, and slippers with buckles on them. There should be lace ruffles in the coat sleeves.

These costumes need not be elaborate but may be easily improvised.

4. *Have a Grand March.*—See Calendar Party, page 21, for the figures of the grand march. It is always well to have a grand march at costume parties, as it gives all an opportunity to see the costumes of others and to show off their own.

5. *Judging Costumes.*—Appoint three judges to decide which has the best costume. Give a prize to the boys and one to the girls. If the group is large, the costumes may be judged by a process of elimination. In conference groups where the company has already been divided into three or four groups, let the group leader and members of the group decide which costumes in their group are best. Then the judges can eliminate all but the best, and so on down to the very best. This judging of costumes will take several minutes of time and at the same time provide entertainment.

6. *Hatchet Snatch.*—Line up so that the boys will face the girls. It is better to do this on a floor that is carpeted or at least have a small rug in the center. A hatchet is made of wood or cardboard. (This may be purchased at the five-and-ten-cent store or the bookstore.) Fasten it in something for a base so that it will stand up. The boys are numbered from one to eight or nine. A similar number of girls play. In this game the numbering is from opposite ends, so that number one would stand opposite to number nine. The leader calls out the number, as "Number Three," and both numbers three, the boy and the girl, are to try to snatch the hatchet. The leader keeps score—that is, gives a point to the girls every time they snatch the hatchet and a point to the boys every time they get it.

7. *Things Associated with Washington.*—Furnish guests with the following things associated with Washington, jumbled:

(1) Thathec. Hatchet.
(2) Mary. Army.
(3) Rechyr erte. Cherry tree.
(4) Leavly Rogef. Valley Forge.
(5) Ratmha. Martha.
(6) Uontm Nervno. Mount Vernon.
(7) Words. Sword.
(8) Veryuosrs hacni. Surveyor's chain.

(9) Raweflle Drdases. Farewell Address.
(10) Oldsier. Soldier.
(11) Mountnem. Monument.
(12) Sidrentep. President.
(13) Antlerp. Planter.
(14) Pamcoss. Compass.
(15) Lawdeare. Delaware.
(16) Galf. Flag.
(17) Steyb Srso. Betsy Ross.
(18) Brefrayu. February.
(19) Potrati. Patriot.

8. *Shaking the Cherry Tree.*—Players stand in a circle, and one in the center is blindfolded. Players step out of the circle and shake the one in the center, who is the cherry tree. If the cherry tree guesses who did the shaking, that one must take the place in the center.

9. *Flag Relay.*—Play like a weaver's relay. Players form two circles of equal number. One player in the circle has a flag. Upon a signal from the leader he starts weaving in and out through the players in the circle. When he has completed the round, he gives the flag to the next one on his right and comes back into the circle. When all have made the circle, carrying the flag, the game is finished. The circle that gets all its players around first wins.

10. *Declaration of Independence.*—Give a prize to the one who can repeat the most of the Declaration of Independence. The first sentences are as follows:

> When in the course of human events it becomes necessary for one people to dissolve the political bands which have connected them with another, and to assume, among the powers of the earth, the separate and equal station, to which the laws of nature and of nature's God entitles them, a decent respect to the opinions of mankind requires that they should declare the causes which impel them to the separation. We hold these truths to be self-evident—that all men are created equal; that they are endowed by their Creator with certain inalienable rights that among these are life, liberty, and the pursuit of happiness.

It is not likely that anyone will know more than the first ten or twelve words. Anyone who can repeat all that is given here should receive a prize, even though there are more than one.

11. *Nothing But the Truth.*—Everyone is required to tell nothing but the truth. For a period of ten minutes (or less), each guest must answer every question asked by another or pay a forfeit. These forfeits may be redeemed later. See "Forfeits" in the Index. Questions that may be asked are: "Who do you think is the prettiest girl in the room?" "Are you engaged?" "Are you in love?" and so forth. A thousand questions will suggest themselves. An evasive answer will require a forfeit as well as a failure to answer. See "Try Your Luck on Telling the Truth," page 94.

12. *Hatchet Hunt.*—Have hatchets cut from colored cardboard hidden about the room. At a starting signal the guests will search for them. Give a prize to the one who finds the largest number.

13. *Washington Crossing the Delaware.*—Place a rug in the center of the floor to represent the Delaware River. The leader says to the first guest: "Washington is crossing the Delaware. How shall he cross?" The player must answer with an adverb that denotes action, as "angrily," awkwardly," "appealingly." The player then must get up and act the part. He must cross the improvised Delaware angrily or awkwardly or appealingly. The next player must cross the Delaware bashfully, blandly, briskly; the next carefuly, cutely, clumsily. So through the alphabet.

14. *Chopping Down the Cherry Tree.*—Players stand in a circle, and the leader stands in the center. The leader has a stick and a hatchet in her hand. She tells the story of the hatchet and of the chopping down of the cherry tree, and as she tells the story each time she says "cherry tree" all players must drop on one knee before the leader can chop three times. The last one down must take the hostess' place.

15. *Old Virginia Reel.*—Some groups may want to do the Old Virginia Reel. If so, it is done best to the tune of "Turkey in the Straw," and in the following manner: The girls line up facing the boys, the lines being about eight feet apart. When the music starts, someone calls the figures as follows, "Forward and back," where-

upon the men lock arms, and the ladies lock arms and take a step or two forward, bowing to each other in the center, then back to their places. Then the man at the head of the men's line comes to the center, meeting the lady on the other end of the ladies' line, bowing to her. The caller should say, "Bow to your partner." When this is done, the man on the other end of the line comes forward and bows to the lady, who meets him from the other end of the ladies' line. The one at the head of the men's line goes forward again, taking the right hand of the lady who meets him, and swings her around. The couple on the other end follows them at all times, doing the same thing that they do. On the next figure, the man takes the girl's left hand and swings her around. The next figure, both hands. The next figure, they both fold their arms and walk around each other. After this has been done by both end couples, the man at the head of the line takes hold of both hands of the girl at the same end of the girls' line, and they promenade together down through the center of the floor and back. When this has been done, the man swings with his right hand the next girl at the head of the line, while his partner swings with her right hand the first man at the head of the men's line. As they swing all the way around, she meets her partner in the center, giving him her left hand. As he swings her around he takes the right hand of the next girl in line, and she takes the right hand of the next man in line, and so on, until they have swung each couple in the line.

After this has been done, they come back to the head of the line, and the man turns to the left and walks around the back of the men's line. The girl turns to the right and walks around the back of the girls' line, meeting her partner at the other end. All others turn and follow the leaders around. The leaders form an arch through which all the others clasp hands and pass. This will put the couple who was second in line at the beginning of the line and the couple which was first in line in the beginning will be at the foot of the line. They proceed in the manner as before—that is, the man at the head of the line and the lady at the foot of the ladies' line meet, bow to each other, swing with right hand, left hand, both hands, fold their arms, promenade, swing each couple in line, and lead their groups around. And so it continues as long as desired.

16. *Refreshments.*—Cherry pie and coffee would be one suggestion. Another would be ice cream and cake with coffee with whipped cream. Waldorf salad with mayonnaise and hot chocolate.

17. *Properties*

(1) Hatchet for Hatchet Snatch.
(2) Carbon or mimeograph copies of Jumbled Things Associated with Washington.
(3) Two small flags for Flag Relay.
(4) Small cardboard hatchets hidden about the room.
(5) Rug for number 13.
(6) Stick and hatchet for number 14.

chapter 8

World-Tour Party

THIS PARTY IS PLANNED IN SUCH A WAY THAT IT WILL BE EDUCATIONAL as well as enjoyable. It is planned to take care of not more than fifty, and would be suitable for almost any average group of young people or adults. It will also be found to be very suitable for intermediate groups.

1. *Invitation.*—The following is suggested for an invitation:

> Have you ever been to Ireland,
>   Where the river Shannon flows?
> Or experienced the spell of the Yukon,
>   In Alaska, the land of snows?
> Then come to our World-Tour Party,
>   Which next Friday evening brings;
> We'll have a good time together,
>   Going places and seeing things.
>   Hour, Place, Date

2. *Decorations.*—Use flags of different countries if obtainable. Have small pictures of flags pinned on the curtains and placed about the room. If it is not possible to get these from a printed book, have them drawn and colored by hand. Many dictionaries and atlases have pictures of the flags of the countries of the world. Fifteen or twenty of these could be reproduced. Use United States flags or bunting in decoration.

3. *Mixing Game: Country, City, River.*—As the guests enter give them each the name of a country, city, or river of the world. Be sure to give these out so that they can form in groups of three by finding the country in which the city and river are located. The following are suggested names to be used:

64

	Country	City	River
(1)	United States	New York	Mississippi
(2)	Italy	Rome	Tiber
(3)	France	Paris	Seine
(4)	Germany	Berlin	Rhine
(5)	Brazil	Rio de Janeiro	Amazon
(6)	Belgian Congo	Leopoldville	Congo
(7)	Ireland	Dublin	Shannon
(8)	England	London	Thames
(9)	Egypt	Cairo	Nile
(10)	Scotland	Glasgow	Dee
(11)	Russia	Moscow	Volga
(12)	China	Canton	Yangtze
(13)	India	Bombay	Ganges
(14)	Turkey	Bagdad	Euphrates

There are several events that will require the party to be divided, and for the relays, and so forth, group all the countries, rivers, and cities together and against each other.

4. *Ireland: Poison Snake.*—When we think of Ireland, we think of snakes, as St. Patrick is supposed to have driven the snakes out of Ireland. Poison Snake is a lively game and quite active. The players all join hands and form a circle. A dozen or more Indian clubs or milk bottles are set around in a smaller circle. The object is to make your comrades knock over the bottles by pulling their hands. Anyone who knocks over a bottle or unclasps hands must leave the circle. The club or bottle is then replaced, and the game continues. The person who is disqualified from the original circle may start another circle with other disqualified players, the players disqualified from that circle may start another, and so on. The player who remains longest in the original circle should receive a prize. Take care that the game does not get too rough. The more bottles or clubs used, the less rough the game will be.

5. *Flag Identification.*—Give paper and pencil to the guests and let them identify the pictures of the flags that have been placed about the room. These flags may be true pictures of the flags cut from a book or reproductions by hand. Only the more familiar flags

should be used, or rather the flags of the larger nations. A number of flags may be borrowed from the local Rotary Club, as they sometimes use a number of small flags on their tables at their luncheons.

6. *First Visit to England: Steeplechase.*—Use about six small horses for each group—Cities, Countries, Rivers. If you do not want to go to the expense of buying toy horses, use something to represent a horse, as a bean bag or a ball. All the countries form a line, all the towns, and all the rivers. Six horses are placed on a chair at the head of each line. When the leader's whistle blows, the horses start moving down the lines. The players must pass them behind their backs, and all horses must be passed down and laid on a chair at the other end of the line before the first one starts back, and they must be passed back in the same way. The second time they go down the line, each one must stoop over and pass the horse around his right leg, and when all have gone down, they must be passed back in the same way. The third time they go down they must be passed around the left leg and back the same way. The fourth time they are passed down one at a time in the regular way. This is the home stretch. The group that gets all six horses back on the original chair first wins.

7. *Scotland: Golf.*—Golf is a Scottish game, and when we visit Scotland we should take our golf clubs. Have a golf game. This may be done in a group competition or just with individuals. Get for the group competition three putting practice boards. These can be purchased or borrowed from any sporting goods store. Also cheap boards with a golf hole in them may be purchased from a novelty store. If the groups compete, give each one three trials, and the group that gets the most balls in the hole wins. Provide three golf balls for each group and a putter.

8. *France: Style Show.*—As France is supposed to set the fashions for the world, a fashion show would be appropriate to represent this country. Have some of the girls bring an extra sport dress, a wedding dress, or an evening dress. They will be asked to model these for the group as in a French style show. It may be made humorous by having some of the boys dress up in girls' clothing

and appear in the fashion show. Some crazy costume, like a bathing suit, rubber boots, and a high silk hat and walking cane, will create a lot of merriment. This stunt can be a very entertaining feature.

9. *The Blind Trainman.*—It will be necessary for the leader to give the names of cities to the players who are not already named with the names of cities. Use the most familiar named cities of the world, as Belfast, Brussels, Istanbul, Cologne, Dresden, Florence, Geneva, Havre, Lisbon, Madrid, Mexico City, Naples, Havana, Venice, Vienna, Warsaw, Tokyo. If this is not enough to go around with what you have already named, use American cities. Towns in your own state would do just as well. The players are seated in a circle, and one is the trainman, and he is blindfolded. He calls out: "I want to go from Paris to Bombay." The players representing these cities immediately change places. As they change they must make the noise of an engine and occasionally the whistle. The leader tries to catch one of them; and if he does, he must tell whether it is Paris or Bombay. If he is right, he takes the seat left vacant by the other player, who becomes trainman. The rules of the game are that a player making the noise of a train may not go back. He may circle or zigzag, but if he backs up he is considered caught.

10. *Chinese Chicken.*—Line up the three groups for a relay race. Place in front of each group a straight row of six or eight rolled newspapers, sticks of wood, beanbags, or even cards. These should be about a foot apart. The person in the front of the line is going to have the most work to do, so someone should be selected who is quite active for the front. The game is as follows: The first player in each line hops forward, hopping over each obstacle, and then turns and hops back. The one on the front of the line is then tipped off, and the first player takes his place at the back of the line. This continues until each player has made the hop, and is concluded by the first men in this way: When all have finished in this group and the first man is again at the front, then he hops forward, and when he reaches the last obstacle he kicks it away and hops back. When he gets to the other end, he kicks away another one of the obstacles,

and so back and forth until he kicks away the last one. The group finishing first, and whose first man gets this done first, wins.

11. *Japanese Crab Race: Boys.*—Pick about six boys for each of two groups, and have them run a Japanese Crab Race. This can be done by having all the boys, or at least an even number of boys from each group, run. A goal is marked off on the floor about twenty or twenty-five feet away. The player stands on all fours with his heels toward the goal. When the whistle blows, first one starts running backward on all fours like a crab. When he has reached the goal the next one starts, and so on until all have run. The group that finishes first wins.

12. *Geography Game.*—The players sit in a circle with one vacant chair in the circle. One player is the World. There should be a rule that the World cannot stand nearer than six feet to this chair. If the room is large, the distance should be greater than that. The World tells a story, calling the names of countries, cities, and rivers. As the players have been previously named, when a name is called the player who represents the name must immediately change to the vacant chair. The World also tries to get the chair; and if he succeeds, the other one must be the World. The World must not take the chair left vacant by the one whose name was called.

13. *Russian Hole Ball.*—Some kind of ball game is played in almost every part of the world. Perhaps this is a new one, but it will be enjoyable for most any group. Use five crocks or jars. Half-gallon crocks would be ideal. Small flowerpots make a good substitute. Set these in a row three or four feet apart. They are numbered from one to five, the one near the throwing line being No. 1 and those farther away 2, 3, 4, 5, the last being at least twenty feet from the throwing line, which should be from eight to twelve feet from No. 1. Players line up as for a relay and are given tennis balls or small rubber balls. A goal is made when a ball enters and remains in a jar or hole. The score is counted according as the jars are numbered. No. 1, or the first jar, counts one point; No. 2, two points, and so on. Each player should be given three throws, and it may be played

by all of one team trying, then all of the other. The final score determines the winner.

14. *Charades on Different Countries.*—Have the three persons that represent a country, a city of that country, and a river of that country get together. Each trio is then asked to do a charade to represent their country. The group that represents England may let London Bridge fall down; those representing India could drape a sheet around one of the boys in imitation of the clothing worn by many men in India; Ireland might sing an Irish song, and so on.

15. *United States.*—Returning home, the guests may play football. See the football game suggested in "Calendar Party," page 26.

16. *Match Partners.*—Match partners for refreshments by giving the boys the names of states and the girls the names of the capitals of the states. When all have been matched, let them find a place that suits them to have their refreshments.

17. *Refreshments.*—Serve tea and cakes. This will represent both Japan and England as well as many other countries of the world.

18. *Properties*

(1) Flags for decorations and games. Draw these or borrow from Rotary Club.

(2) Milk bottles or Indian clubs for Poison Snake. There should be from twelve to fifteen of these, as you will need some for scrub rings.

(3) Papers and pencils for Flag Identification.

(4) Three putting practice boards (one will do) and golf balls. Three putters.

(5) Extra clothing for style show.

(6) Obstacles for Chinese Chicken—newspapers rolled up, sticks of wood, beanbags (any of these will serve).

(7) Five half-gallon crocks or small flowerpots holding about half a gallon. Tennis or other small rubber balls.

(8) Bottles for football game. Use same ones used in Poison Snake. Paste papers on bottom after they have been used in Poison Snake.

(9) Something to represent horses in steeplechase.

chapter 9

Newspaper Party

A NOVEL IDEA FOR AN EVENING OF FUN IS A NEWSPAPER PARTY. VERY little preparation is necessary, and the expense will be negligible. Still there is an opportunity to have a jolly good time.

1. *Invitation.*—The following is a suggested invitation:

Extra! Extra! Read all about it!
The big party's set for next Friday night.
There'll be lots of fun—don't doubt it,
And we must all be very bright.
For it's a Newspaper Party, no less,
And we'll get out the paper together.
"What's cookin'?"—you can't even guess,
So be there in spite of the weather.
Time and Place

2. *Decorations*—Black and white streamers of crepe paper. Newspaper pictures pinned on the curtains and draperies and at other places about the wall and room. These will be needed later for a game.

3. *Dividing into Groups.*—As the guests arrive, they should be given small cards on which are written either Editorial Department, Sports Department, Society Department, Comic Strip Department, or Current Events Department. These groups will work together in the games throughout the evening and then work together in getting out the paper. Someone stands at the door and gives out these cards in order, so that there shall be an equal number of each group. They are told to put these cards in their pockets or some place for safekeeping until they are ready to use them.

4. *Opening Mixer: Making Sentences.*—Pin on the shoulder of each guest a word. These words should be selected so that it is possible to make a lot of sentences from them. For the idea is to have the guests, by grouping together, make sentences. When a complete sentence has been formed, all those who take part in forming it have the privilege of writing it down. The following is an example of some sentences that may be cut up into words and distributed: "A handsome young man took his beautiful sister and mother out riding one afternoon in his snappy convertible. The car stopped. It was found that the engine was broken. A beautiful girl came by in her car and picked them up." It can easily be seen that a number of sentences may be formed by those having these words. For example: "A handsome young man was broke," "A beautiful girl picked up an engine," "A snappy girl picked up a handsome young man," and so on. Continue this game for about five tor ten minutes. Give a prize to the one who has the largest number of sentences.

5. *Newspaper Dresses.*—Ask the five groups—Editorial, Sports, Society, Comic Strip, and Current Events—to get together. Designate places for them to assemble, such as the corners of the room or the dining room or study. Each group is given a large bundle of newspapers and a paper of pins, and told to dress up a couple from their group. This couple then competes with all others dressed by the other groups for a prize.

This game may be lengthened by having each boy dress up a girl, and in case this is done, do not have them divided into groups. Let a boy choose a partner and dress her with newspapers.

It would be helpful to have a number of designs cut from fashion magazines for these dressmakers to copy.

6. *Judging the Winning Costumes.*—Those who have been dressed are then paraded before the judges, who pick the best costume. If all the girls are dressed by the boys, they might have a grand march. For the figures in this grand march see "Calendar Party," page 22.

7. *Current Events.*—Have each guest write down some bit of news he has read in the newspaper recently. Have the longest list

read. Have other items read that are on other lists. This will be both interesting and instructive.

8. *Newspaper Relay.*—Let the girls be matched against the boys in this relay. Have them line up facing a goal, and give each one two newspapers. At a given signal the front one in each line starts toward the goal. They have been told, however, that they can only advance by stepping on newspapers. So they have to place a newspaper down on the floor before they take every step. When the first one returns to the front of the line, the next one starts and the first one takes a position at the back of the line. Do not have the goal very far from the front of the line, as it is difficult to run far in this fashion.

9. *Crossword Puzzles.*—Call together again the five groups—Editorial, Sports, Society, Comic Strip, and Current Events. Give each group a crossword puzzle and a dictionary. Give prizes to the group that finishes first. Do not let this continue more than ten minutes; and if they are not finished, give a prize to the group that has made the most progress.

10. *Funny Paper Charades.*—Give to each group an envelope containing a funny paper. There should be two or three suggestions for charades in each envelope. The group is then to arrange to act out their charades and let the other guests guess what comic strip they represent. Most any of the guests will have his favorite comic strip, and each will be familiar with others. Let each group act out one, two, or three of the comic strip charades, depending upon the amount of time available.

11. *List of Newspapers.*—Have each guest write the names of all the newspapers he can think of. Give a prize to the one who has the largest list.

12. *Chinese Relay.*—Divide into two equal sides for a relay race. This may be done by forming a circle and counting off one and two. All the "ones" form one group and the "twos" the other. Lay down two rows of newspapers, each one of which is folded into a roll and fastened with a wrapper or rubber band, there being eight papers in each row about two feet apart. At a signal from the leader, the

first one in each line must hop over each newspaper without touching it and turn round and hop back over them. He then touches off the person on the front of the line and takes his place at the rear of the line. This continues until all have had a try. The group finishing first wins.

13. *Newspaper Terms in Pied Type.*—Guests are give the following terms in pied type and are asked to straighten out the letters.

    (1) Iroted. Editor.
    (2) Ublisherp. Publisher.
    (3) Wens. News.
    (4) Artex. Extra.
    (5) Sepsr. Press.
    (6) Adyil. Daily.
    (7) Buscribres. Subscriber.
    (8) Itocyse Tedori. Society Editor.
    (9) Ropetrer. Reporter.
    (10) Forpo Aedrer. Proof Reader.
    (11) Icyt Dteiro. City Editor.
    (12) Kame-pu nam. Make-up man.
    (13) Ginistrevda Erganam. Advertising Manager.
    (14) Dtecoiasas Ersps. Associated Press.
    (15) Culicrtanoi Regaman. Circulation Manager.
    (16) Linfa Inotdei. Final Edition.

14. *Newspaper Advertisement Relay.*—Line up the players of the different groups facing tables on which have been placed copies of a local newspaper all of the same date and four pairs of scissors. Give each player in each line the name of an advertisement. Have these written on slips of paper, and pass them out before the whistle blows. When the whistle blows, each one must run to the table, find his ad, cut it out, fold the paper back, run back, and touch off the next player, and take his place at the back of the line. The group that finishes first wins.

15. *Getting Out the Paper.*—Now the time has come to get out the paper. The five groups assemble, and the Editorial Department must produce an editorial on any subject. The Society Department must write up a society column. The Comic Strip editors must

produce some spice, the Sports Department must write all the sport news available, and the Current Events Department must assemble all the local news. While this is being done, reporters may go about from group to group trying to get news, and what is learned may be put in the paper. Allow about ten minutes for the writing of the parts.

16. *Reading the Paper.*—When the paper has been finished, it is then assembled and read. There probably will be a considerable amount of humor in it, and the group will enjoy reading it very much.

17. *Refreshments.*—As such a party as this may be held at any time of the year and has no connection with any particular kind of refreshments, serve any convenient refreshments.

18. *Properties*

(1) Cards on which have been written Editorial Department, Society Department, Sports Department, Comic Strip Department, and Current Events Department. These should be given to each guest so that there will be an equal number of each given out.
(2) Words to pin on guests for mixer.
(3) Plenty of newspapers for dresses and papers of pins.
(4) Papers and pencils for current events.
(5) Five crossword puzzles and five dictionaries.
(6) Five envelopes with two or more funny papers in them.
(7) Typewritten sheets with Pied Newspaper Terms on them.

chapter 10

St. Patrick's Day Party

(*COSTUME*)

IN THE MONTH OF MARCH COMES ST. PATRICK'S DAY, AND THE IRISH motif affords an excellent opportunity to plan for an enjoyable party. St. Patrick was the patron saint of Ireland. The setting and decorations and the atmosphere should be as typically Irish as possible. The pipe, the shillalah, the shamrock, pigs, and snakes should be in evidence, as St. Patrick is supposed to have chased the snakes out of Ireland.

1. *Costumes.*—The boys may wear green ties and shamrocks, while the girls may wear aprons and shamrocks in their hair. If it is not thought desirable to have the guests wear costumes of any nature, the hostess may have them make their costumes on arrival. Provide green and white paper with some cut-out shamrocks, snakes, and pipes, and have the boys make an apron out of the paper, decorating it with the snakes, shamrocks, and pipes; while the girls make a cap for the boys, decorating them in the same fashion. Require that all wear the costumes throughout the evening and that all talk with an Irish brogue.

2. *Invitation.*—The following is a suggested invitation for such a party:

> On St. Patrick's Day at eight o'clock,
> At Dixie Avenue, in the eight hundred block,
> We're giving a party, honoring St. Pat.
> We'll have a big time, we assure you of that.
> At the appointed time, be on the scene,
> With an Irish smile and "wearing of the green."

3. *Mixer: Prize Handshake.*—Prize handshake is a good mixer. Give a dime to a boy and a dime to a girl. Tell them that they are to give this dime to the tenth person who shakes hands with them and tells his or her name. If it is thought best to lengthen this mixer, it could be done by telling the persons who have the dimes to give them to the fifteenth person. However, the handshaking should continue until the leader's whistle blows, so that all will have an opportunity to meet and shake hands with all the others. Then when the whistle is blown, the persons who have been given the dimes can announce who gets them.

If the leader wishes, she may then tell this couple how to get rich in thirty days. "Take this dime. Double it every day. Tomorrow you will have 20 cents. In ten days you will have $51.20. Keep on doubling your money every day, and at the end of fifteen days you will have $1,638.40. Keep on doubling your money each day, and at the end of twenty days you will have $52,428.80. Keep on doubling your money every day, and at the end of thirty days you will have $53,687,091.20 each. All you have to do is just take this dime and double it every day for thirty days."

4. *They Kept the Pig in the Parlor.*—Each boy selects a partner, and all form a circle, the girls taking the boys' left arm. The piano plays the tune, "We Won't Get Home Until Morning," and all sing to this tune as they march:

> They kept the pig in the parlor,
> They kept the pig in the parlor,
> They kept the pig in the parlor,
>> For he was Irish, too.
>
> Stop and bow to your partner
> And take her by the right hand,
> Take your neighbor's left hand,
>> The grand right and left.
>
> Right hand to your partner,
> Left hand to your neighbor,

Right hand to the next one,
And all promenade.

They kept the pig in the parlor,
They kept the pig in the parlor,
They kept the pig in the parlor,
For he was Irish, too.

When they have finished the first verse and start on the second, which starts, "Stop and bow, and so forth," they all stop and bow to their partners. Then they follow the action in the words of the song. They weave in and out, the boys going clockwise and the girls counter-clockwise. They continue doing this and singing until they reach the end of the third verse to "All promenade." Then they start marching again and singing, "They kept the pig in the parlor." This they continue as long as desired, but it will take about three times to do it well. It may help to have the song mimeographed so that all may read it all before the play starts.

5. *The Many-Sided Pat.*—The following writing game is apropos for the occasion:

(1) A Pat that mends.   Patch.
(2) A Pat that loves his country.   Patriot.
(3) A Pat that protects his invention.   Patent.
(4) A Pat used by the dressmaker.   Pattern.
(5) What Pat inherits.   Patrimony.
(6) A Pat we all follow.   Path.
(7) A Pat that is good to eat.   Patty.
(8) A Pat that does sentry duty.   Patrol.
(9) A Pat that is old.   Patriarch.
(10) A Pat that stirs up tender emotions.   Pathetic.
(11) A Pat that the doctor welcomes.   Patient.
(12) A Pat that sounds on the windows.   Patter.
(13) A Pat that is a kind of quilt.   Patchwork.
(14) A Pat that acts fatherly.   Paternal.
(15) A Pat that is part of a Spanish type house.   Patio.

6. *Greased Pig Relay.*—Divide the group into two equal parts. This may be done by counting off one and two, the "ones" forming

one group and the "twos" the other. Have them line up on opposite sides of the room facing each other. At a signal from the leader the ones at the head of the line start weaving in and out through the players in his line. He must go all the way to the foot and back in this way. The second player must then start, being careful to first go around the person at the head of the line and go all the way down to the foot and back to his place. This continues until every player has traveled the full length of his line and back, and concludes when the last player, the one at the foot, makes the run. The side that finishes first wins.

7. *Circle Blarney.*—The girls form a circle in the center and the boys on the outside. Music is played as they march around, the boys clockwise and the girls counter-clockwise. When the music stops, the boy and the girl in front of him must blarney until the music starts again.

8. *Putting the Shamrock in Ireland.*—Have a map of Europe, and have players, blindfolded, try to put the shamrock in Ireland. If there is no large map available, trace one or draw one that will do. Players may be turned around two or three times before they are started and must pin the shamrock at the place where they first touch.

9. *Blowing Bubbles.*—Provide several bowls and pipes for bubble blowing. The following recipe makes a good bubble solution: Fill a quart jar two-thirds full of boiling water, add three ounces of castile soap finely shaven, a teaspoonful of sugar, and four table-spoonfuls of glycerine. When this is shaken thoroughly, it should be strained through a cloth.

Give a prize to the one who blows the largest bubble; the one who can blow the largest number from one dip into the solution; the one who can make his bubble go the highest. Use a cord for a goal at one end of the room and have a race, giving those in the race a fan. See who can fan a bubble across the goal line with the fan.

10. *Shamrock Hunt.*—Have cut-out shamrocks hidden about the room. Give prize to the one who finds the largest number.

11. *Kissing the Blarney Stone Relay.*—Place a stone or something

to represent a stone on the floor. Players line up for a relay in two or more equal groups. At the sound of the leader's whistle the first one runs to the stone, gets down on his knees, kisses the stone, and runs back, touching the person at the front of the line and taking his place at the back of the line. The group that finishes first wins.

12. *Singing Irish Songs.*—Many of the fine Irish songs are familiar, such as "It's a Long Way to Tipperary," "Where the River Shannon Flows," "Mother Machree," "The Last Rose of Summer," "My Wild Irish Rose," "Wearing of the Green," "When Irish Eyes Are Smiling," "Oft in the Stilly Night." Have these songs mimeographed and give a copy to each guest. Have someone play who has been notified in advance and gotten the music necessary, and this will be a very enjoyable part of the evening. Almost anyone can sing a song when they know the tune and have the words on a song sheet.

13. *Green Things.*—Provide each guest with a paper and pencil for this game. Have them write the answers. It will be better to have the questions mimeographed on the sheets of paper given the guests:

(1) A person easily hoodwinked. Greenhorn.
(2) A town in Maine, Kentucky, Tennessee, and other states. Greenville.
(3) Name of a Revolutionary General General Green.
(4) Where actors meet. Greenroom.
(5) A valuable paper. Greenback.
(6) A kind of plum. Greengage.
(7) A good fruit to give you the stomach ache. Green apples.
(8) A house in which flowers are kept. Greenhouse.
(9) A Bible tree. Green bay tree.
(10) A very cold country. Greenland.
(11) A town in Kentucky. Bowling Green.
(12) What kind of a monster is jealousy? Green-eyed.
(13) An internationally famous village. Greenwich.
(14) A dealer in fresh vegetables. Green grocer.
(15) What the moon is said to be made of. Green cheese
(16) The green that beautifies a country home. Greensward.
(17) What you are if you can't answer these. Green.

14. *Potato Roll.*—No St. Patrick's party would be complete with-

out a Potato Relay. Have this in a little different way. Give each person on the front a table knife, and with this he must roll the potato. Mark out on the floor a circle about four inches in diameter, and the potato must roll into this circle and stop. Then the potato is to be rolled back into a circle of similar size near the head of the line. Have each one roll the potato and take his place at the back of the line. The leader will have to insist that the potato actually be rolled into the circle each time. At the beginning the potato must be in the circle each time. This is a game with plenty of life in it.

15. *Green Pig.*—Place a mirror in the bottom of a box and cover the sides of the box with green paper. Use a green light over the box and have it in an otherwise darkened room. Let the players go to see it one at a time. When they look into the box, they will see their picture in green, the Green Pig.

16. *Irish Terms Pied.*—Have these words mimeographed on slips of paper. Guests are to write the correct words:

(1) Okcr. Cork.
(2) Ftselab. Belfast.
(3) Ldunbi. Dublin.
(4) Ilicermk. Limerick.
(5) Lainkelyr. Killarney.
(6) Piyreprat. Tipperary.
(7) Lyenrab Elctas. Blarney Castle.
(8) Nonanhs Vreri. Shannon River.
(9) Etdedsre Avligel. Deserted Village.

17. *Feeding the Pig.*—The St. Patrick's Day party may be turned into a pay social by using the Circulating Pig. This should be started about the first of January. Get an inexpensive china or plastic pig bank. The time to open it will be at the St. Patrick's Day party. Start three or four of these pigs, one in each section of the city. The one who starts it should take it with some money in it and with something she has baked to a neighbor. She should take the poem with it. Some women will prefer to give potted plants or flowers. The pigs should then be opened at the party. The following is a suggested poem to go with the pig:

I am bringing you a pig, perhaps you think it's funny.
The pig was not just given me—in fact, it cost real money.
Now here is how I got the pig, and why it's brought to you:
It is a scheme of raising cash, to see our —————* through.
The one who brought the pig to me brought something for the table,
I just paid what I thought 'twas worth, just what I felt able.
I'm asking you to do the same, for what I've brought to you,
And drop your money in the pig, as all are asked to do.
Then cook something good to eat, and take it to a friend,
And take along the little verse which to you I send.
And please do not keep the pig, but just a day or so,
We want him in every home where he can possibly go.

Someone should be in charge of this plan so that they can see that the pigs are kept in circulation. If this is not done, one of the pigs may get lost or someone may keep the pig a week or two. Open the pigs as a part of the St. Patrick's party and report the money collected.

18. *Irish Jokes.*—Have each guest tell a Pat and Mike joke. If this is thought impractical, select some of the guests and have them tell stories. Others will in all probability take part spontaneously.

19. *Familiar Snakes.*—Have the questions typewritten or mimeographed in advance:

(1) Worn all the year round. Garter.
(2) The baby plays with it and doesn't get hurt. Rattle.
(3) Worn by an Indian. Moccasin.
(4) A snake that consumes our breakfast food. Egg eater.
(5) A snake like a fast horse. Racer.
(6) A name given to northern sympathizers during the civil war. Copperhead.
(7) A snake the color of night. Black.

20. *Refreshments.*—Sliced ham, potato salad, coffee or tea. The host might announce that each guest would be required to pay for his refreshments and that the price is plainly marked on each. The sandwiches may be marked: "One smile each" or "One laugh

---

* Insert name of class or organization circulating pig.

each"; the potato salad, "Four kind words"; the coffee, "One yawn," and so forth. This will prove a very amusing stunt.

21. *Properties*

(1) White and green paper, paste and scissors for making caps and aprons. Also shamrocks, pipes, and snakes to decorate them with.

(2) Two dimes for mixer.

(3) Papers prepared for the Many-Sided Pat.

(4) Map of Ireland. Shamrock to pin on it.

(5) Pipes, solution for blowing bubbles.

(6) Shamrocks for hunt hidden about room.

(7) Irish songs mimeographed. Arrange for someone to play in advance.

(8) Papers prepared for Green Things, Irish Terms Pied, Familiar Snakes.

(9) Potatoes for potato roll.

chapter 11

Progressive Dinner Party

THE PROGRESSIVE DINNER PARTY OR LUNCHEON MAY BE AS ELABORATE or as simple as desired.

A group or a small circle of friends might plan a holiday dinner and progress from home to home for each course. A family who has the custom of dining together on holidays might go to the different homes of the family circle for the various courses; and if the Christmas holiday is being observed, it could be arranged for the family Christmas tree to be at the home where the last course is being served.

The dinner might take the form of an International Progressive Dinner, with the various courses chosen as typical foods of the different countries. At each home or "country" a short talk on current events of that particular country could be given. If the group giving the dinner has a committee on "public affairs," it would be well to turn the program over to such a committee.

Another form of planning a dinner of this sort would be the selection of countries in which a church group has missionary work. At each "country" or home visited the work and workers of that field could be discussed.

The homes should be decorated in the national colors of the country visited, and, in case the missionary idea is used, pictures of the missionaries and of the field where they serve might be displayed about the rooms of the home.

If the homes to be visited are in walking distance of one another, the group should meet and be divided into couples and go to the home where the first course is to be served. After each course new couples should be formed and go together to the next homes. Of course, if the homes are widely separated, it will be necessary to go in cars.

Several methods of forming couples are here suggested:

The girls may be placed behind a sheet with a strong light beyond so that their silhouette is thrown on the curtain. The boys should then be allowed to guess which girl is there and thus secure their partner.

Postcards may be cut in two, and as the couples enter each person should be given one half of a card. Later on these cards are to be matched to form partners for the next course. Care should be exercised in giving out the cards so that the same persons will not be together for the next course.

Again place all the girls behind a heavy curtain. One at a time they raise a hand above the curtain. The boys try to guess the hand, and when successful thus secure a partner.

The same thing may be done with the feet, putting them under the curtain. Of course the girls will attempt to baffle the boys by exchanging rings or shoes. For the sake of variation the girls might be allowed to guess concerning the boys.

The following are suggestions for menus:

SOUP

Italy—Macaroni or noodle soup.
Peru—Lima bean soup.
Scotland—Barley broth.

MEAT COURSE

Turkey—Roast turkey and dressing.
Switzerland—Swiss steak.
China—Chop suey or chow mein.
England—Roast beef.
Mexico or Chile—Chili.
Germany—Pork ribs and sauerkraut.
Hungary—Goulash.

The vegetables should be chosen to conform to the meat course.

SALAD COURSE

France—Lettuce with French dressing.
Russia—Lettuce with Russian dressing.
China—Chinese cabbage salad.
Hawaii—Hawaiian pineapple salad.

DESSERT

United States—Pie (almost any kind).
Japan—Cherry pie.
France—French ice cream.
England—Plum pudding.

AFTER DINNER COURSE

Brazil—Coffee and mints.

The following are suggested as games to be used before the courses: In one of the homes supply guests with slips of paper and pencil. Arrange about the wall pictures of notable places or scenes typical of different countries. Number these and ask the guests to identify them by number. The following are suggested:

Westminster Abbey.   England.
Eiffel Tower.   Paris.
St. Peter's.   Rome.
White House.   United States.
Pyramids or Sphinx.   Egypt.
Leaning Tower of Pisa.   Italy.
Taj Mahal.   India.
Scene in the Alps.   Switzerland.
Eskimo and dog sled.   Alaska.
Cherry blossoms or Japanese house.   Japan.
Kangaroos.   Australia.
Bengal tiger.   India.
Victoria Falls.   Africa.
Picture of geyser.   Yellowstone National Park.

Another game that might be played at one of the homes is the Game of Nations. The following are suggested to us by the *World Outlook*. What nation is the:

Actor's nation?   Impersonation.
Pest nation?   Extermination.
Teacher's nation?   Explanation.
Smallpox nation?   Vaccination.
Soothsayer's nation?   Divination.
A flower nation?   Carnation.
The politician's nation?   Nomination.
Impure nation?   Contamination.
Resolute nation?   Determination.
King's nation?   Coronation.
The deluded nation?   Hallucination.
Writer's nation?   Imagination.
Benevolent nation?   Donation.
Charming nation?   Fascination.
Church nation?   Denomination.
Climax nation?   Culmination.
Start of nations?   Germination.
Astonished nation?   Consternation.
End of a nation?   Termination.

Properties

(1) Pictures of famous or well-known places in different countries; pencil and paper for each guest for country identification game.

(2) Copy of questions for Game of Nations for each guest.

chapter 12

Pirate Party[1]
(*COSTUME*)

A PIRATE PARTY WILL APPEAL TO THE ROMANTIC SIDE OF ALMOST ANY-
one's character. It would be well for those in charge of such a party
to reread Robert Louis Stevenson's *Treasure Island* and refresh their
memory concerning this adventuresome tale.

1. *Invitation.*—The invitation might be written on an old paper
burned around the edges, or it might be on a cardboard dagger,
written in red ink. Another suggestion would be a cardboard copy
of a skull and crossbones with the invitation written on that. Having decided where the party is to be held, a pirate map showing the
location might be sent to each guest to serve as an invitation. The
following is a suggestion for an invitation:

> On Friday the fifteenth we set sail;
> Be here at eight bells without fail.
> We're off seeking treasure of diamonds and gold;
> So come dressed as a pirate most bold.
> The crew is made up of buccaneers of renown;
> No cleverer crew could ever be found.

2. *Costumes.*—This should be a costume party, or how else could
one get into the real spirit of the affair? The boys should wear walking shorts or an old pair of trousers slashed at the knees, colored
shirts, black being the pirate color, bandanas, faces colored with
rouge, mustaches, and penciled eyebrows. An improvised dagger
would finish off the costume. The girls should dress much the same,
with the exception, of course, of dresses, which could be patterned

[1] Prepared with the assistance of Mrs. Roy G. Ross, Indianapolis, Ind.

after a gypsy or Spanish style dress. Judge the costumes and give prizes for the best costume.

3. *Decorations.*—Skull, crossbones, and black flags are emblematic of pirates, and these should be used in decorating for the party. A room might be arranged to resemble a ship, with an entrance in the form of a gangplank. Also a pirate's den might be arranged for, and with colored lights and long cardboard swords and daggers a weird effect might be created.

4. *Mixing Game: Pirate Keeno.*—When the guests enter, they are each given a pirate name taken from Robert Louis Stevenson's *Treasure Island.* Of course all the characters in *Treasure Island* are men; so it will be necessary to put a Miss or a Mrs. before these names. The following is a list of names of these pirates: Black Dog, Billy Bones, Captain Flint, Dirk, Jim Hawkins, Long John Silver, Squire Trewlawney, Dr. Livesey, Tom Morgan, Captain Smollett, Job Anderson, Barbecue, Captain Kidd, Tom, Alan, Ben Gunn, Isreal Hands, Abraham Gray, Mr. John Hunter, Dick Joyce, Thomas Redruth, O'Brien, George Merry. Other pirate names that are familiar to the group may be used, such as Gasparilla.

As the guests come in, a pirate's name which has been written upon a slip of paper is pinned on the guest. After the guests have all assembled, the hostess gives to each one a sheet of paper on which has been drawn sixteen squares about an inch and a half square. There are four squares each way. The guests are then given pencils and told to go to other guests and fill up each one of their sixteen blanks with a pirate name, copying the name on the piece of paper that has been pinned on the guest. After this has been done, these names are taken off and put in a box, and are drawn out one by one, and as the name is called the one who had that name is to stand so that all can see. The guests have been given grains of corn or sixteen lima beans; and when a name is called that he has on his card, he puts down a grain of corn on that name. Whenever he has four grains of corn in a row, either vertically or horizontally, he cries out "Keeno." The game then stops until all grains of corn have been taken off, and they continue as before, calling out the names until someone else has a keeno, or until all the guests have been introduced by their pirate name.

5. *Pieces of Eight.*—To each guest is given a sheet from a magazine which has been cut into a picture puzzle of eight or more pieces. They are to reproduce the picture. Give a prize to the one who does this quickest.

6. *Treasure Hunt.*—Of course a pirate party would be incomplete without a treasure hunt. One may be used that requires quite a good deal of time, or it may be used indoors, having the guests look for the treasure hidden somewhere about the room or about the house. Clues may be given by the leader by reading a letter or furnishing a map.

See "The Treasure Hunt Party," page 155, for additional suggestions. You will also find in this party a number of writing games, such as Hidden Flowers and Hidden Birds, which could be used in connection with a Pirate Party.

7. *Pirate Stagecoach.*—We are giving below an excerpt from Robert Louis Stevenson's *Treasure Island,* in which will be found the names of things associated with a pirate ship. The leader is to read this excerpt after each one of the players has been named. When a player's name is called, he is required to get up and turn around or to walk around his chair. When the leader reads the pronoun "I," all the players must change places. The reader then tries to get a place; and if he succeeds, the one left out must continue the story where he left off. The pronoun "I" is used eleven times in the excerpt given. The following names will be found in the reading and should be given before the reading starts to the players: Bowsprit, keel, jib, deck, forecastle, mainsail, afterdeck, rudder, mast, bulwark, bow, sea, water, schooner, scuppers, wind, main boom, stern, tiller, chest, hands, breeze, island, weather, Hispaniola, wind, handkerchief.

The following excerpt is taken from the first and last parts of Chapter XXV, "I Strike the Jolly Roger":

I had scarce gained a position on the bowsprit, when the flying jib flapped and filled upon the other tack with a report like a gun. The schooner trembled to her keel under the reverse; but next moment, the other sails still drawing, the jib flapped back again and hung idle.

This had nearly tossed me off into the sea; and now I lost no time, crawled back along the bowsprit, and tumbled head foremost on the deck.

I was on the lee side of the forecastle, and the mainsail, which was still drawing, concealed from me a certain portion of the afterdeck. Not a soul was to be seen. The planks, which had not been swabbed since the mutiny, bore the print of many feet; and an empty bottle, broken by the neck, tumbled to and fro like a live thing in the scuppers.

Suddenly the Hispaniola came right into the wind. The jibs behind me cracked aloud; the rudder slammed to; the whole ship gave a sickening heave and shudder, and at the same moment the main boom swung inboard, the sheet groaning in the blocks, and showed me the lee afterdeck.

There were the two watchmen, sure enough: Redcap on his back, as stiff as a handspike, with his arms stretched out like those of a crucifix, and his teeth showing through his open lips; Isreal Hands propped against the bulwarks, his chin on his chest, his hands lying open before him on the deck, his face as white, under its tan, as a tallow candle.

For a while the ship kept bucking and sidling like a vicious horse, the sails filling, now on one tack, now on another, and the boom swinging to and fro till the mast groaned aloud under the strain. Now and again, too, there would come a cloud of light sprays over the bulwark, and a heavy blow of the ship's bows against the swell: so much heavier weather was made of it by this great rigged ship than by my homemade, lopsided coracle, now gone to the bottom of the sea.

At every jump of the schooner Redcap slipped to and fro; but—what was ghastly to behold—neither his attitude nor his fixed teeth-disclosing grin was anyway disturbed by this rough usage. At every jump, too, Hands appeared still more to sink into himself and settle down upon the deck, his feet sliding ever the farther out, and the whole body canting toward the stern, so that his face became, little by little, hid from me; and at last I could see nothing beyond his ear and the frayed ringlet of one whisker.

Then I lashed the tiller and went below to my own chest, where I got a soft silk handkerchief of my mother's. With this, and with my aid, Hands bound up the great bleeding stab he had received in the thigh, and after he had eaten a little and had a swallow or two more of the brandy, he began to pick up visibly, sat straighter up, spoke louder and clearer, and looked in every way another man.

The breeze served us admirably. We skimmed before it like a bird, the coast of the island flashing by, and the view changing every minute. Soon we were past the highlands and bowling beside low, sandy country, sparsely dotted with dwarf pines, and soon we were beyond that again, and had turned the corner of the rocky hill that ends the island on the north.

I was greatly elated with my new command, and pleased with the bright, sunshiny weather and these different prospects of the coast. *I* had now plenty of water and good things to eat, and my conscience, which had smitten me hard for my desertion, was quieted by the great conquest *I* had made. *I* should, *I* think, have had nothing left me to desire for the eyes of the coxswain as they followed me derisively about the deck, and the odd smile that appeared continually on his face. It was a smile that had in it something both of pain and weakness—a haggard, old man's smile; but there was, besides that, a grain of derision, a shadow of treachery in his expression as he craftily watched, and watched, and watched me at my work.

8. *Victim.*—The leader has cards numbered from one to the number of guests in the room. These may be made from any small pieces of cardboard. Each guest is given a number and told to keep his number secret. It is explained that the person who holds number one is to be the "victim," number two the "criminal," number three the "prosecuting attorney," number four the "attorney for the defense," number five the "judge," numbers six to seventeen the "jury," and the rest may be summoned as witnesses.

The lights are then turned out, and the victim, number one, is supposed to play dead, number two is supposed to act like he has killed someone, number three then shows up and begins to question him, number four to defend him, and the judge to preside over the court, and so the case continues. The jury then get together and sentence the criminal.

This may be done a number of times and, if carried out properly, will create a lot of good fun.

9. *Walking the Plank.*—No pirate party could be an orthodox party unless the victims had to walk the plank. Each person is told that he must walk the plank blindfolded and jump over the pan of water at the end of the plank. After he is blindfolded, the pan of water is removed. The unwilling victim jumping wildly in the air

in an attempt to jump over the water will occasion much merriment. In the game of victim suggested above, if nothing else can be thought of as a sentence for the criminal, he may be sentenced to walk the plank.

10. *Chasing the Pirate.*—This is quite an active game and should not be used unless the party is held in a large recreation room or out of doors. One player is the policeman and another the pirate. The policeman chases the pirate; but if any other player runs between the policeman and the pirate, the policeman must then chase that one. If the policeman catches the pirate, the pirate then becomes the policeman, and the former policeman can choose another pirate to be chased, and so the game continues.

11. *Refreshments.*—Serve sandwiches and with them a glass of ginger ale or apple cider.

12. *Properties*

(1) A paper with sixteen squares on it, a slip of paper with a pirate name on it, a pencil, and sixteen grains of corn or beans for each guest. A duplicate set of pirate names in a box.

(2) Magazine pages with pictures cut into eight or more pieces.

(3) Cards for the game of Victim.

chapter 13

Try-Your-Luck Party

IF YOU CAN ARRANGE THIS PARTY ON THE NIGHT OF FRIDAY THE thirteenth, it would be much more effective. But it is not necessary to have it then, as any thirteenth day would be suitable, as Thursday or Tuesday. However, this party may be held on any other day and leave out the idea of thirteen altogether.

1. *Invitation.*—Send guests the following or a similar invitation:

> Are you one of those who like to try your luck?
> Do you blame it on Dame Fortune when you're stuck?
> If you are lucky, you will join us Friday night—
> You will have a chance to try your luck all right.
> Bring your rabbit's foot and be on hand at eight;
> The place is Harry's, and 'twill be unlucky to be late.

2. *Decorations.*—Crepe paper streamers would be sufficient for decorations. As there is no particular color scheme, any kind of decorations, such as potted plants or flowers, would be suitable.

3. *Opening Mixer: Brunswick Stew.*—Pin on the backs of guests the names of the ingredients of Brunswick stew, as beef, potatoes, turnips, carrots, salt, rice, pepper, onions, water, celery, tomatoes, aitchbone, pork, parsnips, butter. There are fifteen ingredients. The guests that gets them all written first wins. Of course this will be difficult to do, as one must try to keep others from reading what is on his back.

4. *Selecting a Partner: Catch as Catch Can.*—Take the boys into one room and the girls into another. Line them up in any way they happen to come and in single file. They march out, and the first boy and first girl become partners. The second boy and the second girl, and so until all are matched.

5. *Try Your Luck on a Shorthand Puzzle.*—Have the following letters written on a blank sheet of paper. Guests are asked to write out common combinations of letters, as F. O. B., and so forth. You will note that there are seventy-seven of these letters—that is, seven times eleven:

U	W	P	A	C	M	U	W	S	U	N
T	I	A	A	B	V	A	O	L	M	K
C	A	N	C	B	A	O	R	E	C	K
S	Y	O	I	O	I	O	F	Y	R	F
S	A	N	R	P	C	O	A	D	W	D
O	S	D	T	S	U	P	D	A	O	A
P	O	C	Y	P	F	O	D	M	B	C

The following are combinations that can be made from these letters. The letters should be checked off as used, for none can be used more than once:

U. N.	U. C. Y. M.	Y. W. C. A.
U. S. A.	W. C. T. U.	B. P. O. E.
M. D.	R. S. V. P.	I. O. O. F.
A. W. O. L.	P. S.	N. B. C.
S. O. S.	P. T. A.	K. P.
C. O. D.	F. O. B.	Y. M. C. A.
I. O. U.	A. A. A.	R. F. D.
A. D.	O. K.	C. I. O.
		D. A. R.

6. *Try Your Luck on Ringing Rosy.*—Divide the group into two parts. This may be done by numbering off one and two and letting the ones form one group and the twos another. Have a boy, preferably a slim one, to dress up in some kind of comic girl's costume and pose as Rosy. Each group is given a large barrel hoop, and from a point about ten feet away each tries to ring Rosy. Give a prize of lillipops to each one of the group that rings Rosy the most times.

7. *Try Your Luck on Telling the Truth.*—Prepare a list of ques-

tions somewhat like the following and ask different ones in the group to answer correctly the question asked them, telling them that they are on their honor to tell the truth:

(1) What do you think is Mary Brown's worst fault?
(2) How much did you pay for your suit of clothes?
(3) How many times have you been proposed to?
(4) What is your pet aversion?
(5) Have you ever met anyone that was as smart as you, and who?
(6) How old do you take John Brown to be?
(7) Would you marry Harry Smith if he asked you?
(8) Who do you think is the handsomest man in the room?
(9) Who do you think is the homeliest man in the room?
(10) If Buddy Thomas were your child, what would you do to him?
(11) Do you like to hear Mabel White sing?
(12) Tell your worst bad habit.
(13) State your age.
(14) Are you in love, and with whom?
(15) When is the last time you went to church?
(16) Have you ever been kissed?
(17) Have you ever been slapped?
(18) What is your greatest talent?
(19) What is your best virtue?
(20) Who in the room do you think would make the most congenial companion?

8. *Try Your Luck at Guessing Slogans.*—Look through a number of current magazines and find about twenty slogans used by companies to advertise their products. It will not be difficult to find well-known slogans in automobile, cigarette, air line, soap, radio, and television advertisements. For example, look for such as: "The instrument of the immortals" (Steinway pianos) ; "When it rains it pours" (Morton's salt). Have this list mimeographed or make enough carbon copies for your guests with a typewriter. The guests are given the lists of slogans and asked to fill in the names of the articles being advertised.

Another way to do this—and by far an easier way—would be to write out these slogans and number them. Pin them on the curtains or drapes. Then give each guest a blank sheet of paper and have them guess the article advertised, identifying it by the number of its slogan. This will eliminate the necessity for preparing the sheets of copy in advance.

A third way to play this game is to cut advertisements from the magazines, cut off or cover up the name of the product advertised, and pin these pictures to the draperies. Each one should be numbered and the guests should be supplied with numbered sheets of paper and pencils. Answers should be written in by number. No matter which method is used in playing the game, the guest who gets the largest number correct should be given a prize or some special recognition.

9. *Try Your Luck on Feminine Wardrobe.*—Have a girl dressed up in all the clothing she can get on. In addition to the regular clothing, there should be a coat, scarf, gloves, veil, hat, overshoes, jewelry, handbag, and anything else that she can have on or pick up. Have the girl stand in a door where all can see her, or walk about the room for one minute. Then she retires, and the guests are given five minutes to write a list of all the things she was wearing. The one who has the largest number should be asked to read his list. You will always find that the girl is credited with having on more than she could possibly have.

10. *Try Your Luck on Gentlemen's Apparel.*—Tell the group to get ready, that you are going to try a similar game with a boy. But when the boy appears, he is to have on nothing but swimming trunks. Ask the guests then to write the names of apparel that he should have or could have worn. Give a prize for the longest list and have it read.

11. *Lucky Spots.*—Have someone play a lively tune. Couples, those that were originally matched, find each other and march about the room. When the leader's whistle blows, or the music stops, all stop and stand where they are. The leader then announces the lucky spot, which should have been picked out and written down in advance. The lucky spots may be as follows: The couple nearest the piano, the couple nearest the front door, the couple nearest the

mantel, and so forth. This could be done a number of times, and each time the couples change partners.

12. *Things That Are Unlucky.*—Have the guests write a list of all the things they can think of that are considered unlucky, such as walking under a ladder, a black cat crossing your path, and so on. For further suggestion look in index under "Bad Omens."

13. *Refreshments.*—"Try your luck on selecting your refreshments," should be written on the top of a fake menu card, such as the one suggested in the April Fish Party. See Index under "April Fish Menu."

After the fake menu any desirable refreshment may be served, such as ice cream and cake or sandwiches and hot chocolate.

14. *Properties*

(1) The ingredients of a Brunswick stew written upon slips of paper in duplicate or triplicate, depending upon the number of guests.

(2) Shorthand Puzzle typed with carbons or mimeographed.

(3) Two or more large barrel hoops for Ringing Rosy.

(4) List of questions or book available for Try Your Luck on Telling the Truth.

(5) Slogans typewritten for each guest or pinned on the curtains. Pencils and papers.

(6) Arrangements made for girl and boy to dress for the apparel stunts.

(7) Papers and pencils for Things That Are Unlucky.

(8) Fake menu cards prepared in advance, and the articles to be served as fake refreshments.

chapter 14

All-Fools' Party

April first. Stunts and pranks are permissible on this day. Funny an excellent occasion for an evening of fun. The day has come to have the idea of backwardness. Meals are served backward or things done backward are frequent on All-Fools' Day. As a person who is foolish is said to be "nutty" or "a nut," the nut idea has gotten into April first, Stunts and pranks are permissible on this day. Funny situations are the vogue.

1. *Invitation.*—The following is a suggested invitation:

> On All-Fools' Night its our intention
> To gather for a Rube Convention,
> The Nuts will gather at the hour of eight;
> We know no more, but don't be late.
> Bring a dime-store toy that makes a noise,
> And leave behind your dignity and poise.

2. *The Setting for the Party.*—One suggestion would be to have everything backward. The hostess will meet the guests at the kitchen door and ask them to come again, and express the hope that they have enjoyed the party. The clock might strike eleven as the guests enter, and the refreshments may be served at the beginning of the party instead of at the close.

If it is not desirable to follow out the above suggestion, another idea would be to put a sign on the front door: "Wet paint; use the back door (or the side door)." Then have another sign on the back door (or the side door) which says "April Fool. Go back and use the front door."

Have some surprises. Put noise-making balloons under the chair cushions and have some jack-in-the-boxes sitting around. Have some candy made out of cotton and covered with chocolate setting on the table marked, "Have one," or perhaps not marked at all.

3. *The Foot That Comes Off.*—Require all the boys, instead of shaking hands with the girls, to shake the girl's foot instead. A row of girls are seated with one leg across the other knee, and the last girl has improvised an artificial leg, which when shaken comes off. This might be made by stuffing a stocking and putting a shoe on it and arranging so that the real foot and leg will be concealed. The room should be dark, and the boys should be brought in one at a time and asked to shake the foot of the girls present. This might be arranged in another way, and the host might put up a sign that, instead of shaking the hand of the host, it is asked that guests shake the foot, and the foot, when shaken, might be arranged so that it will come off.

4. *Fishing for Partners.*—A curtain has been stretched over a door, leaving an opening of about a foot at the top. Small fishing poles with bent pin hook are provided. Two or three of these will be enough. Let either the boys or girls fish for partners. The hook is thrown over the curtain, and the host puts on the name of the fisher's partner.

5. *The Grab Bag.*—Each person has been asked to bring some toy from the dime store that makes a noise. As the guests enter these are put into the "Grab Bag." This bag might be a cloth sack, or even a box. The guest is to put his hand in and take out the first package he touches. These are then opened, and the guests will get much amusement by playing with them.

6. *Threading the Needle.*—Select three or four persons for a needle-threading contest. The leader tells them that the object is to see who can thread the needle quickest with one eye closed. The needle is easily threaded, but the fun comes when the guests see that the ones who have held their hands over one eye of the contestants have had lampblack on them, so that one eye of each is quite black.

7. *Play Mimic.*—Two or three persons are sent into an adjoining

room, and other guests are brought in one by one to guess the name of the game. One person tells them as they enter the door that they are to guess the name of the game that is being played in the room. As they enter those in the room imitate everything they do and repeat everything they say. If they guess the name of the game, or if they do not guess it in just a few moments, they are told what it is and remain in the room, themselves joining in imitating and mimicking others who enter. If the room gets overcrowded, first comers should leave.

8. *The Art Museum.*—While some are guessing the name of the Mimic game, others might be taken to the museum. There they will find the following exhibits:

The Watch on the Rhine. Watch on an orange peeling.
A Diamond Pin. A dime and pin.
A Marble Bust. A broken marble.
A Swimming Match. A match floating on water.
Peacemakers. A pair of scissors.
One-eyed Monster. Sewing needle.
Tamed Groundhog. Links of sausage.
Paradise. A pair of dice.
Slippers. Banana peel.
A Perfect Foot. Twelve inches. A ruler one foot long.
Something to Adore. A doorknob.
Champion American Tumblers. Three glasses.
Ten Carat Ring. Ring made from ten carrots.
Lost Souls. Pair of old shoe soles.
Something Out of King Tut's Tomb. Anything not in it.

9. *Questions and Crazy Answers.*—Have the group seated in a circle with the leader in the center. The leader asks each person a question, to which that person makes some reply, either foolish or serious as he chooses. After the leader has asked a question to each one in the circle, then he informs them that they are to make the same answer as they made the first time to every question asked them during the playing of the game, and that if they laugh when they make their answer, they must take the leader's place. This will create some funny situations. For example, the leader might ask,

"What did you do with that bottle of Coca-Cola?" to which the guest would reply, "Drank it." The next one might ask that person the question, "Where did you get that suit of clothes?" and the answer must be, "Drank it." Suppose the first question asked one player was, "What is the masculine of hen?" to which he would reply, "Rooster." The next question might be, "Which do you like best, brunettes or blonds?" and his answer must be, "Rooster." Anyone laughing must take the leader's place and ask questions.

10. *Jumbled Statements.*—Give each guest the following statements written on a sheet of paper, leaving enough space between the lines to make a correct statement:

(1) Easter Sunday was the wife of Billy Sunday.
(2) The Epistles were the wives of the Apostles.
(3) Helen Keller was a well-known evangelist.
(4) Easter Sunday comes on May 30.
(5) Palm Beach is a fashionable summer resort.
(6) Memorial Day commemorates the ending of the World War I.
(7) Calvin Coolidge was deaf, dumb, and blind.
(8) Lindbergh flew over both the North and South poles.
(9) Will Rogers was an advocate of free silver.
(10) Thomas A. Edison was first to fly the Atlantic alone.
(11) Clarence Darrow was a temperance advocate.
(12) Richard E. Byrd invented the incandescent lamp.
(13) Billy Sunday stopped a police strike in Boston.
(14) Frances E. Willard was a noted criminal lawyer.

Notes for the Leader: Easter Sunday comes on the first Sunday after the first full moon after the twentieth of March; the Epistles are books in the New Testament; Helen Keller was deaf, dumb, and blind; Palm Beach is a Florida winter resort; Memorial Day was instituted to honor the dead of all U. S. wars; Calvin Coolidge stopped a police strike in Boston; Lindbergh was the first to fly the Atlantic alone; Will Rogers was a humorist; Thomas A. Edison invented the incandescent lamp; Clarence Darrow was a famous criminal lawyer; Richard E. Byrd flew over both the North and South poles; Billy Sunday was a famous evangelist; Frances E. Willard was a temperance advocate.

11. *Are You What We Suspected?*—Prepare sheets for each guest marked off as the one illustrated below. They are to fill in these blanks. It will require at least ten or fifteen minutes for this. The leader should explain that the idea is to use words that others will not think about. After the leader's whistle blows and all have

THIS IS TO FIND OUT IF YOU REALLY ARE WHAT
WE HAVE SUSPECTED—AN

	A	P	R	I	L	F	O	O	L
The name of something we eat									
The name of a Bible character									
The name of a girl									
The name of a boy									
An article of clothing									
A city in your state									

stopped writing, grade as follows: Score ten for each person having word no one else has. If two have it, nine each; three, eight each; four, seven each; more than four, it counts one. Take off five for each space that is left blank. This is a good writing game and could easily be made to consume half an hour.

12. *Partners for Refreshments.*—The partners which the guests fish for at the beginning of the party have worked with them through the writing games, and so it would be best to change partners for refreshments. Give slips of paper in duplicate to boys and girls on which are written the name of musical instruments which require some action to play them, such as violin, piano, snare drum, slide trombone, cornet, banjo, bass drum, saxophone, mandolin, Jew's harp, French harp, accordion, cymbals, tambourine, bones, ukulele, hand organ, triangle, xylophone, harp, cello. Boys and girls are to match partners by trying to imitate the motions they would go through in playing these instruments, those who are acting in a similar manner to be partners.

13. *Refreshments.*—Serve a salad in a banana skin. Carefully remove the fruit from the skin and fill with Waldorf salad, potato salad, tuna fish salad, or any other salad. Conceal two olives under the two halves of an English walnut shell. Serve this to the guests, and then later bring in a drink. Hot chocolate with whipped cream or punch.

14. *Properties*

(1) A ten-cent store toy that makes a noise.
(2) Arrange for the foot that comes off.
(3) Equipment for fishing for partners.
(4) A large bag in which to put the toys.
(5) Needles and thread and lampblack.
(6) Articles for the Art Museum.
(7) Papers prepared for Jumbled Statements.
(8) Papers prepared for Are You What We Suspected?
(9) Slips of paper in duplicate on which are written names of musical instruments.

chapter 15

April Fish Party[1]

WE GET THE IDEA OF "APRIL FISH" FROM THE FRENCH, WHO, INSTEAD of saying "April Fool," say "Poisson D'Avril," which means "April Fish." Send out invitations to a fish party to be held on the night of April first; or if it is desired, this party may be held at some other time during April.

1. *Invitation.*—The following is suggested for an invitation:

> Simple Simon went a-fishin'
> For to catch a whale,
> But all the water he could find
> Was in his mother's pail.
>
> We're going fishin' Friday night
> For to catch a sucker.
> At eight bells come to Paul's house
> In your best bib and tucker.

2. *Trading Fish.*—Cut out some small paper fish and give each guest ten. Any time during the evening that one guest can April Fool any other guest, that one must give him a fish. Any time during the evening that anyone says or does something funny that makes others laugh, those who laugh must give him a fish.

3. *Parts of a Fish.*—Give each guest the following parts of a fish scrambled on a sheet of paper. These should be either mimeographed or done on the typewriter with carbon copies:

(1) Ahde.   Head.
(2) Lait.   Tail.

[1] Prepared with the assistance of Mrs. J. C. Woodard, West Palm Beach, Fla.

(3) Ifsn. Fins.
(4) Kocnabeb. Backbone.
(5) Isbr. Ribs.
(6) Lasecs. Scales.
(7) Ehtet. Teeth.
(8) Syee. Eyes.
(9) Lgisl. Gills.
(10) Umtoh. Mouth.
(11) Niks. Skin.

A booby prize of a toy fish might be given to the one who gets done last, or a real prize to the one who finishes first, or it might be better to have all the others give one of their fish to the one who finishes first.

4. *Fishing.*—Use a small piece of cane fishing pole, and on the end of the line about three feet long tie a small magnet. Prepare fish with numbers on them, having them numbered from one to the number of guests at the party. Through these fish stick a pin. By placing the small magnet in the dish, a fish can be picked up. Let each one fish for a number. When all have their numbers, then the leader takes them one by one and has them do stunts. Some of the following are suggested:

(1) Show how you acted when you made your first speech.
(2) Tell what you know about golf.
(3) Show how you proposed (or how you are going to propose).
(4) Draw a picture of yourself.
(5) Say the threes in the multiplication table backward. (This may be done by turning your back to the audience.)
(6) Register supreme joy.
(7) Act as if you were a new stenographer.
(8) Act like you were a successful business man.
(9) Imagine you are a ventriloquist and give a performance.
(10) Imitate a book salesman.
(11) Show how you take your morning exercise.
(12) Act as if you were a Balinese dancer.
(13) Choose a partner and imagine you are playing tennis.
(14) Give a swimming lesson.

(15) Recite "Mary Had a Little Lamb" like a ten-year-old girl.
(16) Tell why or why not you like blonds better than brunettes.

For further stunts, look in the Index under "Forfeits."

5. *Kinds of Fish.*—Give guests a blank sheet of paper and pencil, and tell them that they have five minutes in which to write the names of fish. Give a prize to the one who has written the names of the largest number of fish. There are about eight hundred kinds of fish. It is easy to write the name of forty or fifty in ten minutes' time.

You will find that there will be a lot of variation in this. One player in a party which we attended, in playing this game, wrote Kingfish, Queenfish, Princefish, Bluefish, Redfish, Blackfish, Brownfish, and so on. Another player wrote all the names of fish he could think of, and then he wrote Papa fish, Mamma fish, Baby fish, Fried fish, Boiled fish, Baked fish, and so on. When these lists were read they caused much merriment.

6. *April Fool Relay.*—In order to get some action into the party, we suggest the following relay: Divide the guests into two or more groups and have them stand in line facing a goal. This goal should be twenty or twenty-five feet away. Have them run to the goal in the following manner, both in going up and coming back: They are required to take two steps forward and one step backward. Mincing steps is not allowed. The first one completes the run back and forth to the goal, touches the next one in line, and takes his place in the back of the line. The group that finishes first wins.

7. *Guessing the Names of Fish.*—This game may be used in addition to the other writing games, or instead of either of them.

What fish:
(1) Does the miser love? Gold.
(2) Twinkles in the sky? Star.
(3) Is musical? Bass.
(4) Is part of the human body? Mussel.
(5) Is the royal fish? King.
(6) Is the carpenter's fish? Sawfish.
(7) Is the soldier's fish? Sword.

106

(8) Is a color? Blue.
(9) Will try to swindle you? Shark.
(10) Is like a bird? Flying.
(11) Is another name for a road? Pike.
(12) Is also a frog? Toad.
(13) Serenades you? Cat.
(14) Is immortal? Sole.
(15) Is a flop? Flounder.

8. *April Fish Menu.*—Have the following menu printed on slips of paper and pasesd out to the guests. They are allowed to select any three of the articles on the menu for their refreshments. Of course this is only an April Fool refreshment menu, and after this has been served, the regular refreshments will be served. Bring in the three articles selected on small plates. It will be necessary for each guest to write his name on the menu after he has underscored what he wishes, so that those in charge will know to whom to return the menu and who are to be served the different articles.

MENU

(1) Regular Chicken Dinner

(2) Bell of the Garden
(3) Girl's Delight

(4) Fruit of the Vine

(5) Vital Prop
(6) Nude Colonel

(7) A Chip of the Old Block

(8) Life Preserver
(9) Cool Impudence

(10) Salted Nuts
(11) Spring's Offering

KEY

(1) Mixed cracked grain (a chicken dinner)

(2) Bell pepper (a slice of it)
(3) Date

(4) Cucumber (a slice of it)

(5) Slice of bread
(6) Shelled nut

(7) Toothpick

(8) Salt
(9) Chili Sauce

(10) Nuts off of bolts, salted
(11) Water

9. *Refreshments.*—For the regular refreshments serve sandwiches cut into the shape of a fish, and fruit punch, or ice cream (snow-drift) and cherub's food (angel food cake).

10. *Properties*

(1) Enough paper fish to give ten to each guest.
(2) Papers prepared for Parts of a Fish.
(3) Fishing pole, small magnet, and paper fish with pins in them.
(4) Blank sheets of paper and pencils.
(5) Papers prepared for Guessing the Names of Fish.
(6) Fake menu cards.

chapter 16

Easter Party

EASTER IS NOT ONLY THE TIME OF THE RESURRECTION OF CHRIST, BUT it is also the beginning of spring, the time of the resurrection of nature. The sap begins to rise in the trees, the flowers peep through the ground, the birds sing, and the whole earth takes on the spirit of resurrected life. Easter is the time when spring fever begins to get into the blood, and the time for wholesome recreation to be at a new high. The real significance of Easter must not be forgotten in the spirit of hilarity. The following are some suggestions for an Easter Party:

1. *Invitations.*—The invitations may be written on a cardboard cut into the shape of a chicken, an egg, or a rabbit. The following is suggested for an invitation:

On Thursday evening, we are planning an egg-cellent Easter party. If this invitation is egg-cepted, we are eggs-pecting you to be there eggs-actly at eight. No eggs-cuses will be eggs-cepted. The girls are eggs-pected to bring a chick hat that was chick long ago, the one bringing the oldest and most ridiculous will win a chick prize. 414 Fern Street.

2. *Decorations.*—Use yellow and green crepe paper streamers. Pictures of rabbits and chickens should be in evidence. Baskets of Easter eggs should be on the table and the piano. Use flowers, especially lilies in vases or pots.

3. *Partners: Mutt and Jeff.*—The girls are taken into one room, and the boys remain in the other. The girls are arranged according to height, the shortest in front. The boys are arranged according to height, the tallest in front. They are then asked to number, beginning from the front. When all come together, the boy, the

tall one who was in front and number one, will find the girl who is number one and the short one who was in front, and they will be partners, and so on until all numbers are matched.

4. *Making Easter Hats.*—Provide each boy with crepe paper or tissue paper in various colors, and scissors, pins, and paste. Each boy is to make a hat for his partner, using these materials. After all have finished, a prize is given to the one producing the best hat in the estimation of the judges.

5. *Making Easter Frocks.*—In lieu of making the hat, newspaper may be provided with which to fashion Easter frocks. A stack of old newspapers, among them some comic sheets to lend color. Instead of comic sheets, colored crepe paper may be supplied to decorate the dresses with, to make sashes, or collars, ties, and so forth.

6. *Fighting Easter Eggs.*—Give each guest three hard-boiled eggs which have been colored. These can be the same eggs that are used for decorations. They are to fight eggs—that is, they are to try to break the eggs of opponents by hitting them with their own egg. If they succeed in cracking the shell of the opponent's egg, they are to get the egg. The cracked egg thus acquired may be used to fight with, and it is possible to break a good egg with the other end that is not cracked. Whoever succeeds in winning the largest number of eggs wins a prize.

7. *Easter Egg Hunt.*—Have hidden about the room eggs cut out of colored cardboard or small candy eggs. Upon signal and announcement from the leader, all search for the eggs behind pictures, under table and piano covers, in books, and everywhere that they may be hidden. The one finding the largest number is to receive a prize. If the eggs are candy, they may be divided and eaten.

8. *Rabbit Relay Race.*—Get a number of Easter rabbits from the five-and-ten-cent store. There should be ten of these, although a smaller number will do, even four. In the relay the couples with the even numbers are matched against the couples with the odd numbers. The evens and the odds stand in two lines of equal number facing each other. Five rabbits are placed on a chair at the head of each line. Upon a signal from the leader, the first person in line

110

picks up a rabbit and starts passing it down the line, then another and another until all have gone down the line. When they reach the other end of the line, they must be laid on a chair until all the rabbits have passed down. The one on the other end of the line must then start passing them back one at a time. This game may be lengthened by having the rabbits make two laps—that is, to go down and back twice.

9. *Rabbit Race.*—Select a boy from each group and have them get down on all fours and hop to a goal like rabbits and back in the same way. The one returning first wins for his side.

10. *Making the Most of Easter Sunday.*—Give to each guest a sheet of paper with the words "Easter Sunday" written at the top. Allow them five or six minutes to make words from the letters in Easter Sunday. The guest making the longest list of words wins and should be given a prize.

11. *Flower Stagecoach.*—The guests take the names of flowers, as lily, rose, marigold, carnation, violet. The leader stands in the center and tells about her flower garden. She may say: "I heard that Mrs. Smith was sick, so I went to the flower garden and picked some roses, carnations, and ferns and sent her a bouquet." When she says "rose, carnation, and fern," those who represent these flowers must rise and turn around, or, better, walk around their chair. When she says "bouquet," all must change chairs. There must not be any extra chairs in the circle, and the leader is to try to get a chair when the change is made, the one left out becoming the leader. The new leader then tells about her flower garden in the same manner.

12. *Easter Bonnet Contest.*—The girls have been asked in the invitation to bring an old hat. The older the hat, the better and the funnier. Have them don these hats and parade before the group and the judges. The judges may decide the winner by holding his hand over the contestants and judging by the amount of applause. The one who has the oldest and funniest hat should receive a prize.

13. *Egg Relay.*—Match the even number couples against the odd number and have them stand facing a goal about fifteen or twenty feet in front of each line. The one in front is given a teaspoon with

an egg on it. This egg should, of course, be boiled. One of the colored Easter eggs will do. Upon signal from the leader, the one at the front of the line is to run to the goal, carrying the egg in the spoon, which she holds by the end of the handle. If the egg is dropped, it must be picked up and replaced before the runner proceeds. When the first one is finished, she gives the spoon and the egg to the next one in line and takes her place at the back of the line. The group that finishes first wins.

14. *Refreshments.*—Serve sandwiches cut in shape of chicken or rabbit. A small paper nut cup of candy eggs. Ice cream molded as chicken, rabbit, or lily. Hot chocolate with marshmallows.

15. *Properties*

(1) Crepe paper, scissors, pins, and paste for making Easter hats. Or newspapers, and so forth, for making Easter dresses.

(2) Colored hard-boiled eggs enough for two or three for each guest.

(3) Easter eggs cut out of cardboard hidden about the room, or candy eggs hidden.

(4) Ten toy rabbits for relay race.

(5) Sheets of paper with "Easter Sunday" written at the top.

(6) Teaspoons and eggs for relay.

(7) Prizes for the various contests.

chapter 17

May Day Party

MAY IS THE MONTH OF THE ENDING OF SPRING AND THE BEGINNING OF summer. The flowers begin to bloom, the trees turn to a beautiful green. The birds sing, and the "heart is so full that a drop o'erfills it." Spring fever takes possession of us, and we feel the call of the field and stream. We would like to go and pick wild flowers and wander among the trees. But many of us cannot do this; we live in cities and cannot get away from our work. But in May why not have a lawn party and crown one of your group Queen o' the May?

1. *Invitation.*—Send out the following or similar invitation:

> April showers bring May flowers,
> And May brings sunshine and joy.
> But Friday night brings a jolly time
> For all our bunch—Oh, boy!
> So come at eight to Bob Smith's house,
> For this glorious day
> We're choosin' one to reign o'er us,
> And crownin' her Queen o' the May!

2. *Decorations.*—This party is planned to be held on the lawn and, if possible, among the trees. A home with a large yard in which there are trees, to the limbs of which could be hung Japanese lanterns, would be ideal. Some of the party would be held in the house; at least the refreshments would possibly be served in the house. Decorate the house with vines and flowers. There should be sufficient lanterns with electric lights in them to make the lawn light.

Erect a Maypole on the lawn by putting a pole in the ground, fastening streamers of crêpe paper about ten or fifteen feet long to the top of the pole. There should be enough of these for each guest.

113

3. *Matching Flowers.*—The host should have enough different kinds of flowers, two of each, to pin on the guests as they arrive. It is not necessary to have different species of flowers, but merely different colors. For example, there might be two white roses, two red roses, two pink roses, two white carnations, two red carnations, two dandelions, two daisies. Pin one of these on the girls and another on the boys as they enter. When all have assembled, have them find partners by matching flowers.

4. *Flower Writing Contest.*—Give each couple a blank sheet of paper and pencil. In a given time they are to write all the names of flowers that they can think of. Give a prize to the couple that has the largest list.

5. *Tree, Bird, or Flower.*—Players are seated in a circle. One player is in the center. He points to one in the circle and says, "Tree, bird, or flower—bird." The player must call the name of a bird before the one in the center counts to ten. Otherwise he must take the place in the center. The one in the center, after saying, "Tree, bird, or flower," may call any one of the three, as "tree," "flower," and the player must answer with the proper one.

6. *Making a May Basket.*—Give each couple colored paper, scissors, paste, and pins. This paper should be in several colors. Allow each couple about fifteen minutes to make a basket and fill it with flowers. Give a prize to the couple making the prettiest basket.

7. *Drop the Flower.*—Players form a circle and play drop the flower just like drop the handkerchief. One is outside the circle with a flower, which he drops behind someone in the circle. The one behind whom the flower is dropped must tag the one who dropped it before he makes the circle and enters the place left vacant by the one who chased him. In case the runner drops the flower and makes a complete circuit before the one behind whom the flower has been dropped discovers it, that one must get in the dunce pen—that is, the center of the ring. The only way to get out is to grab the flower from behind someone where it has been dropped before that person gets it.

8. *Are You There?*—Go from Drop the Flower to Are You There? One player is blindfolded and stands in the center with a pole in his hand about eight feet long. Music may be played, although it is not necessary. If music is played, when the music stops, the ones in the circle stop, and the one in the center points his rod toward the circle. The one toward whom he points must take hold of the end of the rod. The leader says, "Are You There?" The player may answer "Yes" or "Uh-huh." The player may try to disguise his voice in any way possible. If the one in the center guesses who it is, that one must change places with him. If no music is played, the one in the center may stop the line marching around by tapping on his pole with a stick.

9. *Flower Relay.*—Divide into two equal sides, and have them form two circles and join hands. One player in each circle is given a flower. When the leader's whistle blows, he must carry this flower in his hand and weave in and out among the players in the circle and in this way make a circuit. He then gives the flower to the next one on his right, and that one must weave in and out around the circle, and so on until all have made the circuit. When all have done this, the game is completed and the circle that finishes first wins.

10. *Dancing Around the Maypole.*—Players stand in two circles, the girls on the inner circle facing clockwise, the boys in the outer circle facing counter-clockwise. When the music starts, they march in opposite directions and wind up their streamers, the boys holding their streamers over the heads of the girls as far as possible, then they face about and unwind them. The girls then form the circle on the outside and the boys on the inside, and the girls raise their streamers over the heads of the boys and wind and unwind in a similar manner.

11. *Hidden Flowers.*—After the games described above are played on the lawn, it would be well to go into the house for the last two games and the refreshments. Have slips prepared for Hidden Flowers. (See Index.)

12. *Identifying Flowers.*—Get from a seed store or flower shop a flower catalogue. Cut this up and pin the pictures of flowers about the room. Give blank sheets of paper to the guests and ask them to number them from one to the last number you have on the flowers. They are to guess the names of the flowers by number.

13. *Choosing the May Queen.*—This may be done by having guests vote by secret ballot for the queen. The two that get the highest number of votes on the first ballot would be voted on in the second ballot, and the one of these two getting the highest number of votes will be crowned queen.

14. *The Popularity Contest: Queen of the May.*—This Party may be made a money-making party by having the Queen of the May's election be the conclusion of a popularity contest. We know of a young people's society that started this popularity contest several weeks in advance and sold votes at one cent each. Fifty votes was necessary to nominate a girl for the contest. Then members of the society could purchase as many votes as they desired for the one they wished to sponsor.

At the time of voting it would be well to have two or three ballots. The three receiving the highest number of votes should have a run-off; and if in the second ballot no one received a majority, there should be a third ballot. The one receiving the largest number of votes is crowned Queen of the May. This could be handled so that it would bring in twenty-five to two hundred dollars, depending upon the financial ability of the group.

15. *Crowning the Queen.*—After the queen has been chosen there should be a coronation ceremony. Attendants for the queen should be chosen by the one in charge of the party, and these should prepare the throne and the crown (which should be made in advance). Have the guests form an arch with their hands, letting the queen and her attendants pass under the arch to the throne. All then come to the throne and bow or kneel before the throne.

16. *Refreshments.*—Serve ice cream and cake. Sliced brick ice

cream with lady fingers makes a dainty refreshment. Another suggestion would be punch and cake.

17. *Properties*

(1) Flowers, two of different species or colors, for matching partners.

(2) Blank papers and pencils for Flower Writing Contest.

(3) Paper of different colors, scissors, paste, and pins for making flower baskets and flowers.

(4) Pole about eight feet long for Are You There? Blindfold.

(5) Maypole prepared in advance as described.

(6) Papers for Hidden Flowers and blank papers for Identifying Flowers.

(7) Crown for the queen.

chapter 18

College Field Day

THE COLLEGE FIELD DAY IS A PARTY SUITABLE FOR LARGE GROUPS, SUCH as United Christian Youth Movement groups, Conference Groups, or Civic Clubs. As many as one hundred could be entertained by these events.

The company is divided into four groups, and each group takes the name of a college, such as Harvard, Princeton, Yale, and Vanderbilt. A leader is selected for each group and also a cheerleader. While the contests are in progress, the other members of a group should cheer their contestants and root for them. This is an important part of the fun and should not be neglected.

1. *Invitation.*—The following is suggested for an invitation:

> Rah, rah, rah, rah, rah,
>> Fifteen rahs for college,
> Fifteen rahs for fun and sport,
>> And forget about the knowledge.
> Well, on next Friday night, let me say,
> We're having a regular College Field Day.
> And I also want to think to remark
> It's going to be a sure-enough lark.
>> Place ....

2. *Decorations.*—Use posters with athletic pictures. Crepe paper colors to suit the college colors may be used by each of the groups to decorate their corner of the room. This would necessitate selecting the colleges in advance and selecting the paper to decorate with. Each group should make a pennant with the name of their college on it. Decorating may be made the first part of the party.

3. *Cross-country Run.*—Groups line up in parallel lines facing the

leader. The leader tells them that this is the cross-country run and that each one must race to a goal, about twenty-five feet in front of each line, with the legs crossed. When the first one returns, he touches off the second and takes his place at the rear of the line. The object is to see which group can finish first. Fifty points.

4. *Shot Put.*—A girl is chosen from each group. They are given a paper bag or a balloon inflated with air. Points can be given for the one who throws it farthest or for the one who succeeds in throwing it across the line. Give 10 points for this.

5. *Chinese Get-Up.*—Two boys are picked from each of the four groups. The two sit down on the floor, back to back, and lock their arms. This may be tried with the two sitting in chairs, back to back, with locked arms. At the sound of the whistle they are to get to their feet without unlocking their arms. The two who can accomplish this quickest win. Give 10 points.

6. *Standing Broad Grin.*—One is selected from each group, either boy or girl. It should be announced in advance that this is the Standing Broad Grin, so that one with a large mouth will be selected. If desired, have the men's contest and then the women's. After they have grinned as broadly as possible, the leader, using a tape measure, measures the width of the grin. The one who grins broadest wins. Give 10 points for this.

7. *High Hurdle.*—One is selected from each group, preferably one who can sing. They are asked, one at a time, to sing the first verse of "America," singing two words and omitting two words. The one who does it most successfully wins. Give 10 points.

8. *Boxing Match.*—The groups line up facing the leader for instruction. The first person in the line is given a penny match box. It is better to use a wooden safety match box for this. They are told that the box must be passed down the line and back by transferring it from nose to nose without the use of the hands. Of course, if the box is dropped, it may be picked up with the hand and replaced on the nose. Use only the outer case of the box. Give 50 points to the group that finishes first.

9. *Shot Dash.*—One boy is selected from each group. They are

119

placed on their knees on a starting line and given a paper bag or balloon inflated with air. They are told to blow this across a goal line twenty or thirty feet away. Give the winner 10 points for his group.

10. *Track Meet.*—One boy is selected from each group. Tell them to select the one with the largest foot. For the track meet the foot is placed on a piece of paper, and the size of the foot is drawn on the paper. The one making the largest track wins for his group. Give 10 points for this.

11. *The Dash.*—Select one from each group. Each one is given two newspapers. They must race to a goal but cannot advance without stepping on the paper. The one who finshes first wins. Give 10 points.

12. *Relay Race: Umbrella and Bucket.*—Select four from each group. The first one in each group is given a folding chair, an umbrella, and a covered bucket with a whistle in it. At the sound of the whistle the contestants are to race, one at a time, to goals drawn on the floor about twenty-five feet in front of each group. They are to unfold the chair and sit in it, raise the umbrella, open the bucket and take out the whistle and blow it, put the whistle back in the bucket and close it, shut up the umbrella, fold the chair, and race back and touch off the next one. The group finishing first wins 20 points.

13. *High Jump.*—Select a girl from each group, preferably one who can sing. The one who can sing the chorus of "Old Black Joe" the highest wins 10 points for her group.

14. *Low Hurdle.*—Place on the floor a folding chair, bucket, umbrella, or other objects. Select some of the group to make a run across the room, and after they have had a good look at the objects scattered on the floor, blindfold them. As soon as they are blindfolded someone noiselessly removes the objects, and it will be very amusing to watch them run, imagining that the objects are still there.

15. *Backward Relay.*—Select two boys from each group. More

than two may be selected, as four, six, or eight. These boys stand back to back at a starting line and are told that they must race to a goal marked on the floor and back. One will run forward on the way up; the other forward on the way back. If more than one pair is used, have the first pair touch off the second, and so on. The group that does this in the quickest time should be given twenty points.

16. *Throwing Contest: Peanut.*—Throwing contest in which all participate with peanuts. Each one is given from one to three peanuts. Vegetable bowls are placed about eight feet from the end of each line. The group that gets the largest number of peanuts in the bowl wins. Give three points for every peanut thrown in the bowls to each group.

17. *Whistle.*—One is selected from each group. Each is given a cracker. He is told that he must eat the cracker and whistle "Yankee Doodle" or "Dixie." The one who first successfully whistles the tune wins. Give 10 points for this.

18. *Aquatic Dash.*—One is selected from each group. The contestants are given a glass almost full of water. They are told to hop to a goal and back to the starting point. The one having the most water in his glass when he returns wins. Give 10 points.

19. *Discus Throw.*—Select two contestants from each group. They are each given a paper plate. The two that can throw the plates the greatest combined distance wins. Give 10 points.

20. *Cord Race.*—Have each group form a circle. Give to each group a ball of twine. The ball is passed around the circle at the sound of the leader's whistle, the first one to start it holding the end of the cord and the others unwinding it. When it comes back to the starting point, it must start back and be wound up as it goes, each person winding his part. The group that can get it back and wound up first wins. Allow 20 points.

21. *Awards.*—Present the winning group with a loving cup made from two tin funnels by sticking the spouts together. Have other equally foolish and inexpensive prizes for the events.

22. *Refreshments.*—Popcorn balls, Crackerjacks, bottled soft

drinks, and hot dogs would make appropriate refreshments for such an event.

23. *Properties*

(1) A score card with the names of the events written in and the number of points to be given the winner. See that a scorer has been selected.

(2) Three judges to decide competitive events.

(3) Paper bags and balloons to be inflated. These are to be used in No. 3 and No. 8. If balloons are used, the same ones will do for both.

(4) A tape measure.

(5) Four penny match boxes. Get wooden safety match boxes and remove the inside part.

(6) Four sheets of white paper and pencil.

(7) Four folding chairs, four umbrellas, four covered buckets, and four whistles.

(8) Enough peanuts to give three to each one. There are about thirty in an ordinary five-cent bag.

(9) Four water glasses.

(10) Four paper plates.

(11) Four balls of twine.

(12) Prizes as suggested.

NOTE.—It will not be possible to have all the events listed above in one evening, as the play should not last longer than one and one-half hours. Select the ones you think will work best.

chapter 19

Aircraft Party

THIS PARTY IS BUILT AROUND THE IDEA OF AIRCRAFT, SUCH AS JETS, propeller type planes, and helicopters. This is a rapidly changing industry and no one knows whether, within a few years, or even months, we will be flying to distant planets. The party must, therefore, be adapted to meet these changes as they come.

1. *Invitation.*—This invitation may be written on a card cut in the shape of an airplane. The following is a suggested verse to use. If it is desirable to use a card or sheet of note paper, airplanes may be cut from magazines and pasted on the invitation card:

No matter how many times you've been in the air,
   You'll be there on next Friday night;
For we're giving a party and want you there,
   And we're going to fly all right.
For the party's an Aircraft Party, you see,
   And each one must take the stick
And fly to the land of fun and glee—
   The thrills will come fast and thick.
                              Time and Place

2. *Decorations.*—Have a sign on the door, "Airport." To give the idea of wind, have some electric fans with paper streamers tied to them blowing the streamers into the room. Picture of airplanes may be pinned on the drapes. These are easily obtainable from the adds of the aircraft industry or the airlines.

3. *Mixing Game: Parts of an Airplane.*—Have written on slips of paper the names of parts of an airplane or accessories needed by the pilot. Here are some suggestions: Motor, stick, radar, compass, defroster, wing, fuselage, landing gear, propeller, cockpit, gas tank,

altimeter, tail, rudder, and windshield. While all the guests are seated in a circle, the leader and his helpers pin a slip of paper on the back of each person. When this is finished, each guest is given paper and pencil and told that he is to write the name of each guest on his paper and the name of the airplane part he represents. He must do this while all are trying to keep their backs turned so that the name of their own airplane part may not be read, and as he writes he must try to protect his own slip from being read. As soon as any player has the names of all guests and the corresponding name of the airplane parts represented, the game is finished. The one who succeeds in getting a full list of names and parts quickest should be given some prize or recognition by the leader.

4. *Airplane.*—After the mixing game just described, the names that are on the backs of the guests are then transferred to the front, and the guests are seated in a circle, with all the chairs filled. The leader starts telling a story in which he uses different parts of the airship. As the story is told the guests having the parts rise and act them out. The propellers may throw their arms around, the motor make a noise like an engine, the wings stand with arms outstretched; and if there is nothing that can be done, merely get up and turn around. Whenever the leader says, "Airplane," all must get up and change places, whereupon the leader tries to get a chair; and if he succeeds, the one left out must continue the story.

5. *Airplane Ride.*—Take a board about six feet long and about ten or twelve inches wide and raise it from the floor by using bricks or blocks on each end. A player is blindfolded and asked to step into the plane for a ride. He is permitted to keep his hand on the shoulder of the pilot while two other players take hold of the board and raise it two or three inches from the bricks or blocks. At this time the pilot stoops down to make it appear that the one on the boards is being lifted. Someone takes a broom, and after crying out, "Look out for the ceiling," touches the passenger on the head with it. Usually the passenger will jump at this time, and it is comical to see how he acts when he finds that he is only six or eight inches from

the floor. This stunt may be done in the yard or in a separate room, and the guests brought in one at a time.

6. *Airplane Race.*—Divide the guests into three groups of equal number and name them the Jets, Propeller Planes, and Helicopters. The three groups line up facing three chairs, on each of which have been placed four toy airplanes. Upon signal from the leader, the player at the head of the line picks up the first airplane and starts it down the line, then the second and third and fourth. The player at the other end of the line must lay down the planes on another chair until he has all four. Then he starts them back up the line. The relay may be lengthened and made more interesting by having the planes make two or three laps up and down. The group that gets all the planes back to the starting point first wins.

7. *The Pilot Has Lost His Hat.*—The players are numbered, and the leader says: "The pilot has lost his hat. Some say that number four has it, others say that number seven has it; but I say that the one who has it is number eleven." The leader then rapidly counts ten. If the leader can do this before number eleven says, "Who, sir; I, sir?" the player must take the leader's place and the leader must take the player's number. But if the player says, "Who, sir; I, sir?" before the leader can count ten, the following conversation takes place between the player and the leader:

Player: "Who, sir; I, sir?"
Leader: "Yes, sir; you, sir."
Player: "No, sir; not I, sir."
Leader: "Who, then, sir?"
Player: "Number seventeen, sir."

The leader then tries to count ten before number seventeen responds with a "Who, sir; I sir?" And so the game continues.

8. *Hidden Airplanes.*—Have airplanes cut out of paper and hidden about the room. Upon a signal from the leader, all hunt for the airplanes. These may have numbers on them, and the person finding them may get a score equal to the total of the numbers on the back of his planes.

9. *Airplanes Fly.*—Airplanes Fly is played somewhat like Birds

Fly. The leader stands in the center of a circle of the players. The leader says, "Airplanes fly, jets fly," and calls other objects that fly, such as rockets, sputnicks, blimps, balloons, and so forth. When something is mentioned that flies, the players must raise their arms and flap them as if they were flying. A player who fails to do this must become "It." Also if a player "flies" when he is not supposed to, he also must be "it." For example, if the leader says, "Dogs fly," "Automobiles fly," "Rabbits fly," "Goats fly," "Cows fly," the players must stand still and not wave their hands. The one who does must be "it."

10. *This Is a Jet Airplane.*—The players are seated in a semicircle. A player on one end has an object; it makes no difference what it is. A spool or a thimble or any kind of a wood block will do. The person on one end of the line turns to the next one in line and says, "This is an airplane." He does not take it the first time, but says, "A what?" to which he replies, "An airplane." The second player then takes the object and turns to the third player and says, "This is an airplane." The third player does not take it, but says, "A what?" The second player then turns to the first and hands him back the object and says, "A what?" He takes the object and immediately hands it back and says, "An airplane." He then passes it to the third player and says, "An airplane," whereupon the third player takes it and passes it to the fourth. Each time it must go all the way back to the first man. But in the meantime at the other end of the line an object has been started in a similar way, except the one who started it has said, "This is a jet," and the jet is passing back and forth at the other end of the line. The fun begins when the airplane and the jet cross each other. It is puzzling which way to send each object and what to say. Try it and see. It is a good stunt.

11. *Ground Work.*—Choose four boys for this stunt. Put three crackers on each of four saucers and set these on the floor about twenty feet from where the boys line up for the start of the race. When the signal from the leader is given, they must hop to the plate of crackers, get down on their two hands and one knee, for they are not allowed to use the foot on which they did not hop or

even to touch the toe or the knee of this leg to the floor. In this position they must eat the three crackers, using only the mouth and tongue to pick them up. When the crackers have been eaten, they get up and hop back and then whistle a tune. The person who first manages to whistle a tune is the winner.

12. *Loop-the-Loop Relay.*—For this relay the two groups, the ones and the twos, divide into two parts each, one half of the group facing the other half of the group and about twenty feet apart. The other group stands in similar formation and about ten or more feet away. When the leader gives the signal, after thoroughly explaining the relay, the first one on one end of each line turns to the left and runs around all the players in his end of the line. He then makes a figure eight, runs to the left, and circles the other end of his side. As he completes the second circuit, he touches off the man on the front of that line, who in turn faces toward the rear of his line and runs around both of his groups, and touches off the first man in his side of the line that is facing his original position. In every case, as in other relays, when a player has completed his run he is to take his place at the back of the line. The group that has every player in both lines around first wins.

13. *Balloon Race.*—Select one or two girls from each group and give to each a rubber balloon. They are to inflate it, and the one bursting hers first wins the prize.

14. *Airplane Take-Offs.*—Of course the airplanes must take-off, and so have some take-offs such as the following:

For the Boys

(1) A man who has lost his collar button.
(2) A man having his picture taken.
(3) A man cooking.
(4) A man shopping with his wife.
(6) A man playing golf.

For the Girls

(1) A girl baiting a fishhook.
(2) A girl playing tennis.

(3) A girl smoking.
(4) A girl making up.
(5) A girl being proposed to.

15. *Refreshments.*—Sandwiches and coffee. Doughnuts and coffee.

16. *Properties*

(1) Papers prepared for Parts of an Airplane, Pencils, Pins.
(2) Board with bricks or blocks for the Airplane Ride; Broom, Blindfold.
(3) Toy airplanes for Airplane Race.
(4) Small paper airplanes for Hidden Airplanes.
(5) Crackers on small plates or saucers for Ground Work.
(6) Balloons for the Balloon Race.
(7) Small object for "This is an airplane."

chapter 20

Shipwreck Party

(*COSTUME*)

HAVE A SHIPWRECK PARTY. IN ONE POPULAR RESORT CITY THIS PARTY was given a number of times and caused much comment and a lot of good amusement. While it is a costume party, the costumes are easy, as one is just supposed to wear what one would pick up hurriedly were he in a shipwreck and all were hastening to get to the lifeboats.

1. *Invitation.*—The invitation will give sufficient information concerning the costume to be worn if the following one is used:

> It is the good ship—Friendship—
> That sails in our social sea.
> But on Friday night we'll make believe
> That the ship no more shall be.
> For we're having a Shipwreck Party,
> And you are just to wear
> What you salvaged from a shipwreck,
> What that is we do not care.
> The ship, of course, met this disaster
> In the still hours of the night.
> So wear what you would first pick up
> Were you forced to sudden flight.

2. *Decorations.*—A few old anchors, ropes, life-preservers, boats, and yacht chairs would make good decorations and furnishings. Also have some steamer chairs or some beach chairs. The host and the hostess may be dressed in sailor suits, as the idea might be that a party of shipwrecked persons was picked up by another boat.

Even the social committee, the judges of the costumes, and those planning the party may be dressed as sailors or in a yachting suit.

3. *Grand March.*—See page 22 for the directions for the grand march. It is always a good plan to have a grand march at a costume party so that all may see the costumes of the others.

4. *Judging Costumes.*—It will be necessary to consume some time in judging costumes. Judges should be selected and the winning costume picked by a vote of the judges, or they might have the contestants march by and hold a hand over their heads one at a time and pick the winner by the applause of the crowd. If the latter method is used, the judges should pick the best ten or twelve and let the audience cheer these.

5. *Four in a Row.*—A good way to introduce the guests and at the same time have a lot of fun is to play Four in a Row, which is somewhat like Bingo. As each guest enters, his name is pinned on him. Each guest is given a card on which have been drawn sixteen squares, four vertically and four horizontally, and sixteen grains of corn. When the leader gives the signal, each guest is to circulate among the other guests and fill his card with sixteen names. The names are then taken off of the guests and put in a box and drawn out one at a time by the leader. As a person's name is called, he must rise, and everyone who has the name of the person on his card is to lay a grain of corn on it. The leader continues in this way until some guest has four grains of corn in a row, at which time he calls out, "Four in a row." All guests then remove their grains of corn from the board, and the leader continues to introduce each one of the guests until someone else has a four in a row, or until all are introduced.

6. *Matching Partners: Eyes.*—Have the women find a partner by finding a man that has the same color eyes as herself. In case there is an argument about the proper matching, the leader must decide the case.

7. *Making the Best of a Shipwreck.*—Give the guests papers and pencils and sheets of paper on which has been written at the top the word "shipwreck." Let the couples work together at this and see

130

which couple can make the most words in a given time. Give a prize for the longest list and have this list read.

8. *Shuffleboard.*—The most common game to be played on ship-deck is shuffleboard. Draw a shuffleboard court on the floor with chalk as illustrated below. Wood disks may be made from blocks of wood more or less round. Shuffleboard sticks may be made by nailing about ten inches of a small wooden barrel hoop to the end of a broomstick or mopstick. Play a tournament as in quoits. The illustration is a shuffleboard court, and the players pitch toward the point of the triangle, or rather slide their blocks on the floor.

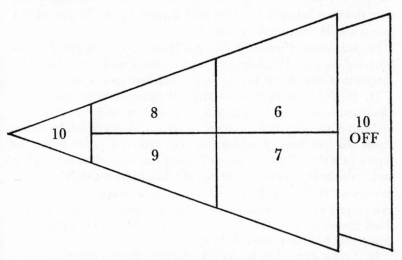

(To play, the player should be about twenty feet from the point of the court.)

9. *Quoits.*—Get rubber quoits from the dime store. Have a quoit tournament. Divide into groups of eight and match two players against the other two, letting them play four at a time. The winners in the first game play the winners in the second game. The two players who win in each of the groups of eight then play off

the tournament. Give a prize to the couple that wins the tournament.

This game of quoits can be played like the game of pitching horseshoes. Each player has two rubber quoits, the one nearest the pin makes one point; and if the player has both of his quoits nearest the pin, he gets two points. A quoit leaning against the pin means three points, and a ringer, five points. Fifteen points is a game. When couples play one should be at one pin and his partner at the other. In this way each player pitches against an opponent, and his partner pitches the quoits back against the other opponent. The distance between the pins will depend upon the size of the quoits and the size of the room.

10. *Shipwreck Crossword Game.*—Have papers prepared as illustrated on page 133. Let the couples work together on this. The couple that fills all the blanks in the quickest time wins.

11. *Marine Warfare Relay.*—Divide the guests into groups, having about ten contestants in each group. They line up for a relay race, and two of the players in each group act as sailors and hold a string about ten feet long on which has been placed a paper funnel to represent a ship. The first player in each line must then act as pilot and blow the ship across the string. He then slides the ship back and touches off the second player, who in turn becomes pilot. The first two players may then relieve the sailors and hold the string for the third contestant as well as for the other members of his group. The group that finishes first wins the race.

12. *Excuse Me.*—The leader asks the first player a question which demands an excuse. The excuse must be given in words beginning with the player's initials. As an illustration—the leader might ask, "Where were you last night?" The player, whose initials are I. M. C., replies, "Excuse me, I was ironing my clothes." The leader asks another player, whose initials are A.M.C., "Where were you yesterday?" He replies: "Excuse me, I was airing my cat." And so the leader goes around the circle. Anyone making a mistake must take the leader's place and ask the questions.

	S	H	I	P	W	R	E	C	K
Something about a ship									
What you thought of when the ship was sinking									
An article salvaged from the wreck									
Where you want to be the next time there is a ship-wreck									

These sheets may be drawn with a pencil and ruler and lettered with a pencil if a typewriter is not available. By using carbons, three or four copies can be made at one drawing. Couples should work together filling the blanks. The couple that fills all the blanks first wins.

13. *Guessing Words Representing Things Done on a Ship.*—In this game one player is sent out of the room. The other players agree upon some word ending in "ing" which represents something done on board a ship, such as sleeping, eating, talking, sailing, commanding, laughing, scrubbing, cooking, washing, bathing, shaving, playing, and so on. When the player comes back into the room, he may ask questions about his word, for example, "Where is it done?" "How often is it done?" "When did you last do it?" "Is it done in the kitchen?" and so forth. When the person who has been sent out guesses the word, the one who gave it away must next go out, and so the game continues.

14. *Refreshments.*—For refreshments serve canned goods, such as might be salvaged from a wreck. For example, each one, or each couple, might be given a small can of sardines with opener, a box of crackers, a bottled soft drink, a jar of pickles or olives. Another suggestion would be to serve canned baked beans, buns, pickles, and coffee in tin cups.

15. *Properties*

(1) A sheet of paper with sixteen squares drawn on it, a slip of paper with his name on it, and sixteen grains of corn for each guest.

(2) Sheets of paper with the word "shipwreck."

(3) Sets of four rubber quoits and two pins for every eight in the group.

(4) Chalk to draw shuffleboard court, shuffleboard sticks, and discs.

(5) Sheets drawn out for shipwreck crossword game.

(6) String about ten feet long and paper funnel for Marine Warfare Relay.

chapter 21

Bride and Groom Party

(*SHOWER*)

THIS CHAPTER WILL FIRST DESCRIBE A SHOWER FOR A BRIDE AND GROOM which was given by a church group, and then suggest additional games and stunts that may be used at such a party.

The party described was arranged by the social committee of a young people's Sunday-school class as a surprise shower for one of the members of the class. The class was accustomed to having regular monthly gatherings for business and for recreation. It was certain that the bride-to-be would be present, for she was one of the officers. It was also certain that the groom-to-be would be present. Such occasions as a shower for a bride and groom are important to the life of such a class, as attention shown to a couple will be remembered by them for years and will tie them to the organization more completely than anything else.

1. *Gifts.*—It is well for a group to decide in advance what shall be given at a shower so that there will be no duplicates. In the case of the shower described in this chapter, the group decided to give a set of china. It had been learned through one of the bride's friends that she did not have china. This friend then found out what pattern the bride would like. The clerk at one of the local stores was asked to keep a list of what was sold, with the idea of completing eight place settings. Those desiring to help with the china went to the store and selected pieces to make up a set of eight, or they selected vegetable dishes, platters, or something else in the pattern. Of course there were those who brought other gifts, such as linen and kitchen utensils.

A very clever idea was carried out by one of the girls. She brought a rolling pin dressed like a baby. The dress was made from crepe paper and was long enough to cover one end of the rolling pin. A face had been drawn on cloth and stuffed with cotton and tied over the other end of the rolling pin, and on this was placed a baby's cap. On the front of the baby was a card which had been pinned with two needles. The following verse was on the card:

> Needles, needles, and rolling pins,
> When a man marries, his trouble begins.

All the gifts were placed in a large clothesbasket, covered with white crepe paper with strips of yellow paper at the top and bottom and around the handles of the basket. This was placed in another room and was not brought in until the party was nearly over. The leader of the party had arranged for the guests to bring their gifts surreptitiously and have them hidden until the time for the surprise presentation.

2. *Decorations.*—The recreation room of the church was used for the party and was decorated with yellow crepe paper made into streamers. Large wedding bells were hung from the ceiling in the center of the room. Potted plants and cut flowers were also used.

3. *Telegrams.*—The leader then told the group that the party was going to be in honor of the couple soon to be married. (This party could be used for recently married couples just as well.) The guests then were each asked to write a telegram of congratulations to the bride and groom on a telegraph blank that had been provided. Some of these were serious and some were humorous. The prospective groom asked the group to please not send the telegrams collect. The prospective bride was asked to read the messages, to which each had signed his name or initials. (Instead of telegrams, a variation of this would be to have the boys write a note of advice to the bride, and the girls write a similar note to the groom. Have these read aloud.)

4. *Presenting the Gifts.*—Sometime near the end of the party the leader announced that the express man was at the door with a package for the class. The president was asked to receive it. He went out and came in with the basket of gifts. A short presentation speech was then made, and the bride was asked to open the gifts. The group was seated in a circle and as the gifts were opened, they were passed around the circle for all to see. The cards were left in the packages so that all might know the donor.

Some of the gifts were arranged so that they were amusing. The rolling pin baby, described above, was in a long flower box. A cupid dressed up like a baby was also passed around the circle. Someone had brought a large safety pin about five inches long, and this caused a lot of comment as it went around the circle.

If you would like to give a shower such as the one described, some games and stunts that may be used by any group at such a function will now be suggested with complete details on how to play them.

5. *Choosing Partners.*—Make a large heart out of red cardboard, leaving a hole in the center. Suspend it from the ceiling. Get a number of pieces of cord—a number equal to half the number of guests expected. Run these cords through the hole in the heart. When the leader is ready for the game, she asks the boys to take hold of the ends of the cord on one side of the heart, and the girls to take hold of the ends on the other side. At a signal from the leader all pull, tearing up the heart. This will leave a boy and girl holding to each end of a cord. These will be partners for the remainder of the games in which partners work together.

6. *Affinities.*—Affinities is an appropriate game for a bride and groom shower. The leader tells the group that a prize will be given to the couple who can write the largest number of affinities. The leader may say that in the future the bride and groom will be thought of together. They will be Mary and John. Suggest some other things that are always thought of together and after giving a few examples, ask the guests to see how many affinities they can write. Below is given a list of things that are usually thought of together.

(1)	Pen and Ink.	(10)	Thunder and Lightning.
(2)	Ham and Eggs.	(11)	Ice Cream and Cake.
(3)	Bread and Butter.	(12)	Hat and Coat.
(4)	Pork and Beans.	(13)	Hand and Foot.
(5)	Knife and Fork.	(14)	Man and Wife.
(6)	Salt and Pepper.	(15)	Shoes and Stockings.
(7)	Peaches and Cream.	(16)	Sun and Moon.
(8)	Pencil and Paper.	(17)	Sugar and Cream.
(9)	Fair and Warmer.	(18)	Comb and Brush.

7. *Two Hearts that Beat as One.*—Paste on a cardboard or pin on a curtain a large heart. Have another heart the same size. These should be made of stiff paper or cardboard. Blindfold the guests one at a time and let them try to pin the other heart directly over the one on the wall. The leader may spin them around once or twice before they start so that they lose their direction.

A variation of this would be to have two quoits made of stiff cardboard in the shape of hearts. Arrange a peg or nail, either elevated or on the floor, and have the guests, one at a time, pitch the two heart quoits and try to get both of them on, so that two hearts may beat as one.

8. *Making the Most of Matrimony.*—The leader should say that as the bride and groom are soon to be married (or, as the bride and groom are now married, as the case may be) they must make the most of matrimony. So the guests, either working together by couples or individually, try to make the most of "matrimony." This is done by each one trying to make all the words he can from the letters in matrimony.

9. *Continuous Love Story.*—The leader may say that we all hope the life of the bride and groom will be a continuous love story. Then the guests are asked to write a continuous love story. Three or four slips of paper are given to the guests seated in a circle. They should be given to every fifth or sixth person. This person is to start a love story, writing two or three sentences, or as many as he can before the whistle blows or the leader stops him with some other signal. When he is stopped, he is to fold his paper so that the

next person cannot see what he has written and pass it on. The next person then has a turn to write. When the five or six have completed their writing and the paper gets to the last person of the five or six, he should be instructed by the leader to write a conclusion. The papers are then collected and read to the group.

10. *Famous Lovers.*—Use scrambled names of famous lovers as a writing game. This game will be found in Famous Lovers Party, page 51, number 4. The couples who were selected by choosing partners should work together for this game.

11. *Mock Wedding.*—For an amusing stunt stage an impromptu mock wedding. Select the following participants: a bride, groom, maid of honor, best man, bride's father, bride's mother, preacher, rejected suitor, ring bearer, and flower girl. While it would be well to have a rehearsal before the party, it is not absolutely necessary. Have the participants assemble in a room for the processional, and let them march in as someone plays the wedding march.

The formation for the procession should be as follows: Preacher, carrying mail-order house catalogue; maid of honor, with mincing steps; flower girl scattering bits of torn-up paper; the bride with the father; the groom and best man, coming through another door and meeting the bride and father at the improvised altar; the bride's mother and the rejected suitor should be weeping as they enter and may carry wet handkerchiefs which they wring out at intervals. Exaggerate all actions. Exaggerated make-up will add to the humor. Ring bearer carries brass curtain ring on large pillow.

The preacher (dressed in long coat and white vest) reads the following ceremony:

Friends and fellow-citizens, lend me your ears. We are not here to bury this couple but to marry them. This occasion is very solemn, yea, almost tragic; for we have gathered together to join this man and this woman into the state of wedlock, from whose bourne no traveler ever returns—except by way of alimony. This event is tragic in that after years of fishing a sucker has been caught. This should teach us all that those who nibble must look out for the hook. This couple comes before me today believing that two

139

can live as cheaply as one—which they can as long as one of them does not eat or buy new clothes. Amen.

If anyone present knows any reason why this honorable mistake should not be made, let it now be known, or ever afterward hold your horses. (The rejected suitor responds with a sob.)

Who gives the bride away?

Bride's Father: I do.

Preacher: Repeat after me these words. (Bride's father repeats:) I gladly give her into the board and keep of this unfortunate man. My gain is his loss.

Preacher: Is there a token to this union?

(The ring bearer brings up the ring, which should be a brass curtain ring carried on large pillow. The ring should be dropped, and all search for it. Then the preacher says:)

Since time immoral brass has been a symbol of wedded love. The bride from the day of the wedding begins to display brass. The groom is found to have plenty of brass. This display of brass will never end, so this brass ring is made in an unbroken circle. Take it, sir, and place it on her thumb and repeat after me these words: "With this ring I thee wed, and with all my earthly possessions I do thee endow, payable in a weekly allowance of four dollars, out of which you must buy the groceries and your clothes, pay for the milk and ice, laundry and gas." Amen.

Preacher: Join your right hands and cross your fingers. Abie, do you take Cutie to be your helpeat, to have and to hold, sink or swim, survive or perish, for better or for worse, and probably worse, promising that you will always obey her, and listen to her lectures unmoved? That you will remain with her in sickness and in health, whenever you cannot think of some excuse to get out with the old gang? And that you will keep yourself as far out of earshot as possible until death or Reno separates you? Do you further promise that you will get up first in the morning (he promises after each item), get breakfast, wash the dishes and sweep, leave your money at home when you go to work, kiss your dear companion when you leave and tell her how young and beautiful she is, get your lunch down in town, buy the groceries as you come home, get supper while she reads the paper, stay at home at night so your wife can go to the bridge club? Do you further promise that you will let her make all the decisions, tell you what to do, buy your clothes, and tell you when to get a hair cut?

(The preacher addresses the bride:) Cutie, do you take Abie to be your husband, promising that you will cultivate his financial ability? Will you see that he walks in the straight and narrow path, that he stays home at night and otherwise helps to develop his tender life until the character sprouts? Do you promise that you will leave father and mother long enough to do this, and that you will cleave unto him whenever he shows an inclination to seek the society of others? Do you promise that you will keep him in hot water all the time, for shaving; that you will help him always, to spend his money, and try to keep him well so that he can work harder and make more money? Do you further promise to remind him when your birthday and wedding anniversary come? And do you further promise that you will completely manage him and at the same time let him feel that he is the boss and the head of the house?

Then, by virtue of the authority vested in me as preacher, I now pronounce you one, which one, only time will tell. May the chain stores have mercy on your pocketbook, and the installment collectors call when you are out; and may the landlord, when he will not give you repairs, give you more time. You are now committed for life, and what we have here joined asunder let no man separate together.

The friends may now come forward and view the victims of the catastrophe and condole the friends. May we all make the best of it.

12. *Refreshments.*—Someone should be asked to bake a large wedding cake. If there is no one who will volunteer to do this, one may be purchased at the bakery. This, with a fruit punch or iced tea, will be appropriate refreshments.

The bride should be asked to cut the cake.

13. *Properties*

(1) A large clothesbasket for the gifts. This should be decorated.

(2) Telegraph blanks or blank sheets of paper and pencils.

(3) Large red heart with strings passing through it.

(4) Two large hearts in stiff red paper or heart quoits and peg.

(5) Paper and pencils for making the most of Matrimony and Continuous Love Story.

(6) Mail-order house catalogue, bits of torn-up paper, and wet handkerchiefs for Mock Wedding.

(7) Mimeographed sheets for Famous Lovers.

chapter 22

An Evening with the Gods[1]

(COSTUME)

IN THE TIME BEFORE "A LONG, LONG WHILE AGO," AND EVEN BEFORE "once upon a time," the peoples of the earth attempted to explain the things of nature, such as the sun, the moon, the stars, the thunder, the Creator, and so on, and out of these explanations there arose the beautiful and strange mythological stories. Everyone is familiar with the gods and goddesses of ancient Greece and Rome, so why not plan to spend an evening renewing acquaintance with them?

1. *Invitation.*—Send out the following or a similar invitation:

> This message comes from Jupiter,
>   And is sent by Mercury with speed,
> To summon you next Friday night
>   For a big party and a feed.
> Wear the garb of a god or goddess,
>   And take care lest you lose your heart,
> For Venus, the goddess of love, will be there,
>   And Dan Cupid with his bow and dart.

2. *Costumes.*—This may or may not be a costume party. If costumes are used, each guest might be asked to represent a certain god or goddess. It would be a good idea for the social committee to send out with the invitations typewritten suggestions as to costumes. The following are some of these suggestions:

[1] Prepared with the assistance of Mrs. Roy G. Ross, Indianapolis, Ind.

142

Suitable Greek costumes may be made of loose pieces of cheese-cloth, draped around the body in various ways and fastened with pins or brooches. The boys might leave the left arm and shoulder exposed by fastening the material under the armpit. Girdles of various colors should be fastened around the waist and any superfluous material pulled up under the girdle and allowed to fall in a baggy fold over it. The girls should dress their hair in Greek style with fillet and psyche. Elaborate earrings, necklaces, bracelets, and hair ornaments should be worn by the goddesses.

If the guests are not asked to come in costume, it would be well for the hostess and others assisting with the games and the refreshments to wear costumes.

3. *Some of the Greek and Roman Gods.*—Most adults will remember some of their mythology, but it would be best to help them dust their memories. The following is a list which may prove helpful in arranging for the costumes:

Jupiter (Zeus).
Minerva (Athens) —Wisdom.
Mars (Ares) —War.
Vulcan—Firebrand, god of metal working.
Apollo—Sun.
Diana—Moon, often represented as a huntress.
Venus (Aphrodite) —Love.
Mercury (Hermes) —Messenger of the gods.
Ceres (Demeter) —Goddess of grain.
Pluto (Hades) —God of the underworld.
Neptune—Sea.
Hercules—Strength.
Atlas—Bearer of great burdens.
Achilles—Warrior who was invulnerable except in the heel.
Janus—God of gates and doors, represented with two faces.
Pandora—The gift of all the gods, beauty, charm, music.
Cupid—God of love, carries bow and quiver of arrows.

4. *Decorations.*—The room should be decorated with streamers of crepe paper in pastel colors. Cardboard with Greek letters printed

on them and hung on the wall would add to the effectiveness of the decorations.

5. *Opening Mixer: Guessing Gods and Goddesses.*—If the guests come in costume, let them begin by trying to guess which god or goddess each individual represents. Some clever or artistic dramatization of familar myths should be given by the guest representing the god of that myth. Supply guests with pencil and paper and ask them to write the name of the guest, and opposite this the name of the god or goddess represented. When all have finished guessing, the leader should read a correct list. The person who has the largest list should be given a prize. As his name is called, each guest should be asked to walk the length of the room, so that all may see the costume. (This will also assist in judging the costumes.)

If costumes are not used, pin the name of a god or goddess on the back of each guest, and let him determine his own identity by questioning others concerning his characteristics. Of course the players will give answers which, though truthful, will puzzle the one trying to learn his identity. As soon as each player finds out who he is, the name is pinned on the front.

6. *Judging the Costumes.*—Judges should be appointed by the leader to determine the best costume and the most beautiful costume. The costumes could be judged by vote of the guests present, or by the judges picking the best six costumes and determining the opinion of the group by holding a hand over the head of each and letting the other guests applaud. The one getting the most applause is declared winner.

7. *Seeds from the Garden of Ceres.*—Secure as many kinds of seeds as possible, and put a small amount of each on separate saucers or small paper plates. Give each kind of seed a number. Any seed store would doubtless be glad to furnish samples of various kinds of seed for this game. Give each contestant a pencil and paper, and ask them to write down all the seeds they know or can guess. The one who guesses the greatest number might be given a packet of seeds as a prize. Some seeds that may be used in this way are the following:

Carrot	Corn	Zinnias
Watermelon	Apple	Prune
Nasturtium	Cowpeas	Peach
Orange	Buckwheat	Millet
Grapefruit	Cantaloupe	Oats
Date		

8. *Atlas Relay Race.*—Secure three or four medicine balls. Divide the guests into a group for a relay race and have them line up in rows facing goals twenty or thirty feet away, if possible. Give a medicine ball to the leader of each group. The leader of the group must place the ball on his shoulder, holding it in place with his arm, in the way Atlas appears to be carrying the world on his shoulders. The leader runs to the goal and back, touches off the next player, who does the same, until all in the group have had a turn. The group to finish first wins.

9. *The Test of Hercules.*—Two tests of strength are given here, one for the boys and one for the girls, though both boys and girls could do either or both. To test the strength of the boys, secure a large size chopping ax and ask the contestant to grasp it by the end of the handle and attempt to raise the ax straight out from his shoulder, keeping his arm straight all the while. This is an old-time method of testing strength, used in the country.

For the girls secure a soft piece of wood about four inches by four inches and either sixteen penny or twenty penny nails, and also a hammer. The object of the game is to see which girl can drive a nail all the way into the piece of wood with the least number of blows from the hammer. Count the blows as the girls drive.

10. *King Neptune's Sea Is Troubled.*—This game can be played by any number of guests. They sit in a circle of chairs, every chair being filled. King Neptune starts the game by calling the names of the Greek gods who are seated in the circle. As he calls these names, those called are to rise from their chair and follow him around. When he says, "King Neptune's sea is troubled," all scramble for chairs. The one who is left out takes the place that King Neptune filled and calls the names of others. When he says, "King Neptune's

sea is troubled," all scramble for chairs as before. Do not play this game more than about five minutes.

Another adaptation of this game is to give the players names of fish, and as the names of these fish are called, they get up and follow the leader.

11. *Paris and the Apple.*—Select two teams of four each. These teams may be composed of four boys each, boys against girls, or two boys and two girls on each team. Give each team an apple and a paring knife. The first one on the team peels the apple, the second one cuts it in quarters, the third one cores the apple, and the fourth one eats it. The team whose apple is first eaten wins.

12. *Cupid's Archery Contest.*—Secure bow and arrows from the dime store. There should be about five arrows. Have the names of guests written on large red hearts mounted on a base so that they will stand up. This could be done by writing a boy's name on one side and a girl's name on the other. Let the girls and boys shoot at any heart they desire. Give candy hearts as a prize for those who hit.

13. *Diana Takes Us All Hunting.*—Tie small objects, such as lollipops, chewing gum, stick candy, or other inexpensive favors, on long strings. Hide these objects in various parts of the room or house, and then wind the rest of the string about various parts of the room, having the strings cross each other frequently until the whole resembles a spider web. All of the strings should converge at one point. Each player is given a string and must then try to find the other end of it. Of course the strings must not be cut or broken, but must be carefully untangled and followed to the end of the prize.

14. *Minerva's Intelligence Test.*—Minerva is the fabled goddess of wisdom. Give guests sheets of paper on which has been written with a typewriter, using carbon copies, or mimeographed, the following intelligence test (without the answers, of course) :

(1) What can run and can't walk, has a tongue and can't talk? Wagon.

(2) What has eyes and cannot see? Potato.

(3) What has legs and can't walk? Table.

(4) What goes all the way around the house and makes one track? Wheelbarrow.

(5) What can be seen when covered? Book.

(6) What would you do if you had a dime and a buggy top? Buy a fine comb and get the bugs out.

(7) What can tell you how you look without talking? Mirror.

(8) What has a face and never washes it? Clock.

(9) What is always found in pairs? Scissors.

(10) What grows larger the more you take from it? Hole.

(11) What is full of holes and yet holds water? Sponge.

(12) Why does a policeman have brass buttons on his coat? To button it with.

(13) What is both a time and a fruit? Date.

(14) What has pains and does not ache? Window.

(15) Why is a Dutchman's pancake like the sun? It rises in the "yeast" and sets behind the "vest."

(16) What is the difference between a woman and an umbrella? You can shut up an umbrella.

(17) Why does a miller wear a white hat? To cover his head.

15. *Atlanta's Relay Race.*—The brief story of Atlanta is as follows: Atlanta, a beautiful girl, had been warned by an oracle that her marriage would be fatal to her, so she fled the society of men and devoted her time to sports. "I will be the prize of him only who shall conquer me in a race, but death must be the penalty of all who try and fail," she declared. Many tried, but all were unsuccessful. Hippomenes, the judge of one of the contests, prompted by her great beauty, decided to enter the contest himself. Atlanta, who had fallen in love with him, decided to let him win. Just before the race she gathered three golden apples and gave them to Hippomenes. At the signal Atlanta and her lover were ready. After they were well started, he dropped the first apple, then the second, and finally the third. As Atlanta stooped to pick it up Hippomenes passed the goal.

The leader might tell this story briefly and then line up the players for a relay race. They should be about thirty feet away from the goal if possible. Draw three circles on the floor about four inches in diameter with chalk. The first of these should be about ten feet from the head of each line, the second about twenty feet, and the third, which is the goal, about thirty feet. Give the ones at the head of each line three apples. When the leader's whistle blows, they must run with these apples, laying one of them in each of the three circles. They then pick them up as they come back and give the three apples to the next one in line and take their position at the back of the line. If a player fails to get the apple in the circle, he must go back and replace it. The side that finishes first wins.

16. *Pandora Will Open Her Mysterious Casket.*—Each player is given a sheet of paper at the top of which is written, "Pandora Will Open Her Mysterious Casket." They are told that out of Pandora's casket escaped all the passions, sorrows, and diseases of the world; that only hope remained in the casket. They are told to write all of the passions and sorrows and diseases that they can think of which can be made by using the letters given above. The one having the largest list is the winner, and this list should be read.

17. *Echo and Narcissus.*—The following is a brief story of Echo and Narcissus: Echo, a beautiful maiden who was fond of the wood and hills, attended Diana in the chase. She, however, displeased Diana by her chatter, so that she was condemned to lose her voice save for purposes of reply. She fell in love with Narcissus, a handsome youth, but she could only mimic what he said. He was unable to understand her, but one day he said, "Let us join one another," she echoed him, whereupon he said: "Hands off. I should rather die than thou shouldst have me." Echo was heartbroken and finally pined away until there was nothing left but her voice.

Using the above thought of Narcissus being mimicked by Echo, play the game of "Mimic," which can be found by looking in the Index.

18. *Refreshments.*—For refreshments serve "Food for the Gods" (angel-food cake). A big freezer of homemade ice cream would go well with this. Another suggestion would be to have a god preside

over the punch bowl and serve punch and sandwiches to the mortals.

19. *Properties*

(1) Pencil and paper for each guest for Opening Mixer.

(2) Many different kinds of seeds for Seeds from the Garden of Ceres. Also pencil and paper for each guest.

(3) Medicine balls for Atlas Relay Race.

(4) Ax for the boys for the Test of Hercules. Wood, nails, and hammer for girls for the Test of Hercules.

(5) Apples and paring knives for Paris and the Apple.

(6) Bows and arrows, large hearts on bases for Cupid's Archery Contest.

(7) Long strings, small favors to be hidden for Diana Takes Us All Hunting.

(8) Papers prepared for Intelligence Test.

(9) Apples for Atlanta's Relay Race.

(10) Papers prepared for Pandora Will Open Her Mysterious Casket.

chapter 23

Treasure Hunt Party

IN THE DAYS OF AUTOMOBILES WHEN IT IS A SMALL MATTER TO GO places, a treasure hunt will be a good idea for an evening of fun. Let the treasure be a large box of candy, or the refreshments for the evening, or a handsome prize. Guests should be sent all over the city and even out in the country searching for it.

We know of one instance where a treasure hunt was a feature at a young people's conference. The conference had been divided into four groups, and a hundred points was promised to the group that found the treasure. Every day some clue was posted on the bulletin board or announced in the dining-room. Toward the close of the conference the award was raised to two hundred points, then to three hundred points, and at last to five hundred points. The treasure was finally found in one of the dormitories where no one had thought to look before.

1. *Map Treasure Hunt.*—The committee in charge prepares a map showing certain points to be visited and certain instructions as to how to look for the treasure at each point. In this case the group would not know where to go first, and each auto load could choose before starting the most likely place. Everyone should be given instructions to the effect that if the treasure is found nothing should be said about it, but those who find it should immediately return it to the place where all are to meet after the search is over.

2. *Letter Treasure Hunt.*—A variation of the above would be to have the group assemble in one place and have the leader read to them a letter giving full instructions as to where to look for the treasure and how it is likely to be found. Have guests take notes on the different clues given in the letter.

3. *One Clue at a Time: Treasure Hunt.*—Have all who are to participate in a treasure hunt come to a starting place for instructions. Here they are informed where they are to go for further instruction. When this place is reached, they find instructions that send them somewhere else. So on until the round has been made. In this case it would be well to hide the treasure near the last stopping place.

4. *Reassembled for Games.*—The Treasure Hunt itself should be planned so that it will last from an hour to an hour and a half, and then the guests should be directed to return to the home of the host for an assembly and refreshments.

5. *Hidden Objects.*—Have objects hidden about the room and give to each guest a slip of paper on which is written some object that they are to find whenever the leader's whistle is blown. These objects might be, for example, a spool of thread, a needle, a spoon, a pipe, a match, and so forth. No one must give information to anyone else, and anyone caught giving this information should be required to pay a forfeit. If these forfeits are paid, see the Index for "Forfeits" for suggestions as to redeeming these.

6. *Hidden Birds.*—The leader should have the following questions written on a typewriter, making carbon copies, or have them mimeographed. Of course, do not underline the letters as they are italicized here:

(1) Moses was found in a smal*l ark*.   Lark.
(2) Have you been to Shad*ow L*awn?   Owl.
(3) A*h, awk*ward fellow, be careful.   Hawk.
(4) In gram*mar tin*y words have important uses.   Martin.
(5) *Can a ry*e loaf of bread be obtained here?   Canary.
(6) I am always up at *daw*n.   Daw.
(7) Tailor, can you fix my coat la*pel? I can,* I'm sure.   Pelican.
(8) Would you try to *rob in* daylight?   Robin.
(9) That sounds as if it might b*e a gle*e club.   Eagle.
(10) I met *her on* Sunday.   Heron.
(11) Ma*j. Ay*ers is our officer.   Jay.
(12) I would like to show he*r a Ven*etian gondola.   Raven.
(13) You certainly *do ve*ry well.   Dove.
(14) Your child looks *wan* and pale.   Swan.

(15) How *rent*s have gone up! Wren.
(16) Whom did they *crow*n Queen of May? Crow.
(17) The children bo*th rush*ed home from school. Thrush.
(18) The baby *swallow*ed his fist. Swallow.
(19) Have you any half *inch* adhesive? Finch.
(20) I believe you are too *gull*ible. Gull.

7. *Are You a Good Treasure Hunter?*

(1) *Sense of smell.* Try out different individuals, blindfolded, to see who can name the largest number of a group of articles by the sense of smell. Use salve, an onion, limburger cheese, castor oil, smoking tobacco, and so forth.

(2) *Sense of hearing.* Blindfold different ones and test the sense of hearing by dropping certain objects which have been previously displayed and letting the person blindfolded guess what it was that was dropped. Use a ball, a book, a bean bag, a sponge, a pencil, a knife, a coin, a shoe, and so forth.

(3) *Sense of sight.* Place a number of objects on a tray and pass the tray around. After the tray has been all the way around, have guests write what they saw. Such objects as a corkscrew, a can opener, a match, a toothpick, a thimble, and a number of small objects may be used.

(4) *Can you see in the dark?* Blindfold about four or five persons for this stunt. Before they are blindfolded, objects are placed on the floor, and they look at them. They are then told that after they are blindfolded, they must walk the length of the room without stepping on any of the objects. When all have been blindfolded and placed in position to walk one behind the other, noiselessly remove the objects from the floor. It will be amusing to see them trying to avoid these objects.

8. *Hidden Flowers*

(1) A charge to remember. Forget-me-not.
(2) Sought by young men. Tulips.
(3) A well-dressed dude and the king of beasts. Dandelion.

(4) Used by the cook in making good cakes. Buttercup.
(5) A flower that won't tell. Daisy.
(6) Often between two thorns. Rose.
(7) Most young women aspire to wear it. Orange blossoms.
(8) Worn on the lady's foot. Lady's-slipper.
(9) What we throw in winter. Snowball.
(10) What we used to call Dad. Poppy.
(11) Son's morning reveille. Johnny-jump-up.
(12) Good for a sad heart. Heart's-ease.
(13) One way for a man to get rich quick. Marigold.
(14) How can you tell if she will have you? Aster.
(15) An hour in the afternoon. Four-o'clock.
(16) Two very familiar girls' names. Rosemary.

9. *Refreshments.*—Perhaps the hidden treasure was a large box of sandwiches. At any rate, sandwiches and coffee or sandwiches and cocoa would be good for refreshments.

10. *Properties*

(1) A treasure hidden in advance, with map or letter or clues describing places where it might be found.
(2) Objects hidden about the room, enough for each guest, and these written on slips of paper to be given out to the guests.
(3) Carbon copies or mimeographed copies of hidden birds.
(4) Articles for blindfold test, for smell and hearing. Also articles on tray for sense of sight. Objects for Can you see in the dark?
(5) Hidden Flowers, carbon or mimeographed copies.

chapter 24

Bible Party

A BIBLE PARTY WOULD BE APPROPRIATE FOR A SUNDAY-SCHOOL CLASS, a United Christian Youth Movement group, or young people's conference group. This party is planned, not for study, but for an evening of fun. At the same time no one can play the games given here without getting a lot of Bible knowledge that will be helpful.

1. *Invitation.*—The following is a suggestion for an invitation:

> Come to our Bible Party,
>   Don't think it will be dry.
> We will have a lot of fun,
>   Or know the reason why.
>   We'll have laughter, games, and stunts galore,
>   And you'll have a better time,
>   Without spending a single dime,
> Than you've ever had before.

2. *Decorations.*—Bible pictures would make a good decoration. These can be used for a game later.

3. *Opening Mixer: Bible Questions.*—Give Bible questions to the boys and the answers to the girls. Let them match questions and answers and find partners in this way. The following are some suggested questions and answers.

(1) How many books in the Old Testament? Thirty-nine.
(2) How many books in the New Testament? Twenty-seven.
(3) What are the first words in the Bible? "In the beginning God."
(4) What is the golden text of the Bible? "For God so loved the world, that he gave his only begotten son, that whosoever believeth on him should not perish, but have eternal life."
(5) In what town was Christ born? Bethlehem.

(6) By whom was Christ baptized? John the Baptist.

(7) In what river was Christ baptized? Jordan.

(8) In what city did Christ perform his first miracle? Cana of Galilee.

(9) On what body of water did Christ walk? Sea of Galilee.

(10) Who betrayed Christ? Judas.

(11) Near what city was Christ crucified? Jerusalem.

(12) On what day was Christ resurrected? Sunday.

(13) From what mountain did Christ give the great commission? A mountain in Galilee.

(14) What are the first four books of the New Testament called? The Gospels.

(15) What is the Golden Rule? "As ye would that men should do unto you do ye even so to them."

(16) What are the first words of the twenty-third Psalm? "The Lord is my shepherd."

(17) What is the shortest verse in the Bible? Jesus wept.

(18) What apostle made four missionary journeys? Paul.

(19) Who wrote the Ten Commandments? Moses.

(20) Who preached the Sermon on the Mount? Christ.

(21) What is the love chapter of the Bible? 1 Corinthians 13.

(22) Who wrote the greater part of the New Testament? Paul.

(23) What disciple denied his Lord three times? Peter.

(24) What disciple was a doubter? Thomas.

(25) What disciple was a tax collector? Matthew.

4. *Bible Pi.*—Slips of paper with a typewritten list of the following names of books of the Bible jumbled are given to the guests. They are to write the name of the book by unjumbling the letters:

(1) Karm. Mark.

(2) Cats. Acts.

(3) Honaj. Jonah.

(4) Hajsou. Joshua.

(5) Nessige. Genesis.

(6) Napsehies. Ephesians.

(7) Loje. Joel.

(8) Lemonphi. Philemon.

(9) Kule. Luke.

(10) Soam. Amos.

(11) Sutti. Titus.

(12) Nedlai. Daniel.

(13) Numah. Nahum.

(14) Smalps. Psalms.

(15) Whettam. Matthew.

(16) Hacim. Micah.

(17) Hertes. Esther.

(18) Morans. Romans.

(19) Levantoire. Revelation.

(20) Rubmens. Numbers.

(21) Reza. Ezra.

Couples should work together on this game and the next one.

5. *Identifying Bible Pictures.*—Get a series of Bible pictures from one of the teachers of small children of the Sunday school. Hang these from the window curtains and draperies, and lay them on the tables or piano, or hang them on the wall. Have these numbered and give each guest or couple a sheet of paper and ask them to number the paper with as many numbers as there are pictures. Let them guess what the picture represents by number. Give a prize to the one having the largest number correct. New Testaments or small Bibles make good prizes. Other suggestions would be small storybooks like the stories written by Van Dyke, or the *Greatest Thing in the World,* by Henry Drummond.

6. *Bible Character Race.*—Print the names of the following Bible characters on large squares of cardboard: Adam, Boaz, Caleb, Daniel, Esther, Festus, Goliath, Herod, Isaac, Jonah, Kish, Luke. This is a relay race, so have the party divided into two groups. This may be done by counting off one and two and having all the ones form one group and the twos the other. They form two lines facing each other. The first one in each line is given the twelve cards so that the letters do not come alphabetically. They must be passed down each line one at a time, and the last man must lay them on the floor and arrange them alphabetically. When this is accomplished, he must start passing them one at a time back, passing back Adam first, Boaz next, and so on. The first group to have all the cards back alphabetically arranged wins. This could be prolonged by making a race out of it and having the cards go down and back two or three times and then have them arranged the last time.

7. *Bible Alphabet.*—Give each guest or couple the following prepared list of questions, which should be written out on a typewriter or prepared with a mimeograph machine. They are to give the answer as indicated below:

A was a traitor found hung by the hair.   Absalom (2 Sam. 18:9).
B was a tower built in the air.   Babel (Gen. 11:49).
C was a mountain rising into the skies.   Carmel (1 Kings 18:42, 43).

D was a woman heroic and wise.   Deborah (Gen. 35:8).
E was a firstborn, bad from his youth.   Esau (Heb. 12:16).
F was a Roman who trembled at truth.   Felix (Acts 24:25).
G was an angel sent with good word.   Gabriel (Dan. 9:21).
H was a mother who lent to the Lord.   Hannah (1 Sam. 1:27, 28).
I was a name received at a ford.   Israel (Gen. 32:22, 28).
J was a preacher who fled from the Lord.   Jonah (Jonah 1).
K's son was taller than him by a head.   Kish, father of Saul.
L was a pauper begging for bread.   Lazarus (Luke 16:20, 21).
M was a leader who wrote down the law.   Moses.
N made a large boat ages ago.   Noah (Gen. 6:13).
O was a slave acknowledged a brother.   Onesimus (Philem. 1:16).
P was one Christian greeting another.   Paul (2 Tim. 1:1, 2).
Q was a Christian saluted by Paul.   Quartus (Rom. 16:23).
R heard Peter's voice and ran and told all.   Rhoda (Acts 12:13).
S was a judge exceeding strong.   Samson (Judg. 14:5, 6).
T was a seaport where preaching was long.   Troas (Acts 20:6, 7).
U was a man whose widow became David's bride.   Uriah (2 Sam. 11:27).
V was a queen whom the king set aside.   Vashti (Esther 1:9-16).
Z was a place where a man wished to hide.   Zoar (Gen. 19:22).

8. *Bible Relay.*—Use the same groups as for Bible Character Race. Have them all stand facing a goal marked out on the floor, about twenty or thirty feet in front of each line. The person on the front of each line is given a stiff-backed Bible (another book may be substituted). At a signal from the leader he balances this Bible on his head and runs to the goal and back. He must not use hands except to replace the Bible if it falls. When he returns to the line, he gives the Bible to the next one, who in turn runs to the goal, the first player taking his place at the back of the line. The group that finishes first wins.

9. *Bible Riddles.*—Have the following riddles written on slips of paper with a typewriter. The guests are asked to write the answers. Give a prize to the one having the largest number correct:

(1) When is baseball first mentioned in the Bible?   Gensis 1:1. In the beginning (in the big inning).
(2) Who is the first man mentioned in the Bible?   Chap. 1.
(3) At what time was Adam born?   A little before Eve.

(4) Why should Adam have been satisfied with his wife? She was cut out for him.

(5) How do we know that Adam used sugar? Because he raised Cain.

(6) In what order did Noah come from the ark? He came fourth.

(7) How long did Cain hate his brother? As long as he was Abel.

(8) How do we know that Samson was an actor? He brought down the house.

(9) When was paper money first used? When the dove brought the green back to Noah.

(10) Who was the first woman mentioned in the Bible? Adam. The Bible says he was first made (maid).

(11) Who are the two smallest men mentioned in the Bible? Bildad the Shuhite and Nehemiah (Nehi-miah).

(12) What are the two smallest things mentioned in the Bible? The "widow's mite" and the "wicked flee."

(13) Why did they not play cards on the ark? Noah was on the deck.

(14) Who was the first electrician? Noah; he made the ark light on Mount Ararat.

(15) Who were the three Tom Thumb apostles? Peter, James, and John. They slept on a watch.

(16) Who were the two noblemen of Bible times? Baron Fig Tree, Lord How Long.

(17) In what place did the rooster crow so all the world could hear him? The ark.

(18) Who was the first great financier? Noah. He floated a company when the whole world was in liquidation.

(19) How do we know that St. Paul was a cook. The Bible says he went to Philippi (fill a pie).

(20) When are preserves first mentioned? When Noah preserved the pairs in the ark.

(21) Who was Jonah's guardian? The whale brought him up.

(22) How do we know that there will be no women in heaven? The Bible says that there was silence in heaven for one minute.

10. *Oral Bible Alphabet.*—The leader stands in the center of the room with the players seated in a circle. The leader calls a letter of the alphabet, omitting to call Q, U, W, X, Y, and Z, and as he calls he points to a player and slowly counts to ten. If the player can name a Bible character whose name begins with that letter, he must do so or take the place of the leader. So the game continues.

11. *Bible Dramatics.*—Divide the party into four or five groups, having from four to eight in a group. Tell each group that they are to dramatize a Bible story. Let them go into other rooms or into corners of the room and plan their drama. The leader should visit each group to be sure that there are no duplicates. Some suggestions would be: Ruth, Esther, David and Jonathan, David and Goliath, Samson and Delilah, Christ cleansing the temple, the raising of Lazarus, healing of a blind man, stoning of Stephen, conversion of Saul of Tarsus, the beheading of James.

12. *Bible Baseball.*—One of the best Bible games known is Bible Baseball. This can form the major part of an evening entertainment. Nine or more players are chosen from each side, as they have been previously divided. There should be a pitcher and an umpire selected. They ask the questions and make decisions as to correct answers. Bases are drawn on the floor, and a player takes his place at home plate, the pitcher asks a question, which, if the batter answers, he (the batter) goes to first base. If he misses the question, it is one out for his side. Players on bases can only be advanced by others on their side answering questions. Scores are made when bases are full and another question is answered, forcing the man on third base home. Suggested questions follow:

OLD TESTAMENT QUESTIONS

(1) Name the first three books of the Bible. Genesis, Exodus, Leviticus.

(2) Name the last book in the Old Testament. Malachi.

(3) Name two of Adam's sons. Cain and Abel.

(4) Who said, "Am I my brother's keeper"? Cain.

(5) Who was translated to heaven? Enoch.

(6) How many people were in the ark? Eight.

(7) Name two sons of Noah. Ham, Shem, Japheth.

(8) Who was told that his descendants should be as numerous as the stars? Abraham.

(9) Who was Abraham's wife? Sarah.

(10) What son was Abraham commanded to sacrifice as a burnt offering? Isaac.

(11) Who sold his birthright? Esau.

(12) Who was Rebekah's favorite son? Jacob.

(13) Who saw a ladder reaching from earth to heaven? Jacob.

(14) Who waited fourteen years for a wife? Jacob.

(15) What Hebrew was sold into Egypt by his brothers? Joseph.

(16) Who was found in a small ark by Pharaoh's daughter? Moses.

(17) What land was given to the Hebrews? Canaan.

(18) Who wrote down the Ten Commandments? Moses.

(19) From what mountain was God's law given? Sinai.

(20) Who followed Moses as leader of the Hebrew people? Joshua.

(21) What river flowed between the wilderness and Canaan? Jordan.

(22) What city was it whose walls fell after the Hebrews had marched around it for seven days? Jericho.

(23) What woman was a judge in Israel? Deborah.

(24) What Hebrew leader dismissed an army of 30,000 and beat the enemy with 300? Gideon.

(25) Who tied firebrands to foxes' tails and turned them loose in the Philistines' grain fields? Samson.

(26) What child was dedicated by his mother, Hannah, to service in God's house? Samuel.

(27) Who was the first king of Israel? Saul.

(28) What shepherd lad was anointed king of Israel? David.

(29) Who slew a giant with a sling shot? David.

(30) Who was David's intimate friend? Jonathan.

(31) Who built the first temple at Jerusalem? Solomon.

(32) Who told Ahab that it would not rain until he said so? Elijah.

(33) Who wished that he might die under a juniper tree? Elijah.

(34) To whom did Jehovah appear in a still small voice? Elijah.

(35) Who was Elijah's successor? Elisha.

(36) What king of Israel was a fast driver? Jehu.

(37) What two books in the Old Testament are named for women? Ruth and Esther.

(38) What Hebrew did Ruth marry? Boaz.

(39) Who was noted for his patience? Job.

(40) Who was sent to Nineveh to preach? Jonah.

(41) What queen risked her life to save her people? Esther.

(42) Who was hanged on the gallows he built for another? Haman.

(43) Who saw the handwriting on the wall? Belshazzar.

(44) Who rebuilt the walls of Jerusalem? Nehemiah.

(45) Name two great prophets of the Old Testament? Isaiah, Jeremiah, or any other two.

(46) Who refused to eat dainty food and drink wine? Daniel.

(47) Who was thrown into a den of lions?   Daniel.

(48) Quote the first sentence of the twenty-third Psalm.   "The Lord is my Shepherd; I shall not want."

(49) Quote the first four words of the Bible.   "In the beginning, God."

(50) How many books in the Old Testament?   Thirty-nine.

New Testament Questions

(1) How many books in New Testament?   Twenty-seven.

(2) Name first four books in New Testament.   Matthew, Mark, Luke, John.

(3) Name fifth book in New Testament.   Acts.

(4) Who wore camel's hair and ate locust and wild honey?   John the Baptist.

(5) Who pointed to Jesus and said, "Behold the Lamb of God"?   John the Baptist.

(6) In what town was Jesus born?   Bethlehem.

(7) Who brought gifts to Jesus?   The wise men.

(8) In what city was Jesus reared?   Nazareth.

(9) How old was Jesus when he was found in the temple talking with the doctors and lawyers?   Twelve.

(10) What was Jesus' trade?   Carpenter.

(11) Who were the first two disciples?   Peter and Andrew.

(12) Who was called the "disciple whom Jesus loved"?   John.

(13) What disciple was the doubter?   Thomas.

(14) What disciple made a feast for Jesus?   Matthew.

(15) What disciple was the treasurer of the group?   Judas.

(16) To whom did Jesus say, "Ye must be born again"?   Nicodemus.

(17) What two women were friends of Jesus at Bethany?   Martha and Mary.

(18) What man did Jesus raise from the dead at Bethany?   Lazarus.

(19) Who climbed a tree that he might see Jesus?   Zacchaeus.

(20) What disciple objected to Jesus' washing his feet?   Peter.

(21) What disciple cut off an officer's ear with his sword?   Peter.

(22) What disciple denied Christ three times?   Peter.

(23) Before what Roman governor was Jesus tried?   Pilate.

(24) In whose sepulcher was Jesus buried?   Joseph of Arimathea.

(25) Give two of the Beatitudes.   Any two (Matt. 5).

(26) What is the Golden Rule?   "As you would that men should do unto you, do you even so to them."

(27) On what day did the Spirit come with the sound of a mighty wind?   Pentecost.

(28) Where was the first Christian church?   Jerusalem.

(29) Who was the first Christian martyr? Stephen.

(30) What apostle was first beheaded? James.

(31) What apostle was led forth from prison by an angel? Peter.

(32) Where was Paul's birthplace? Tarsus.

(33) Of what race was Paul? Jewish.

(34) What was Paul's citizenship? Roman.

(35) What was Paul's trade? Tentmaker.

(36) Where was Paul converted? On the Damascus road.

(37) Who converted an Ethiopian treasurer as they rode in a chariot? Philip.

(38) What man and his wife told a lie about the sale of their property? Ananias and Sapphira.

(39) Who was Paul's first missionary partner? Barnabas.

(40) Who was Paul's second missionary partner? Silas.

(41) Where were the people called "noble" because they searched the Scriptures? Beroea.

(42) Where was Paul stoned? Lystra.

(43) What couple did Paul meet at Corinth who were tentmakers and Christians? Aquila and Priscilla.

(44) Who appealed to Caesar and was sent to Rome? Paul.

(45) Who was the "beloved physician"? Luke.

(46) What preacher did Paul call his son? Timothy.

(47) Where were the disciples first called Christians? Antioch.

(48) Who wrote the Acts of the Apostles? Luke.

(49) Who wrote the Revelation? John.

(50) What is the love chapter of the Bible? 1 Corinthians 13.

13. *Hidden Books of the Bible.*—The following is a writing game, and the story may be written out, using a typewriter and making carbon copies, or the story may be mimeographed. The object is to mark all the books of the Bible that can be found in the story as they are in italics here.[1]

While motoring in Palestine I met Chief Me*jud, g*esticulating wildly. His *fez, r*aiment, and features were odd. I never saw so dis*mal a chi*ef. On *mark*et days he pum*ps alms* from everyone, *a mos*t common practice. A glance shows that he *acts* queerly. Excuse me spea*king so*, but he was showing a crowd how they used to *revel at Io*nian bouts, when *the brew s*eemed bad.

[1] From the *Christian Endeavor World.*

A fakir was seated *on a hum*mock, minus *hose a*nd shirt, and wearing as *comic a h*at as they make. He pointed u*p eter*nally toward a rudely carved letter *J on a h*igh cliff.

My companion excitedly cried: "See that *J. Oh, n*ow I know we are near the ancient Ai. Was th*is Ai a h*oly place?"

*From answ*ers given elsewhere I'll say not.

We asked the age of the big stone *J*. "*O, el*even centuries at least."

I knew that in such a *jam esc*ort was necessary. Besides, our car stuck in a *rut h*ere. So, leaving the s*edan, I el*bowed nearer the fakir. A toothless *hag gain*ed access to his side, and paused to *rest her*self. She hinted, "You have treasure?" To which I retorted: "No*t I. Moth, y*ou know, and rust, corrupt earthly store."

Me*jud ex*pressed a wish to accompany us, but I decreed, "Thy party we will not an*nex, O dus*ky chief."

"I a*m at the w*ork of tracing a cargo of lost tobacco. That's my *job*." To the chief's expression of sorrow over the toba*cco loss I answ*ered, "It would all have gone up in smoke, anyway."

My brother is a tram*p (rover)*, *B.S.*, from Harvard, too. His name is Eu*gene. Sis*ter is nursing him now. They asked, "Where is the prodi*gal at?*" I *answ*ered tha*t it us*ed to be incorrect to use "at" that way, but that the *flu ke*pt Eugene at home this year. It really is too *bad, I a h*ome body, roaming the Orient, and he, a tramp, at home in bed.

13. *Choosing Partners for Refreshments.*—Give each boy the name of a male Bible character, written on a slip of paper which he is to pin on his shoulder. The girls are given the names of female Bible characters—the wives of the male characters which have been given to the boys—which they too pin on their shoulders. The couples match by finding the person who wears the name of his or her Bible husband or wife.

(1) Adam and Eve.	(9) Mary and Joseph.
(2) Abraham and Sarah.	(10) Ananias and Sapphira.
(3) Isaac and Rebekah.	(11) Priscilla and Aquila.
(4) Jacob and Rachel.	(12) Zebedee and Salome.
(5) David and Bathsheba.	(13) Lot and Lot's wife.
(6) Ruth and Boaz.	(14) Peter and Peter's wife.
(7) Ahab and Jezebel.	(15) Cain and Cain's wife.
(8) Zechariah and Elisabeth.	(16) Noah and Noah's wife.

14. *Refreshments.*—Ice cream and cake or iced tea and cake. If cold, serve hot chocolate or coffee and sandwiches.

15. *Properties*

(1) Bible questions and answers for opening mixer, written on typewriter.

(2) Jumbled Bible names for Bible Pi, written out with typewriter.

(3) Bible pictures numbered and placed about the room. Papers and pencils.

(4) Large cardboards for Character Race.

(5) Typewritten papers for Bible Alphabet.

(6) Two Bibles with stiff backs for Bible Relay.

(7) Papers prepared with typewriter for Bible Riddles.

(8) Questions prepared for Bible Baseball.

(9) Bible couples written on typewriter and cut apart for choosing partners for refreshments.

(10) Mimeographed sheets for Hidden Books of the Bible.

chapter 25

Aquatic Party

(*OUT OF DOORS*)

CONDITIONS UNDER WHICH THIS PARTY IS HELD MAY MAKE IMPOSSIBLE the using of all the things suggeseted. An ideal setting for such a party as this would be a swimming pool near the beach; however, it could be given at any lake, river, or swimming place. It would be better to have the guests come about five-thirty or six o'clock and have plenty of food on hand so that they need not have dinner before coming. It would be better to pick a moonlight night, but this is not necessary as a fire can be built which will give light enough for the games that are to be played after dark.

1. *Invitation.*—The following is a suggested invitation for such a party:

<blockquote>
In the good old summer time
It's just the season prime
To get into the water cool
With your friends and mine.
So bring your suit and water wings,
For the water will be fine,
And we'll sizzle good old hot dogs
By the silvery moonshine.
</blockquote>

2. *What Each Must Bring.*—Each person should be asked to bring something. A committee should designate someone to bring five pounds of weiners, or perhaps several will have to bring weiners if the group is large. Someone else will be asked to bring buns or rolls. Someone will be asked to bring some wood if it is not to be found where the party is held. Old wire coat hangers straightened

out make good roasters for wieners. Cabbage slaw goes well with wieners. Someone should be designated to handle the aquatic events, and someone to look after the properties.

3. *Aquatic Events*

(1) Diving Contests. Judges should be appointed in advance.

(2) Have a dash the length of the pool. Contestants may use any desired stroke. Give a prize to the winner.

(3) The Plunge. Contestants plunge off the edge of the pool, and the object is to see how far they can go without moving the body. Contestants try this one at a time and the distances are recorded. The one who plunges the farthest wins. Judges should see that after the plunge there is no body movement.

(4) Fancy Stroke. Have a race in which the contestants use the different fancy strokes, as the back stroke, the breast stroke, the crawl, and so on.

(5) Balloon Race. Get six or seven toy balloons of different colors. Line up all swimmers at one end of the pool and give them each a balloon. They are to lay the balloon on the water and swim to the other end of the pool, knocking their balloon along as they swim. Give a prize to the winner.

(6) Turtle Race. All contestants are placed on one side of the pool. The swim is to be the short way of the pool. This is a strenuous game, and the girls should not compete against the boys, but should have a separate contest. At a signal from the leader all plunge in and swim to the other side of the pool. The five to reach there last are eliminated. If the number is large, it is better to eliminate a larger number. Then the leader's whistle is blown again, and they swim back. Five more are eliminated. So they swim back and forth until there are only two left. They make a final try, and the winner receives the prize. It is a good idea to let contestants rest a minute between each try. When the boys have tried this, let the girls have a try. It is better with the girls to eliminate a larger number so that no girl will have to swim the width of the pool more than four times.

4. *Aquatic Games.*—Perhaps it is needless to say that there should

be plenty of rest between these games. Not all will take part, and while those who do take part have a period of rest, others can be swimming, diving, or just playing in the water.

(1) Water Polo. Choose five men on a side. The referee stands about the middle of the short end of the pool. He tosses the ball up so that it will come down about the center of the pool. When the ball is tossed up the men are lined up on the edge of the pool. The object is to swim out and get the ball and bring it back to their goal. When the referee drops the ball in the water, the fight is on. One or two men may be sent to the opponents' goal to keep them from touching the ball to their side of the pool. A goal is made when a player is able to hold the ball and touch his side of the pool.

(2) Water Basketball. Rig up some goals about four feet above the water. Barrels or large garbage cans or washing tubs would make good goals. These could be set on each end of the pool. The game is played just like regular basketball and the points scored in the same way.

(3) Water Baseball. Lay something as a marker for the home plate, first, second, and third bases on the edge of the pool. Choose nine players on a side. The game is played in the same manner as baseball, using a large paddle for a bat and a rubber ball about the size of an indoor baseball. This game may be played on the beach or in the surf if the water is not too deep and the sand is smooth.

5. *Stunts.*—Either of these stunts suggested will cause much merriment:

(1) Terrapin Race. Have some of the boys catch two or more terrapins and keep them until the time of the party. Mark off a starting place and a finish line. Put them on the starting line and number them with chalk and see what happens. This is very funny.

(2) Duck Race. Get a duck, cut off the feathers on its wings so that it cannot fly, and put it in the water. Give a prize to the boy who can bring the duck to the shore. Many times by the flapping of his wings the duck will force the swimmer to release him when he is almost to the shore.

167

(3) Three-Legged Swimming Race. This game requires four, six, or eight boys who are good swimmers. Pair the boys off according to height and weight and tie the right leg of one boy in the pair to the left leg of the other boy in the pair. Designate a finish line and the pair of boys who swims to this line first, while tied together, is the winner.

6. *Refreshments.*—The events suggested above should take place before dark or just as it is getting dark. As soon as dark comes, move from the pool to the beach and make a fire. Roast wieners by the fire and serve with cabbage slaw and mustard on buns. It would be well also to have some marshmallows to toast. It is well to have sandwiches, also, and watermelon for dessert. Cold soft drinks can be easily served. After the meal is over, play games by the firelight or the moonlight.

7. *Snap Answers.*[1]—The players are seated in a circle. One who is "It" stands in the center.

"It" asks a question of each player, who must answer with words beginning with his own initials. For example, a girl whose initials were B. R. G. might be asked, "What is your favorite flower?" and she would answer quickly, "Bright red geraniums." The next man, named Charles W. Smith, when asked, "What is your ambition?" would answer, "Chasing wild steers." Those who fail to answer pay a forfeit when the game is over. If the group is large, the leader might find it helpful to write out a list of thirty or forty clever questions.

8. *Pom-Pom Pull Away.*—Two lines are drawn on the beach fifty or seventy-five feet apart. All players line up on one line except the leader, who stands in the center. Then the leader or "It" calls out "Pom-Pom pull away" and all run across the clear space to the other line while the leader or "It" tries to tag some of them. Those who are tagged stay away and help catch the others. When all are caught, the game starts over, the first caught being "It." This is an old game and very popular.

[1] Written by Mrs. Elizabeth Coffey Bailey, Denver, Colo. Used by permission.

9. *Three Deep.*—Players form two circles, that is, one circle within another circle so that one player is directly in front of another player. Two players are not in the circle; one of these is the runner and the other the chaser. The chaser tries to catch the runner. The runner may save himself from being tagged by stopping in front of any couple, thus making the circle three deep. The player in the back circle then becomes runner and is chased by the chaser. When the runner is tagged, he then becomes chaser. He must remain chaser until he tags someone else. The runner has the privilege of taking his place in front of another couple, but the chaser does not. This is a very old and popular game.

10. *Farmer in the Dell.*—See "Kid Party," page 322.

11. *Around the Fire.*—After the games have been finished, sit around the fire and tell stories or have a brief program of entertainment. Have someone recite or tell a story. Have someone sing to accompaniment of ukulele or some other musical instrument. A song sheet may be prepared in advance and some of the familiar songs sung. A group that is tired of play will enjoy sitting around the fire for a few moments after the games.

A good trick to teach the group around the fire and first to surprise them with is a Matchbox Trick. The matchbox lies on the back of the right hand, and the one who does the trick tells the group that when he whistles, the matchbox will rise and stand erect. They are surprised when it actually does this.

It is done in the following manner: Get a box of safety matches in a wooden box. Take about half of the matches out of it, as it is better to have it heavier than the empty box. Open the box about half an inch and turn it upside down so that the open place will be on the right wrist. Wrinkle the wrist and catch a small bit of skin in the box opening and push the box shut. By closing the fingers and slightly dropping the hand and tightening the muscles in the forearm the box can be made to move up and down at will.

12. *Properties*

(1) A refreshment committee should instruct each one what to bring in the way of refreshments.

(2) Toy balloons for Balloon Race.

(3) Large rubber ball for Polo and Basketball.

(4) Small rubber ball for Baseball.

(5) Two or more terrapins.

(6) A duck with its wings cropped.

(7) Several pieces of rope for Three-Legged Swimming Race.

(8) Small wooden matchbox for Matchbox Trick.

(9) Ukulele, or some similar instrument, song sheets, for **Around the** Fire.

(10) Barrels, large garbage cans, or tubs for Basketball.

chapter 26

Fourth of July Party

OF COURSE WE WILL WANT TO CELEBRATE THE FOURTH OF JULY WITH a party. Build the party around the thought of our country and our states, characters of history, and the modern way of celebrating the Fourth—fireworks.

1. *Invitation.*—Send out an invitation similar to the one given below, written upon a cardboard cut in the shape of a flag, or upon a bell to represent the Liberty Bell. The following may be written on the flag or bell:

> On the birthday of our country,
>   We're having a party to celebrate.
> At eight o'clock on the Fourth of July,
>   Come to Pilcher's, and don't be late.

2. *Decorations.*—Use flags and bunting and red, white, and blue streamers for decorations. Pictures of great American characters may be hung on the walls. The decorations will be easy.

3. *Matching Partners.*—As the boys enter, pin on them the names of the states. On the girls pin the names of state capitals. When the guests all arrive, have them find partners by matching states and capitals. The leader should take care to give out only the capitals of the states that are given out, and of course all the states and capitals will not be required for most parties.

4. *The Names of the States.*—Give guests blank sheets of paper and pencils. Let couples work together. Ask them to write all the names of the states. This may look easy, but it is doubtful if any will finish writing the names of all the states in ten minutes. Give a prize

to the one finishing first, unless the game is too long, in which case give a prize to the one having the longest list.

5. *The National Anthem: Do You Know It?*—Give to each guest the words of the "Star-Spangled Banner" written with the italicized words blank. Let them see which couple can fill the blanks correctly in the quickest time:

O say, can you see by the *dawn's* early light,
   What so proudly we *hailed* at the twilight's last *gleaming?*
Whose *broad* stripes and *bright* stars, through the *perilous* fight,
   O'er the *ramparts* we watched, were so *gallantly* streaming?
And the *rockets'* red *glare,* the bombs bursting in air,
Gave proof through the night that *our flag* was still there.
O say does the Star-spangled Banner yet *wave*
O'er the land of the *free* and the home of the *brave?*

On the *shore* dimly seen thro' the *mists* of the deep,
   Where the *foe's* haughty *host* in dread silence *reposes,*
What is that which the *breeze,* o'er the towering steep,
   As it fitfully *blows,* half *conceals,* half *discloses?*
Now it catches the *gleam* of the morning's first *beam,*
In full *glory* reflected now shines on the *stream;*
'Tis the *Star-spangled Banner,* oh, long may it wave,
O'er the land of the free and the home of the brave!

Oh, thus be it ever when *free-men* shall stand
   Between their lov'd *homes* and the *war's* desolation!
Blest with vict'ry and peace, may the *heav'n-rescued* land
   Praise the Pow'r that hath made and *preserved* us a *nation!*
Then *conquer* we must, when our *cause* it is just,
And this be our motto: *"In God is our trust!"*
And the Star-spangled Banner *in triumph* shall wave
O'er the land of the free and the home of the brave!

6. *Washington Surveying Relay.*—It is a well-known fact that Washington was once a surveyor. Line up the players for a relay race. They may be divided into three groups, the Reds, Whites, and Blues. This may be done by pinning on red, white, and blue ribbons, having an equal number of each. The three groups face a

goal about fifteen or twenty feet away. Give to the player at the head of the line a yardstick. They are to measure the distance to the goal and back with a yardstick, laying it down and picking it up each time. The players, as soon as they have finished, give the yardstick to the next one in line and take their places at the back of the line.

7. *Post Office.*—Each guest is given the name of a city. Inasmuch as the girls already have the names of state capitals, it would be well to ask the boys to take the name of another large city in the state they represent. The players sit around in a circle. There are two ways to play this game.

(1) The postman may be blindfolded. He stands in the center of the circle of guests and calls the name of two cities by saying, "I have a letter from New York to Jacksonville." When he says this the players who represent New York and Jacksonville must get up and change places. The blind postman tries to catch one of them, and if he does, that player becomes the postman and the postman takes his seat. After several tries, if the postman fails to catch any one, the leader of the party should call out the names of four cities, and have them all change at the same time.

(2) Another way to play this game is to have one player stand in the center who is not blindfolded. When he calls the names of the different cities, he does not try to catch the players, but tries to get a chair. The one whose chair is taken must become the postman. Occasionally the leader of the party may call out, "General Delivery," at which time all must change chairs. The player that fails to get a chair must become the postman.

8. Geography.—A mixing game, adaptable to this party. Country, city, river, may be found on page 64.

9. *Spin the Plate.*—Play the old game Spin the Plate in a little different way. Have one player spin the plate and call the name of a state or capital. The boy who represents the state or the girl who represents the capital must catch the plate before it falls. If she fails to do this, she must pay a forfeit. However, let us do this in a different way. Let us have a number of forfeits written out, and as soon as she fails to catch the plate, she draws out one of the forfeits

and must do the stunt indicated. After she has finished her stunt, she spins the plate and calls the name of a state or capital, and the game proceeds as before. The following are some forfeits which would be suitable for this party:

Impersonate—
    (1) Paul Revere mounting his horse.
    (2) Benjamin Franklin flying his kite.
    (3) Washington chopping down his cherry tree.
    (4) Pocahontas saving Captain John Smith.
    (5) Patrick Henry making a speech.
    (6) Andrew Jackson fighting a duel.
    (7) Daniel Boone killing a bear.
    (8) Abraham Lincoln splitting rails.
    (9) The Statue of Liberty.

For additional forfeits that would be suitable for this party, look in the Index under "Impersonations."

10. *Ringing the Liberty Bell.*—Cut a large piece of cardboard into the shape of a bell. If it could be drawn with a crack in it to look like the Liberty Bell, it would be much better. Fix this bell up over the opening of a door. Cut in it a circle about six inches in diameter. Behind this hole hang a small bell. Use three tennis balls and let each group, the Reds, Whites, and Blues, try ringing the bell. Each player is given three throws, and a score for the whole group is kept. The side that rings the bell the most times should be given a prize.

11. *Fireworks: John Brown's Alive.*—Of course in a Fourth of July party there must be some fireworks. Matches are used for this stunt. The leader strikes a match and gives it to a player, telling him that he has the privilege of passing it as long as it is alive, that is, as long as it is burning or is a live coal. He merely is to say, "John Brown's alive," and pass it on to the next player; but if it is not alive, the next player does not have to take it. Whoever has it when it is dead must have a mustache painted on them with the burned match. Also they must start another match.

12. *As You Were.*[1]—The girls and boys form two circles, the boys on the outside and the girls on the inside. It is necessary that there be an equal number of boys and girls. If there are not, it will be necessary for some of the girls to act the part of boys, or vice versa. A girl taking the boy's part can be designated by a handkerchief tied around her arm. The leader gets in the center of the circle and gives the commands. He might start out with "Promenade," which means that they are to march around the circle. He next says, "Halt." After this he may say, "Girls outside, boys inside." Then, "Girls in front of boys." Then, "Halt and face your partners." Then the command may be given, "The grand right and left." This is done by the boy taking with his right hand the right hand of the girl in front of him. They both move forward and swing halfway around, taking the left hand of the next girl in line with his left hand, and so they weave in and out around the circle, each girl and each boy swinging with the right hand and next with the left hand the next one in line. When the leader calls, "As you were," they all try to get back to their original positions and find their original partners.

Vary this by getting the circle in single file and having them clasp hands. The leader than winds them up until he himself is in the center of several circles of guests joined by the hand. He unwinds this by simply turning around and letting the line follow him back until they are in their original positions.

13. *Taxation without Representation.*—The guests are seated in a circle. The leader tells them that he is going to organize a Revolutionary Club. In order to become a member one must be initiated. The leader says "the initiation ceremony consists in saying what I tell you and doing what I do." The leader then says, indicating one of the guests, "Say, 'Taxation without representation.'" In saying this the leader makes some peculiar gesture with the hands, as if to emphasize what he says. Usually the guest will imitate the gesture and say, "Taxation without representation," when the point is to

[1] Adapted from *Phunology*, by Harbin. Abingdon Press. Used by permission.

merely imitate the gesture and say, "Taxation," as he has been told to say taxation without (saying) representation.

14. *Teakettle.*—The game of Teakettle is played in this way: One player leaves the room and the other players decide on two words which are pronounced alike and yet have different meanings, such as "son" and "sun." Others that might be used are "write" and "right"; "present" (meaning at this time) and "present" (a gift); "type" (what the printer uses) and "type" (an emblem); "sight" (to see) and "site" (a place for a building).

When these words have been decided on by the group, the one who was sent out of the room is recalled. He may ask questions, and the players must use sentences in which the word decided upon should occur, but instead of saying the words in each case they must say "teakettle." Instead of saying, for example, "The mother's young son went out to play in the sun," they would say, "The mother's young teakettle went out to play in the teakettle." Instead of saying, "The linotype operator was setting type, but he did not like the type of machine he was using," one would say, "The linotype operator was setting teakettle, but he did not like the teakettle of machine he was using." The player who gives away the words or who furnishes the clue that enables the leader to guess must be the next one to go out, and so the game continues.

15. *Refreshments.*—Serve red, white, and blue brick ice cream with cake. Another suggestion would be fruit punch and cake.

16. *Properties*

(1) Names of enough states and capitals to pin on the guests.
(2) Blank sheets of paper and pencils.
(3) The National Anthem written out, leaving spaces blank.
(4) Three yardsticks.
(5) Game of Geography written on sheets of paper.
(6) Number of forfeits written out and plate for Spin the Plate.
(7) Matches for John Brown's Alive.
(8) Blindfold for Post Office.
(9) Cardboard Liberty Bell, small bell, and three tennis balls for Ringing the Liberty Bell.

chapter 27

Stunt Night

THE FOLLOWING PROGRAM IS SUGGESTED FOR SUCH GATHERINGS AS young people's conference or summer camp where there are groups from different sections of the state or nation. It is always a good idea, when groups like this come together and have evening programs, to have those from each city or state put on a stunt.

This also might be used by a church or school, the different Sunday-school classes or young people's societies putting on stunts. It could be used as a pay program, using the recreation room of the church.

It has plenty of other possibilities. In a city of about thirty thousand people a woman's club has started having annual stunt night and giving a cup to the organization putting on the best stunt. On this stunt night the civic organizations, such as the Women's Club, Kiwanis, Rotary, Lions, and American Legion, compete. They charge one dollar admission, and it has been the means of raising money for the organization for several years.

1. *Publicity.*—Such programs as this should be given publicity through the newspapers, or public announcement should be made of it. We are only suggesting a few stunts that might be used. At the close of the chapter you will find a list of books which you will find helpful for such a program as this.

2. *Living Pictures.*—Living pictures make a very beautiful and impressive stunt. We are assuming that these stunts will be on a stage. Have a large frame constructed about eight feet high and about ten feet wide and hidden lights around the border. Raise this frame up a foot or more from the floor on a platform. A hidden chorus or quartet furnishes the music while the pictures are given

in tableau. Between each song that is given in tableau the quartet or chorus sings "Memories."

(1) "School Days." The tableau would be a small boy and a small girl holding hands, the girl carrying in her hand a slate on which is written "I love you, Joe," and thus they stand while the chorus or quartet sings.

The curtain is then drawn and the picture is changed, but the chorus continues singing "Memories."

(2) "Rock-a-bye Baby." This picture might be a mother with her baby. If an old-fashioned cradle can be obtained, have a doll or a baby in the cradle. The mother rocks the cradle while the chorus sings.

(3) "When You and I Were Young, Maggie." An old couple are on the stage holding hands.

(4) "Always." A couple dressed as bride and groom are in the picture. A quartet sings "Always," while the couple poses as if plighting their troth. As the curtain closes, a recessional is played.

(5) "Mother Machree." An old lady dressed in black or lavender with white lace and cap is seated in a rocker. A young man stands by her. He looks down at her as the song is sung.

(6) "My Wild Irish Rose." A girl with summer dress, wide-brimmed hat, garlanded with roses, and a boy are on the stage. The boy is dressed in a white suit or sport coat and trousers. The girl takes a rose and puts it in his buttonhole during the singing of the music. The action should be carefully timed to fit the scene.

Other songs that might be used are "Let Me Call You Sweetheart," "Auld Lang Syne," "Comin' Through the Rye," "Gypsy Love Song," "I Want a Girl Just Like the Girl That Married Dear Old Dad," "Silver Threads Among the Gold."

3. *A Trick with Cards.*—This trick is done with a deck of playing cards. They have been divided so that the hearts and diamonds, the red cards, are all together, and the spades and clubs are all together, and they are also divided so that each set is separate. The one who is doing the trick takes a piece of paper. We will suppose that he writes on it "King of Hearts." He takes this piece

of paper, folds it up, and puts it under the glass tumbler on the table. Then he takes a deck of cards and says: "There are twenty-six black cards and twenty-six red cards in this deck. Which will you take?" If someone says, "The red cards," then he says, "You have taken the red cards, so I will throw away the black," and he lays down the black cards. But if someone says, "I will take the black cards," then the black cards are laid down and he says, "That leaves me the red." He then says: "Now I have twenty-six red cards. Thirteen of them are hearts, and thirteen of them are diamonds. Which will you take?" If someone says, "I will take the diamonds," he says, "All right, you may have the diamonds," and he throws them into the discard. But if someone says, "I will take the hearts," then he says, "All right," and throws away the diamonds and keeps the hearts. He then says: "Now, I have ten numbered cards and three face cards. Which will you take?" If someone says, "I will take the numbered cards," he says, "All right, you may have them," and he throws them into the discard, or he may say, "That leaves me the face cards." But if someone says, "I will take the face cards," he says, "We will use the face cards," and throws the numbered cards into the discard just the same. Then he says, "Now I have three face cards, which will you take?" And suppose they say, "The king of hearts." If they do, he throws away the queen and jack, lifts up the glass, and shows them that he has written "King of Hearts" on the paper. But if, on the other hand, they choose the queen of hearts, he must continue and say, "Well, you may have the queen of hearts," and throws the queen of hearts into the discard. Then he says, "I have two cards, the jack and the king; which one will you take?" If someone says, "The king," he says, "The king is the very one we are looking for, and he throws away the jack. But if someone says, "The jack," he says, "Very well, you may have the jack," and he throws the jack into the discard. The trick is in the use of language, but is nevertheless hard to catch on to.

4. *Booking Office Auditions.*—This stunt may be carried out by having the performers come for tryouts before the booking agent. The acts may be announced by the performers themselves, or by the

booking agent's secretary, or by his partner, or by the doorman, who, of course, is the master of ceremonies.

5. *Brain-Testing Machine.*—Construct brain-testing machine as follows: Make a box with boards about nine inches wide and about one foot square and as high as the width of the boards. Put a board over the top and on the bottom, boring a hole about a half inch in diameter through the top and bottom boards. It is necessary for this box to set about two inches off of the table, so around three sides of it there should be a board one by two nailed up edgewise, so that the bottom of the box will appear to be on the table. Get a piece of small rubber hose at the dime store about a half inch in diameter. This should be ten or twelve feet long. Put this through the holes in the bottom and top of the box, so that one end of it just projects over the top of the box. It will be necessary to get a small tube, glass or brass, which may be procured either at a hardware store or a plumbing shop. This should be just large enough to slip the end of the rubber hose over and to make it fit tight in the hole and in the box. Then get a toy rubber balloon and slip over the end of the tube. This box is placed on the table with the tube sticking out on the back side, and then the tube is placed behind the curtain, with one person behind the curtain to make the balloon large or small at will by inflating it. It would be well also to have some sort of a dial either drawn on the side of the box or purchased and put on the box. Also have some kind of a crank that will turn other little apparatuses on the box. On the top side there should be driven a nail on each corner and a small wire tied around the entire edge of the box also, tying it to the top of the nails. One person stands on the stage and announces that very recently a wonderful machine has been invented which will test brain capacity and that it operates electrically. He puts one hand on the head of an individual and the other hand on the wire of the brain-testing machine, and the balloon will indicate the capacity of the brain. This is a very humorous stunt if carried out properly. As soon as the hand is placed on the wire, if it is desirous to indicate that the person is a

man of brain capacity, the balloon is immediately made large. If not, it might be made to just barely move, and perhaps just to flop over.

Another variation of this is to get a bald-headed man and put lampblack on the fingers and make some black spots on his bald head. This will cause much merriment. If it is desirous to especially honor someone, the one who is blowing the balloon might blow it until it bursts, or the one on the stage might puncture the balloon with a pin or touch it off with a cigarette.

6. *Style Show.*—This stunt is better done on a stage. Any sort of background will be all right. The scene is supposed to be laid in fashionable ladies' shop. The characters should be:

The shopkeeper.

The French maid, assistant to the shopkeeper.

The bride-to-be.

Mother of the bride-to-be.

The shopkeeper and her assistant are on the stage busy at anything they desire when the bride-to-be and her mother come in. The bride-to-be is shopping and the shopkeeper displays different kinds of dresses. These are worn by models, who should be boys dressed up as girls.

First there should be a street dress, then an afternoon dress, an evening dress, and a sports outfit. There might be two or three of each displayed, depending upon the number of boys available to take part.

Do not have too much conversation or let the stunt last too long. The main feature will be the laughs when the models enter. This is a very effective stunt and one that needs very little rehearsal.

7. *Black Magic*

(1) The equipment necessary for this trick is a table, preferably with a tablecloth on it, four balls all alike, and two felt or soft straw hats. The balls should be exactly alike, and if the table is covered so that they will not rattle, four marbles all alike would be good. Four white moth balls would also be good, or four grapes of the same size and color would do.

The trick is done in the following manner: Place the four balls on the table, which is otherwise bare. The one who does the trick says the following or similar words as he displays two hats: "When my great-grandfather died he willed me these two magic hats. With them he said I would be able to do wonderful things. He told me to take this hat and place it over this ball." When the performer says this, he places the hat down over one of the balls, holding the hat with the fingers on the inside, and as he places the hat down, he picks up the ball which is under the hat, using his first and second fingers to pick it up from the table, and pulling it into the palm of his hand. This is done with the right hand. He then says, as he transfers the other hat which he is holding in his left hand to the right hand, "He told me to place this hat over this ball," and he places the hat over the second ball and at the same time drops from his hand the ball that he picked up from under the first hat. The performer then picks up one of the balls which is not covered by a hat and says, "My great-grandfather then told me to make this ball go through this hat by saying, 'Aggremento, presto, chango, hokus-pocus!'" He then takes the left hand and picks up the hat under which he has already placed two balls. It looks very much from the audience as if he has made the ball go through the hat. This hat should be picked up with the left hand, picking it up by the top. When he places the hat back down over the two balls, he does it with the right hand as before and drops a third ball under the hat. He then picks up the other ball which is not covered by the hat and says, "My great-grandfather told me to make this ball go through this hat by saying, 'Aggremento, presto, chango, hokus-pocus!'" He then picks up the hat again with the left hand, picking it up by the top, and there are three balls under it. He lays the hat down again with his right hand as before, dropping the fourth ball. To the audience it appears that there is still a ball under the first hat, and so the performer says, "My great-grandfather told me to then make this ball [touching the first hat] go out of this hat and go into this hat [touching the second hat] by saying, 'Aggremento, presto, chango, hokus-pocus!'" He then picks up both hats and all four balls will be found to be under one hat.

This has been done in the presence of people who have been watching everything, and not one person in one hundred will catch on. It is better done on the stage, or the crowd should be kept back a few feet, so that they will not interfere.

(2) The same performer might do also this trick with cards, which is a very clever trick and never fails to excite the curiosity. Take out from a deck of playing cards one full suit. Arrange the cards in the following manner, and this is counting from the table up, if the cards are lying on a table in a stack: 3, 8, 7, ace, queen, 6, 4, 2, jack, king, 10, 9, 5. The one who does the trick then turns the cards face down in his hand and begins to take them off one by one as he spells out the numbers. He spells o, and takes off a card, n, and takes off another card, e, and takes off a third card, putting these cards at the bottom and then he pronounces "one" and throws off the ace, which is on top. Then he spells t, w, o, and each time he calls a letter he places a card at the bottom of the pack, then he throws off the two. And so he goes right on through the set, spelling each number and also spelling jack, queen, and king. If they are arranged as indicated above, it will work out perfectly.

8. *Kitchen Cabinet Orchestra.*—The kitchen cabinet orchestra is a good stunt, but some care should be exercised in selecting those who have good voices, and there should be some rehearsing. Each player in the orchestra is provided with an instrument, to which has been attached a kazoo. This is a small, inexpensive instrument which can usually be purchased at a novelty or music store in any city. Imitations of the sounds of instruments can be made on the kazoo, and a number of good voices, especially mixed voices, give a very pleasing result.

Someone who is very clever at improvising should be asked to make the instruments. A cornet could be made from a rolling pin, with a funnel on one end and the kazoo attached to the handle on the other. A clothesbasket with a mop stick and some old wires could be made into a bass viol. A bass horn can be improvised out of an inner tube attached to a funnel and some other kitchen utensil. A long-handled frying pan might be made into a violin. A washing tub would make a good bass drum, and a small dishpan would make a good snare drum. The leader could use a dish mop for a baton.

It would be better to have each one improvise his own instrument. In this way you would get a variety of ideas.

The program should be given from a stage. There should be some old tunes such as "The Old Gray Mare, She Ain't What She Used to Be," "Dixie," "Yankee Doodle," "Carry Me Back to Old Virginny," "My Old Kentucky Home" and " 'Way Down Upon the Swanee River." Then use some current popular songs. Close with "God Be with You Till We Meet Again" or "Perfect Day." These songs are only suggestions, and the leader should feel free to make his own selection. A program of familiar and popular music will be pleasing.

9. *Upside-down Quartet.*—This stunt could be put on by any quartet. The quartet is to perform behind a curtain. The leader might pull the following wisecrack in introducing the quartet: "This is a fish quartet. Mr. Brown, first tuna; Mr. Smith, second tuna; Mr. White, barracuda; and Mr. Young, bass." When they start singing, they put their shoes on their hands and stick their hands up over the curtain. The curtain should be just about six feet high, and it might be well to have something for them to sit on, so that it will be just natural for them to stick their hands up over the curtain. Have them render one or two numbers in this manner.

10. *The Questionable Well.*—This is a good stage stunt and will long be remembered. Construct out of old boards a box about three feet square and about two and a half feet high. Have board extending into the air from each side and a board nailed across the top from which is hung a rope with a hook on it, so that a bucket can be hooked on the rope, and a small part of the top of the bucket can be seen from the audience. Get about two or three pounds of rice and put in the bucket. Fill a dipper about half full of water and set it in the bucket and on the rice.

When the curtain is pulled, no one is on the stage, but a couple enters. The girl says: "I am thirsty. Look, here is a well." They go to the well, and the boy picks up the dipper and hands it to her. She smells the water and says, "I do not believe that water is good," and sets the dipper back in the bucket, taking care not to spill the water. This couple retires, and another couple enters immediately. This couple goes to the well, and the boy says to the girl, "Will you have a drink?" to which she says, "No, thanks." The boy then takes the dipper and tastes the water and says, "My gracious, that water isn't fit to drink," and throws the water on the floor. This couple passes on, and a third couple enters and goes to the well. The boy dips down as if to get a dipper of water, puts it to his nose and smells it, and says, "I do not believe that water is fit to drink," and hands the dipper to the girl. The girl smells it ands says, "Good gracious, no." The boy then takes the bucket from the hook and throws the rice into the audience.

As all have received a very vivid impression of there being water in the bucket, there will be much dodging to get out of the way of the water and a very amusing surprise when it is found that the bucket contained rice.

This may be done by three persons instead of three couples, and could be done quite as effectively by two persons.

11. *Womanless Wedding.*—In "The Bride and Groom Party," page 135, will be found a wedding ceremony. If all the characters are men, this could be put on as a womanless wedding, having the wedding procession come down the aisle of the auditorium and then having the ceremony on the stage. This makes a good stunt.

For additional Stunt Night suggestions see *The Cokesbury Stunt Book,* by Depew (Abingdon Press) and *Phunology,* by Harbin (Abingdon Press).

chapter 28

Gypsy Party

(COSTUME)

THE GYPSY PARTY AS DESCRIBED AND OUTLINED IN THIS CHAPTER WAS planned by the writer and used successfully in a young people's conference group of about one hundred and fifty. In this case the conference was already divided into four groups or tribes, and preparation was made in advance for the storytelling feature. Also the groups vied with each other in the arrangement of costumes, as points were given for the best costume for the boys and the best for the girls. The costumes and the stories were, in this case, the best part of the party. Each group was allowed to select a boy and girl to compete for the best costume. By a process of elimination the best boy's and the best girl's costume were selected by the judges.

Storytellers, two from each group, one boy and one girl, competed for the storytelling prize, for which prizes in points were also given. These eight sories around the campfire were an important part of the party. In arranging a party of this nature it would be best to have some storytellers selected in advance.

1. *The Setting for the Party.*—The ideal setting for a Gypsy Party would be a picnic ground on a moonlight night. The beach would also be a good place for such a party. Another suggestion would be the back yard of a residence. The spot should be lighted with flares, or electric lights, or lanterns. There should also be a large campfire, over which hangs a large pot on a tripod, to be used for the gypsy goulash, the recipe for which will be found at the conclusion of the chapter. In a party of this nature informality should reign, and no one should expect to be entertained or served,

as each should depend somewhat on his own ingenuity in helping to provide entertainment for himself, and each should serve himself goulash and coffee.

2. *Costumes.*—Costumes may be made from red or yellow cheesecloth. Or at least headbands, sashes, and scarfs can be made from these materials. Further suggestions for the girls would be Spanish costumes, with hair loose or braided down the back. A timbrel would add to the effect. Use plenty of beads, earrings, bracelets, or other jewelry. Boys could wear colored shirts, bandana handkerchiefs, slouch hats, large earrings, such as brass curtain rings tied on to the ears, mustaches pasted on, or masks. Plenty of color should be put on the cheeks with rouge or cocoa.

3. *Initiation.*—Guests should be met at the door or entrance to the place where the party is held by rough-looking gypsies with knives or revolvers. Each guest is kidnapped and taken before the gypsy king and initiated. To do this he is made to get on his knees, put his head to the ground, and say:

> I know my mind,
> And I know my heart.
> I know I have a foolish part.

This should be repeated three times as the guest bows before the king. He is then initiated into the order of gypsies.

4. *Bartering.*—Each guest has been notified in advance that he is to bring some article wrapped in a package. A price limit should be set on this of ten cents or twenty-five cents. After all have been initiated, the leader then tells the guests that, as they are now gypsies, they must trade, for gypsies trade. Each person is to talk up the article in his package without revealing its identity. When the trading has been going on for about ten minutes, the leader blows the whistle, and all open their packages to discover the misfits. Usually there will be noisemakers, mechanical toys, teething rings, candy with salt and pepper in it, and so forth.

5. *Stealing.*—The leader should announce that another characteristic of gypsies is that they steal, and that, as they have been initiated

into the order of gypsies, they will have the privilege during the evening of stealing. Also a prize will be given to the one who can display, at the close of the evening, the largest number of articles stolen. The leader should explain that stealing does not mean taking by force, but that the gypsies have light fingers. This stealing should continue while the games are being played, and later in the evening after the games are over, there should be a time to return stolen property.

6. *Storytelling.*—The leader should then say that another characteristic of gypsies is that they tell stories; that a prize will be given by the king for the one who tells the most ridiculous story. Instead of ridiculous, the leader might use the adjectives interesting, funny, realistic, and so on. This will work better if some have been selected in advance to start off the stories and then have others from the group tell something if they will. Also recitations, readings, and travel stories may be used.

7. *Singing.*—The leader will then say that another characteristic of gypsies is that they sing. A leader has been selected in advance, and a song sheet typewritten or mimeographed for each one. This is important, for many know the tune of a song but do not know the words. There will probably be someone in the group who plays a stringed instrument or a ukulele, and these should have them ready to play during the singing.

A soloist or quartet should be asked to sing "Slumber On, My Little Gypsy Sweetheart."

8. *Gypsy, Gypsy, Don't You Laugh.*—The players stand in a circle, and the leader tells the others that they are to do as he does to the one on his left. The leader then reaches up with his right hand, and with his thumb and forefinger he pinches the one on his left on the right cheek, and says, "Gypsy, Gypsy, don't you laugh." This one then is supposed to do the same to the one on his left. The joke is that the leader had lampblack on his thumb and forefinger and has blacked the cheek of the one on his left. If he does not catch on to what the others are laughing about, the leader starts again by pinching him on the left cheek and saying

the same words. This can continue on the nose, chin, and so on until he catches on.

9. *Handkerchief Chase.*—The leader stands in the center of the circle with a bandana handkerchief in his hand. He throws the handkerchief in the air and calls the name of a player in the circle. If the player fails to catch the handkerchief before it falls to the ground, he has to be "It" and take the leader's place in the circle. Another manner of playing this game is to have each of the players numbered, and "It" throws up the handerchief and calls a number instead of a name.

10. *Handkerchief Laughs.*—The leader throws the handkerchief into the air and calls the name or number of a person in the circle, and that person must laugh while the handkerchief is in the air and cease immediately when it falls to the ground. If that person fails to laugh while the handkerchief is in the air, or laughs when the handkerchief is not in the air, he must be "It." In order to accomplish this end "It" may make a motion as though he were going to throw the handkerchief and then fail to throw it. The game may be varied by designating certain kinds of laughs, such as nervous laugh, coquettish laugh, boisterous laugh, horse laugh, silly laugh, stage laugh, giggle, or others.

Another way to play this game, possibly a better way to start it, is to have all the circle laugh while the handkerchief is in the air. The leader could say that another characteristic of gypsies is that they laugh. Then tell them that they are to laugh while the handkerchief is in the air, and whoever is caught not laughing at the proper time or laughing when they should not will have to be "It" or pay a forfeit.

11. *Gypsy Firefly.*—The following game is quite an active one. A circle is formed by couples—that is, each boy holds the hand of a girl partner. One couple is outside the ring with a flashlight. They walk around the outside of the circle and suddenly flash a flashlight on one of the couples. This couple must immediately leave the ring and run around the circle to the right while the couple that is out must race around the circle to the left. Both

couples are trying to get back to the open space in the circle. The couple that gets back first occupies the space, and the other couple is out with the flashlight.

12. *Fortunes.*—After playing a game as active as the above sit around the fire for a while for the fortunes. The easiest way to accomplish this is to have the fortunes prepared in advance and placed in capsules. These capsules should be about one inch in length and the fortune typewritten and rolled up and placed inside. Players draw for their fortunes, and at the signal open the capsule and read aloud. These fortunes may be written with a pen, using lemon juice for ink. This makes an excellent invisible ink, and this may be passed to the Gypsy Queen, who holds it over the candle, and the words of the fortune will appear on what seemed a blank piece of paper.

The following are suggestions for written fortunes:

For the Girls

You are going to keep house in a bungalow,
With a cat—and a husband, too, you know.

You're going to study art two years in some academy;
And if you study hard enough, quite famous you will be.

In far-off Africa you'll spend your life
As a much-loved missionary's wife.

You'll be a globe-trotter and travel quite a heap,
Till you get a little house of your very own to keep.

As a business woman you'll win renown,
With a great big office in a great big town.

The profession of a nurse is the happiest you will find,
Till you meet a man who'll make you change your mind.

Before you are twenty you'll wear a wedding gown,
And have a nice home in a neighboring town.

You're going to live alone, just as happy as can be,
With your cat and your parrot, and your little cup of tea.

Gypsy Party

You'll never be as famous as others have planned,
But you'll have the happiest home in the land.

To a large fortune you soon will be heir,
Your life will be happy and free of care.

You'll be a music teacher,
And all the men will want to meet yer.

You'll pass up the youths who seek your hand,
And be an old man's darling—with money and land.

You'll try for motion pictures and make good,
And live in a large house in Hollywood.

You'll be a lady lawyer and read law books,
And attract a lot of clients with your good looks.

You are going far away to a university;
When you return a teacher you will be.

If you study and work hard, with toil,
You will write many a story and tale.

For the Boys

You'll go to college and get a degree,
And a brilliant man you'll surely be.

You'll be a lawyer and plead well a case;
You'll go into politics and win every race.

You will be a sailor lad, a-sailing on the sea;
And if you work your very best, a captain you may be.

You'll go to West Point and learn to be a soldier,
But you'll have to work hard to get an eagle on your shoulder.

You'll be a preacher, a man good and true;
You'll fall in love with a girl named Sue.

You'll be a farmer and sow and reap and mow;
You'll be a hayseeder, but have lots of dough.

You'll forget all the things you learned in the schools;
You'll start working as a plumber and forget to bring your tools.

191

A very famous doctor you are going to be,
With a great big practice and a great big fee.

You'll pilot a spaceship to the moon,
And have the reputation of being a loon.

Some day you will have renown;
You'll be elected mayor of your town.

You'll play tennis when you grow up,
You'll win the famous Davis cup.

A great deal of money you are really going to get,
But you'll have to work hard for it—twenty years yet.

Study hard and work while you wait,
And you'll be the governor of the state.

You're going to be a farmer and raise corn and wheat,
And when you are old you'll live on Easy Street.

You're going to be a railroad man,
And be the superintendent if you can.

Musical Fortunes—Girls

In the key of A your life will be;
You'll marry a sailor, and he'll go to sea.

In the key of B your life is cast;
You'll marry a rich man and live very fast.

In the key of C your life is pitched;
The man you marry will get ditched.

We find your life in the key of D;
An old maid schoolteacher you'll be.

Your life in the key of E we find;
Your hubby will be poor but very kind.

In the key of F your fate we read;
Your mate will be famous indeed.

In the key of G we find your place;
You'll win your fortune by your face.

192

MUSICAL FORTUNES—BOYS

Your life falls in the key of A;
You'll be president some day.

To the key of B your life is set;
You love a blond, but will marry a brunette.

We find your life in the key of C,
Which indicates you'll a bachelor be.

Your life-music is set to the key of D;
You'll go to seminary and a preacher be.

Your life's in E, and we suspect
You'll be a great architect.

Your life in the key of F we see,
You'll shine as a star of T.V.

In G we see your future clear;
You'll make your mark, so never fear.

13. *Run, Gypsy, Run.*—Run, Gypsy, Run is played much the same way as the old game Run, Sheep, Run. Two captains are chosen, who choose players and divide the group into two parties. One party remains at the goal, and the other party is taken by the captain and hidden. When the captain has hidden his party and arranged signals with them, such as the ones described below, he returns to the goal and takes his place with the searchers. The captain of the searchers must leave the goal and take his group on the search. The captain of those hidden calls out signals to members of his party, who try to keep hidden and at the same time get nearer the goal. The game is won by the side whose first player reaches the goal after the proper signal. No one, however, can run for the goal until his own captain calls out, "Run, gypsy, run." The captain of the hiding party is generally the first one to give this signal and start one of his men to the goal. The captain of the

searching party then calls the same signal to his group. The player first reaching the goal wins for his group.

Some such signals as the following may be prearranged between the captain and members of the hiding party: Red, danger; green, advance; yellow, caution; blue, go around the house; purple, keep on going in the same direction and get nearer the goal.

14. *Secrets.*—Gypsies have secrets. Divide crowd into groups. The same division as that used in the preceding game may be used. If the party is large, however, it would be best to divide into four groups. Each group selects a captain. Each group selects some object to be stolen while on some imaginary raid to town. Each group keeps this object a secret from the other band. A member of each camp is sent over to the rival camp to be questioned. They try to get out of him the name of the object he is going to steal. The visitor must answer the questions by "Yes" or "No." If the group guesses the object after five questions, they retain the visitor in their camp. If they fail to guess after five questions, the visitor returns and a visitor is sent to his camp from the rival group. In case the object is guessed, another object must be selected for the second visitor.

15. *Last Couple Out.*—Couples form a line facing the leader, who stands about ten feet in front of the line with his back to the line and calls, "Last couple out." The couple in the rear separate, one running toward the leader to the right and the other toward the leader to the left. The object is for the couple to run around the leader to the front and join hands before the leader catches one of them. If the leader is a boy, he tries to catch the girl for his partner; and if he succeeds, he goes with her to the front of the line, while the other boy becomes the caller. After the boys have been the callers for a while, change and have a girl call, "Last couple out," and try to catch a boy for her partner. If the caller fails to catch a partner before they encircle him and join hands, he must continue calling until he does catch a partner.

16. *Returning Stolen Property.*—This should be given some time, and all stolen articles should be identified and returned to the owner and a prize given to the one who can show the largest collection.

17. *Refreshments.*—Refreshments should consist of gypsy goulash and coffee, to which each one serves himself. Paper cups and plates may be used. The following is a recipe for the goulash, which, of course, must be cooked before the party and just heated up on the fire at the party:

Cook a large piece of beef or veal in a fireless cooker or over a slow fire until about half done. Season this with salt, pepper, onions, and bay leaf. Remove from the fire and cut meat into pieces suitable for serving and return to the fire. Add about one half can of tomatoes with additional seasoning, if necessary, and enough uncooked rice to absorb the stock and the tomato juice. Cook until rice has had time to thoroughly cook. If cooked on top of the stove, care must be taken that it does not stick to the bottom of the kettle. A little red pepper and more onions may be added if desired.

18. *Properties*

(1) A package containing some article not to exceed in cost ten or twenty-five cents for bartering.

(2) Song sheets mimeographed or typewritten.

(3) Small quantity of lampblack. Ten cents' worth, obtainable at a paint store, will last a lifetime.

(4) Bandana handkerchief.

(5) Flashlight.

(6) Fortunes prepared in capsules.

(7) Refreshments prepared according to recipe, arranged in pot over fire.

(8) Stringed instruments to accompany in singing.

19. *Story of the Gypsies.*—To add something of a more worthwhile nature to the party someone may be asked in advance to tell something of the gypsies—their origin, language, customs, and characteristics. The following brief sketch will form a basis for such a story. If additional material is desired, it may be found by consulting a good encyclopedia. It is best to have someone who is a good storyteller to take this part, and by all means it should not be a long-winded person:

Perhaps all of us have seen Gypsies. A half century ago they used to roam over the United States practicing magic, trading horses, telling fortunes, and practicing certain skills, such as tinkering, mending pots and pans, shoeing horses, and other small jobs. With the coming of the automobile they changed their mode of transportation from the covered wagon to the automobile, but they continued to wander.

Where do they get the name Gypsies? This is, in all probability, a misnomer, as they quite likely came from India rather than Egypt, from which country is derived the name Gypsy. The main body of their language has a close affinity with the Indian language. It is thought that they left India about A.D. 1300 and wandered through the Middle East and reached Europe about 1500. Their personal traits and customs still show much of the Hindu character. There have been many dissimilar ideas concerning the Gypsies, however. The French used to call them Bohemians, believing that they had been driven from Bohemia and were Hussites. The Gypsies call themselves Rommany, from their word "rom," which means man.

The Gypsies seem to be a vanishing race. Those that remain and segregate themselves, living nomadic lives, probably number not more than a quarter of a million. These are scattered through Turkey, Hungary, Rumania, Czechoslovakia, Spain, and smaller numbers in France, England, and the United States.

The Gypsies are remarkable for the yellow, brown, or rather olive color of their skin, the jet black of their eyes and hair, the extreme whiteness of their teeth, and the symmetry of their limbs.

The Gypsies are musical. Some of their melodies have become the loved property of the nations in which they have wandered. Their stories and their music have been incorporated in some of our favorite operas. The Gypsies have about them a certain amount of romance. Who has not been touched by the beautiful little melody, "Slumber On, My Little Gypsy Sweetheart"?

All attempts to make the Gypsies settle down have been futile. On the merest excuse they will travel thousands of miles. Many times a member of the family, possibly a distant relative, will be lost. This will form an excuse for wandering all over the world in search of the lost one.

One of the fundamental teachings of the Gypsies is that the wife must be loyal to her husband. This does not work both ways, however. The man is permitted to put his wife out without ceremony if he becomes tired of her. The Gypsies' world is a man's world. The three commandments of Rommany are:

Separate not from the husband.
Be faithful to the husband.
Pay your debts to the husband.

While this law seems to favor the male sex, it has been largely responsible
for the maintenance of the tribal spirit and language.

20. *Ridiculous Stories That May Be Told at Party*

THE CAT AND THE CREAM PITCHER [1]

(Crying all through the Story)

I wonder what Ma will say when she gets home?
She went to visit Mrs. Jones an' ain't got back yet.
Susie and John and Mary and I thought we'd surprise Mama and set
the table.
Susie climbed upon a chair so she could reach the cupboard where Ma
keeps her *bestest things.* [Crying very hard.]
Susie got Ma's very best linen table cover what was given her when she
was married.
And she got the best silverware that's been in the family for years.
And then—and then—[pausing and crying] they got down Ma's best—
[pausing and crying] Ma's best china dishes.
Uncle Josh gave them to her many years ago—and we used them only
when we had company. [Crying.]
But we wanted to surprise Mama [crying]; so we put the extra leaves in
the table, and put on Ma's best tablecloth, dishes, and silverware. [Crying.]
Then we waited and waited, and [crying] still Ma didn't come.
So Mary put on some water for the tea—and still Ma didn't come.
Then all of us went on the porch and looked up the street [crying] and
looked down the street [crying], and Mama was nowhere to be seen.
But when we turned round what do you suppose we saw?
There was that big black cat of ours a-smelling the butter on the table.
[Crying.]
And before we could ketch him, he walked right up and stuck his head
in the cream pitcher [crying very hard], Ma's very best cream pitcher.
[Almost breaking down in large sobs.]
And there we were with the cat's head in the cream pitcher, and we
couldn't get it out, and we didn't know what to do. [Crying very hard.]
So John said the best thing to do was to cut the cat's head off.

[1] Written by Mrs. Lawrence Derthick, Washington, D. C.

So we got the great big butcher knife—you know, the great big knife you use to cut bread with.

Then we crept over softly to the table—then—ooohhhh—[Cut very quickly and cry.]

And there we were with the cat's head in the cream pitcher, and it wouldn't come out. So we decided the best thing to do was to break the cream pitcher.

And we did. [Crying very hard.]

I wonder what Ma will say when she gets home.

How We Hunted a Mouse

It was in the evening after dinner, and I was dozing comfortably in my easy chair and dreaming of the good times which I hoped were coming, when there fell upon my ears a most startling scream. It was the voice of my Maria Ann in agony. The voice came from the kitchen, and to the kitchen I rushed. The idolized form of my Maria was perched upon a chair, and she was flourishing an iron spoon in all directions and shouting, "Shoo, shoo," in a general manner at everything in the room.

To my anxious inquiry as to what was the matter, she screamed: "Oh, Joshua, Joshua; a mouse, a mouse. It run right out of the cupboard. Kill it, Joshua; kill it." All this fuss over one little harmless mouse. Some women are afraid of mice. Maria is.

So I got the poker and set myself to poke that mouse. The first time I hit it I didn't poke it any, for I got my poker tangled up in the dishes in the sink, and I didn't poke it any more, for it wouldn't stay still. It ran right toward me, and I naturally jumped as anybody would; but when the horrid thing ran right up the leg of my trousers, I screamed for Maria, who had already fled from the kitchen. I was afraid the mouse would gnaw a hole in my garment. Now, there is something real disagreeable about having a mouse up the leg of one's trousers. Its toes are cold, its claws scratch, its fur tickles, its tail feels crawly, and there is nothing real pleasant about it. That mouse was next to me. I could feel its every movement with clear and startling distinction. Therefore I yelled for Maria, and, as the case seemed urgent, I may have yelled with some vigor; but I deny that I yelled, "Fire," and if I catch the person who said I did, I will inflict punishment upon his person.

When Maria came in she was as white as a sheet. She asked me what I had thought of doing, as though I could hold the mouse and plan a campaign at the same time. I told her to think of something. She thought she would throw things at the mouse. But as there was no earthly chance of her hitting it and every shot took effect on me, I told her to stop after she had tried two smoothing irons, the meat mill, and the rolling pin. I told her to think of something else. She thought she would get some cheese and coax the mouse down. But I was afraid to let loose for fear it would run up. Then she wanted to get some boiling water and scald the mouse, but I objected to this process except as the last resort. Then she exclaimed: "Oh, Joshua, I wish you had not killed the cat." I submit that this thought was born of the weakness of woman's intellect. How on earth could a cat get where the mouse was? Rather have the mouse there alone than to have a cat prowling around after it.

Maria paused for breath, but I kept bobbing around. It seemed that I had no inclination to sit down anywhere, when finally from mere exhaustion I tripped over a smoothing iron, lost my balance and my hold on the mouse, and it fell to the floor very dead. I had no idea a mouse could be squeezed to death so easily.

But that was not the end of the trouble. Before I had recovered my breath a fireman broke through the front window. He was followed by his whole gang, and they dragged hose and mussed things all over the house. Then the fire chief wanted to thrash me because the house wasn't on fire. We had hardly gotten him pacified when a policeman rushed in and arrested me. Someone had phoned in and reported that I was drunk and was killing Maria. It was all that Maria and I could do by combining our eloquence to prevent him from carrying me off in disgrace.

Now when mice come out of the cupboard, I just let Maria shoo them back. I can kill a mouse, but the fun doesn't pay for the trouble.
—*Anonymous.*

The Overthrow of King Gastric Juicibus [2]

There was a mighty monarch called King Gastric Juicibus.

He ruled over a kingdom called Stomach-i-ti-cus.

And the only way to his kingdom was through a long, long lane called Aesophagus.

One day when King Gastric Juicibus sat on his throne enjoying peace and plenty, he looked down that long, long lane and beheld approaching one of his bitter enemies—Lobster Saladibus.

King Gastric Juicibus arose quickly from his throne, girded on his armor, strapped on his sword, and prepared himself to do battle.

They fought for hours and hours. Finally King Gastric Juicibus was victorious, and he overcame Lobster Saladibus and tied him up in a knot and threw him over into one corner of his kingdom.

[2] Written by Miss Cynthia Pearl Maus.

But hardly had he sat down again on his throne when, looking down that long, long lane, he beheld another enemy approaching. This time it was his deadly enemy, Chicken à la Kingibus.

He arose again from his throne and buckled on his armor and strapped on his sword. They fought for hours and hours and hours, and finally when the strength of King Gastric Juicibus was almost exhausted, he prevailed and overthrew his enemy, Chicken à la Kingibus, and tied him up in a knot and threw him over into another corner of his kingdom.

But King Gastric Juicibus had hardly sat down again on his throne till, looking again down that long, long lane, he beheld approaching his most deadly enemy, Mince Pie à la Modibus.

King Gastric Juicibus again buckled on his armor and strapped on his sword and prepared himself to do battle. They fought for hours and hours and hours and hours. But this time King Gastric Juicibus was not the victor. He was overthrown by Mince Pie à la Modibus. And Mince Pie à la Modibus tied up King Gastric Juicibus into a knot and threw him over into a corner of his kingdom.

Then Mince Pie à la Modibus went over to Chicken à la Kingibus and untied him and set him on his feet.

Then he went over to Lobster Saladibus and untied him and set him on his feet.

Then Mince Pie à la Modibus said to Chicken à la Kingibus and Lobster Saladibus, *"Come on, boys, let's go upstairs."*

WHY THE CHINESE HAVE SHORT NAMES [3]

Long, long ago, in far-away China, there lived two little boys. One was named Choy, and the other Tinky-tuky-timbo-no-si-nembo-hooy-booy-bousky-peooy-pen-do-hickey-pon-pon-nickey-no-me-on-don-peooy-eo. He was named this because it was a custom in those days for the mother to name her child a long name just according to how much she loved him.

One day little Choy and Tinky-tuky-timbo-no-si-nembo-hooy-booy-bousky-p e ooy-pen-do-hickey-pon-pon-nickey-n o-me-on-don-peooy-eo were playing beside the well, when all of a sudden little Choy fell in the well. Little Tinky, and so on (this full name must be repeated each time by the one giving the recitation), was so very frightened and ran. "Mother, Mother, Choy has fallen into the well. Come quickly and get him out." She said: "Little Choy fell in the well? Oh, little Choy fell in the well. Well, darling, run tell the gardener to get little Choy out of the well."

So little Tinky, and so on, ran to the gardener and cried: "Oh, Gardener,

[3] Written by Mrs. J. G. Deriso, Jacksonville, Fla. Used by permission.

Gardener, poor Choy has fallen into the well. Come quickly and get him out."

"Huh, what's that you say?" he asked.

"Oh, come quickly. Choy has fallen in the well."

"Oh, Choy has fallen into the well. Well, we will get Choy out right away."

So the gardener ran and put a ladder in the well and climbed down and got little Choy and brought him out of the well.

Many weeks after that when Choy got well enough to play, the two boys were playing beside the well again, when all of a sudden poor little Tinky, and so on, fell into the well.

Little Choy ran to his mother and cried: "Oh, Mother, Mother, little Tinky-tuky-timbo-no-si-nembo-hooy-booy-bousky-peooy-pen-do-hickey - pon - pon-nickey-no-me-on-don-peooy-eo has fallen into the well. Come quickly and get him out."

She said: "Little Tinky, and so on, fell in the well? Oh, little Tinky, and so on, fell in the well. Run, darling, and tell the gardener to get little Tinky, and so on, out of the well."

Little Choy ran to the gardener and cried: "Oh, Gardener, Gardener, poor little Tinky, and so on, has fallen into the well. Come quickly and get him out."

"Huh, what's that you say?"

"Poor little Tinky, and so on, has fallen into the well. Come quickly and get him out."

"Oh," he said, "little Tinky-tuky-timbo-no-si-nembo-hooy-booy-bousky-peooy-pen-do-hickey-pon-pon-nickey-no-me-on-don-peooy-eo has fallen into the well. We will get little Tinky, and so on, out right away."

So the gardener got a ladder and climbed down and down and down and got little Tinky, and so on, out of the well, but poor little Tinky, and so on, was almost drowned. He didn't grow up to be a strong man like Choy, so that taught the Chinese mothers a lesson, and ever since that time they have been naming their children real short names like Choy, Tu, Chong, Wu, and Fu.

---

4 "And so on," after the name of Tinky is used in the printing only for brevity. The person giving the recitation must repeat the full name each time it is used. This is, in effect, the real point of the story.

chapter 29

Celebrities Party

WE ALL ADMIRE FAMOUS PEOPLE, SO FOR ONE EVENING LET US PLAY
that we too are celebrities. This party is built around famous people
of the past and present. Celebrities of past history, as well as present
outstanding persons will be present in spirit at the party. The same
is true of famous people from the screen, stage, and television. Stars
of sports of all kinds, famous people in aviation, religion, politics,
and music will all be a part of this gathering.

1. *Invitation.*—A suggested invitation is given below:

> If your name is not in Who's Who,
> > You can be great just the same.
> You can act like celebrities do—
> > Be alive in a Hall of Fame.
> So come to Smith's on Saturday night
> > It's no fun to stay on the shelf.
> You'll live in the past and present both.
> > We believe you'll enjoy yourself.
>
> Give Hour of Party and Street Address

2. *Decorations.*—Most of the characters who will be present "in
spirit" will be great Americans. They will have won their fame or
fortunes in our country. It will, therefore, be appropriate to use the
national colors in the decorations. Use crepe paper streamers of red,
white, and blue, with bunting and flags. This will be very appropriate setting for such a gathering.

3. *Opening Mixer: Who's Who.*—The leader has arranged in advance a number of names of famous persons from American life,
and has had these typed on small slips of paper to be pinned on

202

the guests. The following are suggested as examples, but the leader should add a lot of currently famous celebrities to the list:

George and Martha Washington.
Abraham and Mary Todd Lincoln.
James and Dollie Madison.
Captain John Smith and Pocahontas.
The President of the United States and the First Lady.
Current stars of baseball, tennis, football, and golf.
Great Leaders of Industry such as Henry Ford and John D. Rockefeller.
Inventors like Eli Whitney, Thomas A. Edison.
Stars of stage, movies, and television.
Popular musicians or composers.

It will not be difficult to get enough names from this list for every boy and girl in attendance, unless the party is very large.

After the guests arrive and it is time to start the games, the leader asks the guests to seat themselves in a circle. As they are seated in this circle, the leader and his helpers pin on the backs of the guests the names of the famous persons they are to represent for the evening. They do not know what name is pinned on their backs, and they are supposed to try to prevent the other guests from finding out. When the leader has finished pinning on the names, she gives each guest a paper and pencil. All are then invited to rise and attempt to get the name of each of the other guests and to write it on their paper, together with the name of the person he represents for the evening. Later the person who has the longest list of names of guests, with the names of the famous person they represent, will be asked to read his paper and should be given a token prize.

In the meantime, however, and after the leader has declared that the name-seeking phase of the game is over, each guest must try to learn the name of the person he represents by asking questions. His questions must always be answered by the other guests with a "Yes," or "No." For example he may ask: "Am I a celebrity of the present?" The answer will be "No." "Am I a statesman?" Again, "No." "Am I a soldier?" The answer will be, "Yes." "Am I General Robert E. Lee?" The answer will be, "Yes," for that is the name that was

203

pinned on his back. When a guest learns what famous person he represents, he may remove the name from his back and pin it in front to be worn the remainder of the evening.

4. *Impersonations.*—The leader should then ask certain of the guests to impersonate the famous person they represent or to perform some act that is a part of his history. George Washington may be asked to chop down the cherry tree, or Pocahontas may be asked to save Captain John Smith from being killed by the chief. Abraham Lincoln may be asked to read the Gettysburg Address. Characters representing current stars of sport may be asked to demonstrate how to knock a home run or how to pitch a curve. Stars of movie, stage, or television may be asked to do or say something for which that character is noted. This could go as far as asking a guest to sing or play an instrument like some current musical star.

At the time that this part of the program concludes, the person who was able to write the largest list of guests with the names of the characters they represent, should be asked to read his list, and should be given a token prize.

5. *Taxation Without Representation.*—One of the guests is selected to be the leader of this game. (Perhaps the one who wrote the longest list of names in the game above should be given this job.) He is given a list of the famous persons the guests impersonate, or he is told to read these names from the slips of paper pinned on them. He begins to call these names, perhaps taking a girl and then a boy. He calls the names, as, Dollie Madison, George Washington, Pocahontas, Captain John Smith, and so forth. These persons rise and follow him as he walks around inside the circle. There must be no vacant chairs in the circle when the game starts. When a half dozen or more have been called, the leader says, "Taxation without representation." Whereupon all scramble to get a chair. The person who fails to get a chair becomes the new leader and must call the names and follow the same procedure. Let this game continue until seven or eight guests have had a try as leader.

6. *Can You Remember?*—This game could be played by either giving the guests the list of questions given below and having them write the answers, or by conducting it like a spelling match. The leader asks one player the question and tells the others to remain silent. If this one cannot answer the question, it passes on to the next one, and so on around the room. The following questions are suggested:

(1) Who said, "Give me liberty, or give me death"? Patrick Henry.

(2) Who was called "Old Hickory"? Andrew Jackson.

(3) Of whom was it said, "There is [he] standing like a stone wall"? T. J. [Stonewall] Jackson.

(4) Who said, "We must all hang together, or assuredly we shall all hang separately"? Benjamin Franklin.

(5) Who was king of England during the Revolutionary War? George III.

(6) Who made the first American Flag? Betsy Ross.

(7) What do the stars in the American flag represent? The states.

(8) What do the stripes in the American flag represent? The 13 English Colonies.

(9) What country presented the Statue of Liberty to the United States? France.

(10) Who took a twenty-years sleep on a hillside? Rip Van Winkle.

(11) Quote the first line of "The Raven." Once upon a midnight dreary.

(12) Who said, "I only regret that I have but one life to lose for my country"? Captain Nathan Hale.

(13) Who said, "Four score and seven years ago"? Abraham Lincoln.

(14) What was the battle cry during the Spanish-American War? "Remember the Maine!"

(15) What event started the war with Japan? The bombing of Pearl Harbor.

(16) What president was noted for his honesty? Abraham Lincoln.

(17) Name three presidents of the United States who were assassinated. Lincoln, Garfield, and McKinley.

(18) Who served the longest as president of the United States? Franklin Delano Roosevelt.

(19) What American is associated with a hatchet? George Washington.

(20) Who wrote,

"Lives of great men all remind us
We can make our lives sublime"?

Longfellow.

(21) What American is associated with a rail fence? Abraham Lincoln.

(22) What organization has the slogan, "Be prepared"? Boy Scouts and Girl Scouts.

(23) Who said, "Go West, young man"? Horace Greeley.

(24) Who said, "Sir, I would rather be right than be President"? Henry Clay.

7. *Spelling à la Chinese.*—The guests are given slips of paper on which have been written sentences with the words that are in italics blank. These blanks must be filled with words which can be spelled both backward and forward. The word spelled backward fills one blank and spelled forward fills the other.

(1) The *dog* regards man as his *God.*

(2) I read of a man who would *flog* his wife because he couldn't shoot par *golf.*

(3) The *dam* was used to hold back the *mad* waters.

(4) You must *stop* throwing trash into the flower *pots.*

(5) On this *spot* the boys always came to spin their *tops.*

(6) I told him that it did *not* weigh a *ton.*

(7) She told him to *nip* the bud (flower) and *pin* it on.

(8) The *strap* was cut in two *parts.*

(9) The *deer* was standing in the water by a tall *reed.*

(10) I put the dog in the *tub, but* he jumped out.

(11) From this *spot* one can see the *tops* of the city's skyscrapers.

8. *Sail the Ship.*—Guests are seated about the room in a circle. The leader takes a sofa pillow and says, "I'm going to sail my ship with a dog." He says this because his name is John Doe, and he sails the ship with something that starts with the first letter of his last name. The next player, whose name is Brown, should say, "I am going to sail my ship with a banana." Players who do not sail the ship correctly must sit on the floor. They can still play the game, however, and from time to time the pillow should be thrown to them; and if they sail it correctly, they may take their seats again. This game should not be played for more than five or ten minutes.

9. *Rescue the Flag: Relay.*—The guests should be divided into equal groups—there may be celebrities of the past and celebrities of the present. If there is not an equal number, drop off some of those in the larger group to make the sides equal. Take a small American flag and place it in something that will hold it up. There should be one flag for each side, and it should be from twenty or thirty feet away from the head of the line. The first player in this line runs up and gets the flag. He brings it back and gives it to the next one in line, who runs up and replaces it. Each player, after running, takes his position at the back of the line. The side that finishes first is declared winner.

10. *The Head of George Washington.*—Give guests a half cake of soap and a paring knife. The boys, of course, may use their pocketknives. Any kind of sharp instrument could be substituted for a paring knife. Give a prize to the one who can sculpture the best head of George Washington. Newspapers should be provided so that the scraps of soap will not get on the floor.

11. *Refreshments.*—Serve ice cream and cake and Boston tea. Another suggestion would be a salad of cottage cheese, covering the cheese with crushed pineapple, and topping it with mayonnaise. Serve with crackers and coffee.

12. *Properties*

(1) Slips of paper on which to write names of celebrities.
(2) Impersonations written out and numbered.
(3) Papers prepared for Spelling á la Chinese.
(4) List of questions for Can You Remember?
(5) Sofa pillow for Sail the Ship.
(6) Two flags and vases for Rescue the Flag.
(7) Half cake of soap and paring knife for each guest.

chapter 30

King Neptune's Carnival[1]
(A WATER CARNIVAL OR PAGEANT)

AN IDEAL SETTING FOR SUCH A PAGEANT OR WATER CARNIVAL AS THE one described in this chapter would be a pool where guests could be seated on the edge to watch the proceedings. It might be presented as a money-making program and admission charged or merely as an entertainment program. Such a program would be ideal for a civic club picnic program or a church Sunday-school picnic. If the pool was lighted, it would be better to have it at night.

1. *Invitations.*—If such a program is to be given as a benefit and the public is to be invited, it would be best not to send invitations but to give publicity to it through the papers. In case it is to be a Sunday-school picnic, it should be announced rather than invitations sent. Civic clubs using it will send out their usual bulletins.

2. *Preparation.*—Such a program as this will need careful preparation and rehearsal. It will probably be necessary to get someone outside the group giving the carnival to demonstrate some of the swimming strokes and fancy dives.

3. *Characters and Costumes*

King Neptune—Long gray beard and hair; greenish draperies; gold crown; trident.

[1] The pageant or water carnival given in this chapter was adapted from the pageants "King Neptune's Carnival" and "How Swimming Grew Up," issued by the American Red Cross First Aid and Life-Saving Service. The former was produced under the direction of B. Dean Brink, assisted by Mrs. A. L. Gillette, at Huntingdon, Long Island, N. Y., while the latter bulletin was written by Commodore W. E. Longfellow, Assistant National Director of First Aid and Life-Saving, American Red Cross. Used by permission of Commodore W. E. Longfellow and the American Red Cross.

Mermaids and Mermen—In bathing suits.

Tree Princess—Green costumes.

Sea Prince—Sea green draperies, and so forth.

Mr. World, Mrs. World, Sister World, Brother World—Typical family in street costumes.

Davy Jones—Rakish sailor suit; black patch over eye; red nose; cocked hat.

Swimming Instructor—A typical pool swimming instructor in beach robe and wooden clogs.

Mr. Stonehatchet, Mrs. Stonehatchet, Sammie Stonehatchet, Susie Stonehatchet—Cave dwellers of the stone age; simulated animal skin costume over bathing suit; man carries stone ax or club.

Greek Youth and Maiden—Short white slips; girl has ribbon-bound hair; sandals.

Cassius and Caesar—Roman soldiers; silver cloth suit over bathing suit; silvered helmet. (May be made of gauze hat frame painted with aluminum paint.)

William Trudgeon—Old-fashioned English bathing suit; with sleeves (short) and skirt; has sideburns or long chop whiskers.

Richard Cavill and Two Opponents—Dressed in old-fashioned bathing suits.

Dignified Swimmer—To swim side overarm stroke.

Crawl Swimmer—To swim crawl.

Two Backstroke Swimmers.

4. King Neptune's Carnival

Episode No. 1—Synopsis: Mr. and Mrs. World come to the pool to find out about getting swimming lessons for their children. They begin to discuss the origin of swimming and are surprised by Father Neptune, who appears suddenly in the center of the pool. Neptune declares that he has a wonderful manuscript compiled by Davy Jones, which gives the history of swimming. He calls Davy Jones, who brings the manuscript. While Neptune reads aloud the history of swimming, shades of the departed swimmers he mentions appear and go through the actions and events credited to them in the manuscript.

Episode No. 2—Synopsis: King Neptune is joined by a large company of mermaids and mermen, who emerge from the water at the end of the first episode. The King ascends his throne, and the mermaids and mermen pass before him in review and pay tribute to him. Tableau.

Episode No. 3—Synopsis: Demonstration by mermaids and mermen.

Episode No. 4—Synopsis: The romance of the Tree Princess and the Sea Prince.

Episode No. 1: The Swimming Pool

Mr. and Mrs. World come to bring their children to the new pool for a series of swimming lessons. The diving board is draped in white cloth, or sheets, which hang clear to the water's edge in order to conceal Neptune and Davy Jones, who are hiding there. (Some place should be curtained off for mermaids and mermen.) To insure their not being seen, it would be well to keep the audience out until at least fifteen minutes before the performance is to be given; also, so that all the players can be ready in their places.

Mrs. World: So this is the swimming pool?

Instructor: Yes. We have a very fine pool here, sterilized water, tested, found to be purer than the water we drink.

Mrs. World: Do you have many good swimmers?

Instructor: Yes. We have more than fifty who can swim a mile.

Mr. World: How could anybody swim a mile in that pool? I do not believe it is over seventy-five feet long.

Instructor: Oh, they swim back and forth the same as a squirrel does in his revolving cage. It is much handier for the instructor. We can criticize them without walking a mile to keep up and watch the safety of the others at the same time.

Mrs. World: I am glad to see you have a man around here, because I should hate to think of our children falling in with only a woman to take care of them.

Brother World: Who ever invented swimming, anyway? I wish you would tell us about it.

Instructor: It just happens that I have an hour of free time, and I will tell you all about it. But I hope you will sit over here while I do, because it is apt to be a long story.

(The World Family take seats designated by the Instructor, and he is about to begin when a voice from the middle of the pool is heard.)

Neptune: Hello there.

Instructor: Hello yourself! Who are you? How did you get in?

Neptune: Swimmers the world over call me their Daddy. I am Father Neptune, who is given dominion over the seas and waterways. I have with me a very ancient manuscript which will tell these people of the World Family how swimming grew up.

Mr. World: Where is the book? Where did he get it?

Neptune: Davy Jones has been compiling it in his hang-out at the bottom of the sea. Ho, Davy! Bring up the documents in the case.

(Davy Jones makes a surface dive under the springboard and emerges in the middle of the tank alongside of Neptune. He has a roll of oilcloth with ancient characters painted on it.)

Davy: Help me. Father Nep, haul this up.

(Both pull on a rope and pull the end of the scroll out of the water, and hand it to the Instructor. Both men climb out, take the scroll, and hang it over the doorway from which the swimmers will enter.)

Neptune: Swimming is quite general all over the world. But there was a period when, probably because of the fearsome monsters that lived in the water, humans kept out of it as much as possible. This resulted in their losing their ability to swim. One day when a family of cave dwellers by the name of Stonehatchet were traveling in the forest looking for berries and fruit, they heard in the jungle behind them the sound of the roar of the saber-toothed tiger. Now they were afraid of the water, but they were more afraid of the tiger. When they struck the water, they were still running, and they kept up their running until they ran clear across the stream, looking back occasionally to see if the tiger was coming after them. It happened like this.

(A roar is made by pulling a rosin string attached to a tin can. Then Mr. Stonehatchet, dressed in animal skins and leaves, carrying a stone battle-ax, emerges from a dressing-room door, jumps into the water, fol-

211

*lowed by his wife and three children similarly clad. The hair of the girls
is flying loose and bound with leaves and flowers. They swim to the shallow
end of the tank and look about them. They congratulate one another on
escaping the terrible tiger.)*

Neptune (continuing) : After resting a bit, they decided to return
home the same way they had come and then wait a few days to
see if anybody died from getting wet all over. No one did. So
about a week later they all went in the water again. This happened on a Saturday and was the beginning of that custom, which
seems to have taken root all over the world, of a Saturday night
bath. Mother Stonehatchet was not sure of herself this time, so
she walked around and entered the water at a shallow place. Sammy
Stonehatchet swam by splashing his arms alternately in the water,
but Sister Susie lay over on her side and, resting her head on the
water, managed to stay up with her mouth and nose above the
surface. These accomplishments they proudly displayed to Mother
Stonehatchet. She was so interested that she fell over backward and
thrashed her arms alternately in a sort of back stroke which carried
her clear across the stream. When she stood up again, the children
were delighted and laughed themselves sick. But she was very in-
dignant because no one helped her. "I might have drowned," she
said. "Why didn't someone pick me up?" "But, Mother," they
cried, "you were swimming. Do it again." After thinking a moment,
Mrs. Stonehatchet, who was a broad, heavy lady, thought what they
said was true, and she tried it again, which was the beginning of
the backstroke.

(The Stonehatchets retire.)

Neptune: Pictures on the walls of ancient tombs and on pottery
show that very early in the world's history swimming was practiced
by various peoples. In fact, an alternate overarm stroke was practiced by the Assyrians. Records also show that these people crossed
streams on inflated goatskins, which they called "musseks." It is con-
ceivable that this stroke was developed because they found them-

selves better able to pull themselves along by alternate strokes than by the rowing motion. It is quite possible, too, that others slipped from their inflated skin bags, which were the early water wings, and in reaching for them alternately developed the ability to do without them. So we will picture for you a group of Assyrians crossing a river in the early days.

(*Sound of oriental music is heard from behind the scenes—use a record player in one of the dressing rooms. A group of three persons, with water wings painted to represent inflated goatskins or "musseks," enter the water. Two of these paddle across on their wings, towing a raft with their packs. The third slips off his wings, and they float away from him. He swims after them with the crawl stroke, pushing the wings ahead of him.*)

(*When the Assyrians depart, Neptune continues.*)

Neptune: The early Greeks, who were all-round athletes, did not overlook swimming in their endeavor to attain physical perfection. They found swimming an ideal exercise to achieve their purposes. Their swimming was not confined to heated baths, but they practiced in the open sea.

(*From the portal come a Greek Youth and Maiden wearing the short Greek robe over their costume. In playing ball they lose the ball and both laughingly plunge in to recover it, catching it back and forth with much laughter all the way down the tank until they disappear. If desirable, several girls could play this, instead of a boy and a girl. Appropriate music should be played during this episode.*)

Neptune: From the Greeks the Romans got many ideas about swimming and bathing which they utilized in their marvelous system of baths, ruins of which are found all over Europe. You will remember the episode in the life of Caesar which Cassius tells of in the words of your poet and dramatist, Shakespeare. Mark where he says:

I was born as free as Caesar; so were you;
We both have fed as well, and we can both

213

Endure the winter's cold as well as he;
For once, upon a raw and gusty day,
The troubled Tiber chafing with her shores,
Caesar said to me, "Darest thou, Cassius, now,
Leap in with me into this angry flood,
And swim to yonder point?" Upon the word,
Accoutred as I was, I plunged in
And bade him follow; so indeed he did.
The current roar'd, and we did buffet it
With lusty sinews, throwing it aside
And stemming it with hearts of controversy;
But ere we could arrive the point proposed,
Caesar cried, "Help me, Cassius, or I sink!"
I, as Aeneas, our great ancestor,
Did from the flames of Troy upon his shoulder
The old Anchises bear, so from the waves of Tiber
Did I the tired Caesar.

(*As Neptune declaims these lines, Cassius and Caesar enter through the portal in light armor and swords and enact the scene in the water, Cassius rescuing Caesar, towing him to shallow water and bringing him out with the saddleback carry.*)

Neptune (continuing): It is almost as bad to overdo a thing as not to do it at all, and the Romans put too much stress on bathing in their *natatoria* throughout their world-wide domain. These pools were the scenes of excessive luxury and great licentiousness, reflecting the tendency of the time. So in the dark ages the peoples themselves were dark because they renounced even the cleansing bath as well as the swimming, and so for a time the art was lost, or nearly so. From the continent of Europe comes the stroke known as the breast or broad stroke. It was the stroke which grown-ups—powerful, lusty men—swam in facing the rough sea. It was also called, for this reason, man fashion or sailor fashion as opposed to the boy or dog fashion, for boys even then learned to swim by the dog paddle. So we have a group of European swimmers doing the breast stroke, a stroke which was taught to the soldiers of Germany many years ago.

214

(Demonstration of the breast stroke.)

Neptune (continuing) : You have seen how, 'way back in the Stone Age, the children varied from the breast position to the side to avoid getting water in the face. So it has been in every nation which has taken up swimming, and when it the period 1875 to 1890 swimming had a great revival in England and Scotland, the side stroke was much used in competition.

(Demonstration of side stroke.)

Neptune (continuing) : It was natural enough for the person who liked canoeing and who took up swimming to adapt the canoe paddle idea to his side stroke, reasoning that there would be less friction if the arms were recovered entirely out of the water each time, as the canoe paddle is lifted at the end of the pull. So we have the English overarm or single overarm stroke, a much faster stroke than the breast stroke. It was the development of this stroke that put to rest the contention of the breast-stroke swimmers that they had a faster stroke than the side stroke.

(Here side-stroke and breast-stroke swimmers demonstrate their respective strokes, in which the side strokers should finish first to make good Neptune's argument.)

Neptune: 'Way back in 1859 an English swimmer, W. Payton, used the stroke which we now know as trudgeon in a breast-stroke race in the famous Lambeth Baths and was disqualified for it. The stroke, however, was named for William Trudgeon, a seafaring man, who is said to have picked it up in Buenos Aires, where the natives used it. Trudgeon swam a short-arm pull with the double-overarm pull, the hands entering the water almost level with the shoulders, using the legs as in the breast stroke or frog kick. Later one of the Cavill family of Australia used this and won the race with it. So we have William Trudgeon's original stroke.

(Enter William Trudgeon. Does the Trudgeon stroke.)

Neptune: The crawl stroke, as we first heard of it, came from the swimming baths at Melbourne, Australia. The Australians, as did their English cousins, took their swimming very seriously, and when young Richard Cavill used to plow along in the bath with his head in the water, working both arms like the paddles of a side-wheel steamer, they voted him rather a nuisance. But when he entered a 220-yard free style race, which usually meant the English overarm, and won his heat, his opponent, a dignified swimmer of the old school, refused to go against him, saying that splashing about in the water like that was not swimming. So Cavill was the winner. His "funny crawling stroke" won him more and more fame. Later he was sent to England and made a wonderful showing there with the stroke, which was then known as the Australian crawl. But first from the pages of history let us show that epoch-making race in which Cavill won his heat.

(Show heat of two lengths with three side strokers, and second heat showing two side strokers and one crawl swimmer who uses only the arms in his stroke. Then argument between winner of each heat, ending with the awarding of the race to Cavill, who swims an exhibition length of the legless crawl.)

Neptune: The Australian crawl had but two scissor kicks. It was in trying to perfect this early crawl stroke that Charles M. Daniels, who was America's first world champion, hit upon the American flutter crawl. He did not know just how the Australian crawl went, but found that he could go faster by working his legs rapidly with a slower arm beat. He soon won most of the world's speed championships.

(Following Neptune's discussion of the Australian crawl, this is demonstrated by a swimmer for two lengths; and then the American crawl stroke is shown by a swimmer who covers the length of the tank with legs alone, attaching the arm motion on the return trip.)

Neptune: Through the years there have been many improvements in the crawl stroke, making it even faster. Next we have, in its wonderful rhythm, the crawl as it is performed today.

(Demonstration of crawl is now given by several swimmers.)

Neptune: From the time that Mother Stonehatchet fell over on her back and paddled along, the backstroke has had favor with many people. There are several types of backstrokes. The European backstroke is a co-ordinated stroke very much like the breast stroke upside down. Then we have the inverted crawl, which, next to the crawl itself, is the fastest stroke known. One of the foremost exponents of the racing backstroke was Miss Sybil A. Bauer, a celebrated swimmer. We will now see these different types of backstrokes.

Episode No. 2
King Neptune ascends his throne. Mermen and mermaids appear from the water. He calls mermaids and mermen, who pass in review before him and pay tribute. Tableau.

Episode No. 3
(1) *Mermen compete in races.*
(2) *Mermaids do likewise.*
(3) *King Neptune's children race across the lake in mortals' washtubs.*
(4) *Mermen compete in umbrella and nightshirt race.*
(5) *All members of the court in the mortals' game of pushball. Substitute polo, basketball, or baseball from Aquatic Party, page 165.*
(6) *Mermen and mermaids compete in canoe novelty race and tilting.*
(7) *Mermen and mermaids demonstrate graceful aquatic accomplishments.*
(8) *King Neptune's children indulge in water potato race.*

217

(9) *Mermen and mermaids show King Neptune their ability in fancy diving.*

King Neptune gives brief explanation of dives:

(1) *The Fear Dive.* The fear dive was the dive of the primitive man when he was chased into the water by the wild beast. (*Demonstration.*)

(2) *The Long Dive.* The primitive man soon learned that the body would travel faster through the air than through the water, and he soon learned to do the long dive. (*Have someone demonstrate.*)

Other dives may be demonstrated, as follows: Plain front dive with height, running front dive, swan dive, front jackknife dive, the bat dive, the back jackknife dive, and all others that can be demonstrated.

Episode No. 4: The Tree Princess and the Sea Prince

Mermen and mermaids resting on an enchanted island. The Tree Princess descends from her tree castle and is discovered by the surprised sea nymphs. Sea nymphs welcome her and invite her to her castle beneath the sea.

Prince Neptune, heir to the sea throne, falls in love with the Tree Princess who scorns his advances. Frightened by his pursuit, the Tree Princess flees in anger. In her haste she falls into the waters of the lake. Having lived her life in the trees, she is unfamiliar with the art of swimming and sinks beneath the waves. Prince Neptune immediately dives and in making the rescue demonstrates the holds, breaks, and carries used in saving drowning persons. After bringing the apparently drowned Princess to the shore, the Prince restores her to consciousness, using the latest method of resuscitation.

Grateful for her rescue, she accepts the proposal of the Prince, and, accompanied by the sea nymphs, the Prince takes the Tree Princess to his father, King Neptune, who bestows his paternal blessing. They then go to his castle beneath the sea and live happy forever after.

5. *Refreshments.*—Box lunches may be served. If the affair is given for a benefit, additional money may be made by selling these box lunches to those in attendance. A good box lunch would consist of a ham sandwich, pimento cheese sandwich, a cup of potato salad, a deviled egg, and a cup cake. Watermelon may be served as the dessert instead of the cup cake. If this carnival is given as a Sunday-school picnic, it would be better to have a refreshment committee to arrange for different individuals to bring certain articles of food. Ice cream and drinks may be served by the group giving the picnic.

6. *Properties*

(1) Characters in costume, taking care to have all the parts taken and rehearsed.

(2) Instructions for King Neptune to read. These may be placed in a jar and taken out of the water. Have a large piece of oilcloth wrapped around the jar. Have the book handy in case the paper in the jar gets wet.

(3) Have each character bring the properties needed for his part.

(4) Some large washtubs.

(5) Umbrellas and nightshirts.

(6) Pushball if obtainable. Substitute rubber ball about the size of basketball for polo or basketball or smaller rubber ball for baseball.

chapter 31

Old-Fashioned Party

(*COSTUME*)

THERE ARE SO MANY GAMES PLAYED A GENERATION AGO THAT ARE
rarely ever used now that to use them would be the equivalent of a
new game. So why not have an old-fashioned party and wear old-
fashioned costumes and play old-fashioned games?

1. *Invitation.*—The invitation may read in this manner:

> Twenty-year endowments,
> We hear of every day;
> They're always in the future—
> Let's look the other way,
> Twenty years behind us,
> And maybe twenty more,
> And practice all the pleasures
> They liked so much of yore.
> So borrow grandma's petticoat

(Grandpa's flannel underwear for boys)

> And find yourself a mate,
> And come to 14 Macy Street
> On Friday night at eight.

2. *Costumes.*—Hoop skirts and tiny hats would be appropriate
for the girls. They might wear their hair pompadour. Boys wear
the most antiquated cut of clothing that can be obtained. Costumes
should be judged, and the one having the best or funniest costume
should receive an appropriate prize. There should be prizes for
both boys' and girls' costumes.

3. *Circle Confab.*—An old-time game is Circle Confab. The boys form a circle by joining hands around the circle of girls joining hands. When music is played, they start marching in opposite directions. When the music stops, the boy must become acquainted with the girl in front of him in the circle. When the music starts again, the march continues, and when the music stops again, the boy and girl thrown together must converse until the music starts again, and so on.

4. *Shouting Proverbs.*—One person or couple is sent out of the room. The group decides on a proverb that they are going to shout. Suppose they decide on the proverb, "All is not gold that glitters." This is given out one word at a time to the circle; the first one is to shout, "All," the second, "is," and the third, "not," and so on around. The proverb may go around three or four times—that is, three or four in the group may have the same word. When the person or couple that has been sent out returns, at the signal from the leader all shout their words at the same time. If it is not guessed the first time, two other trials may be allowed. If not guessed in three trials, the proverb is told and another person sent out. The following are some proverbs:

All is not gold that glitters.
A stitch in time saves nine.
Honesty is the best policy.
A friend in need is a friend indeed.
A word to the wise is sufficient.
Half a loaf is better than no bread.
When angry, count ten before you speak; if very angry, count a hundred.
A bird in the hand is worth two in the bush.
A penny saved is a penny made.
Procrastination is the thief of time.
Make hay while the sun shines.
Never put off until tomorrow what you can do today.
Every cloud has a silver lining.
Appearances are often deceiving.
Make the best of a bad bargain.
Never count your chickens before they hatch.
A rolling stone gathers no moss.

Plow deep while sluggers sleep, and you'll have corn to sell and keep.
Faint heart never won fair lady.
No news is good news.
A cat may look at a king.
It never rains but it pours.
A drowning man will catch at a straw.
Never look a gift horse in the mouth.
After dinner sit awhile, after supper walk a mile.
A watched pot never boils.
One good turn deserves another.
Look before you leap.
A creaking door hangs long on the hinges.
Out of sight, out of mind.
A bad workman quarrels with his tools.
Birds of a feather flock together.
A new broom sweeps clean.
A fool and his money are soon parted.
Waste not, want not.
Who steals my purse steals trash.
Better late than never.
A barking dog never bites.
It's a long lane that has no turning.
There's many a slip 'twixt the cup and the lip.

5. *Clap In, Clap Out.*—All the boys retire to another room, and the girls stand behind vacant chairs. The boys are brought in one at a time. They take a seat. If everybody claps, they are in the wrong seat. That means that the girl who asked for him was not the girl in whose chair he seated himself. If desired, two trials may be given each one. If he gets the right chair, he remains in the room and is privileged to sit in the chair. After the boys have all come in, the girls may go into the adjoining room and be brought in one at a time in the same manner.

6. *Wink.*—The boys are seated in the chairs, and the girls stand behind. One girl's chair is vacant. She winks at a boy who sits in another chair, and he tries to go to her chair. If his partner succeeds in tagging him before he gets away, he has to remain, and the girl must wink at another. After this game has been in progress for a while, the girls take the chairs with the boys standing.

7. *Jumbled Proverbs.*—Write out on the typewriter several proverbs. Cut each of the proverbs into four or five parts, mix up the parts, and give out the pieces. Select the proverbs that have some action in them, like "A new broom sweeps clean," or, "Make hay while the sun shines," or, "A stitch in time saves nine," "Look before you leap," "A drowning man will catch at a straw," and so forth. Some time will be required for the guests to find the persons having the other words or phrases of their proverb. But when those having different parts of the proverb have gotten together, each group is to act out its proverb and let the others guess what it is.

8. *Identification of Photographs.*—Have each guest bring to the party a photograph taken twenty years ago. In case the party is given by young people, ask them to bring a baby picture. These pictures are numbered and placed about the room or pinned to the curtains. Each guest is given a slip of paper which is numbered with as many numbers as there are pictures. They guess the name and write it opposite the corresponding number. Give a prize to the one who has the largest number correct.

9. *Fruit Basket.*—The leader goes to each guest, giving him the name of a fruit, as apple, peach, pear, plum, prune, strawberry, and so on. One person is "It" and stands in the center of the circle seated in chairs. All vacant chairs should be removed. The leader calls out, "Pear and prune change places," whereupon the two who have those names have to change places. The one in the center tries to get one of the places while this change is being made; and if he succeeds, the one who is left out becomes "It," and the game continues. If the person in the center calls the name of a fruit and no one has that name, he must call again.

10. *Charades.*—Divide the party into two or more groups. Let them put on charades representing the names of famous people, songs, books, plays, words, or famous places. The following are some suggestions for charades:

Famous People—Samson (Sam-son); Jackson (Jack-son); Dante (Dan-T); Shakespeare (men shaking improvised spears); Longfellow (a tall man).

Songs—"Let Me Call You Sweetheart" (acted by a couple); "Comin'
Through the Rye" (stepping high and going through motion of kissing);
"Singin' in the Rain" (with umbrella or raincoat); "Carry Me Back to Old
Virginny" (carrying someone; "Where are you going?" "To Virginia");
"Blest Be the Tie That Binds" (someone bound with a cord); "Drink to
Me Only with Thine Eyes" (start to drink to other's health, is stopped, and
eyes indicated).

Books and Plays—Bible (By, Bill); Edward the Second (Edward, Jr.);
Almanacs (awl, man, ax).

Places—Yellowstone (a yellow stone); the Rhine (watermelon or orange
rind); Reading (Pa.), (a person reading book); Florence (girl by that
name); Caesar (seize her); Panama (pan, a ma).

Words—Cupboard (cup board); paradox (two doctors or two men who
address each other as "Doc"); misunderstanding (a girl under a table with
someone standing on table); bookcase (a book and a spectacle case);
eyelash (strike someone with a lash); hornpipe (a horn and a pipe);
broomstick (a broom and a stick); paradise (a pair of dice); menace
(men, ace); parapets (two pets, cats, dogs, two people who pet each other);
buttercup (butter, cup); ragamuffin (rag, muffin); woman (a man walks
out, the others yell "Whoa!"); ingratiate (in, gray, she, ate); antarctic
(ant, ark, tick); anti-climax (anty, climb, ax); handcuff (hand, cuff);
cutlass (girl with butcher knife); billboard; campbell; blackboard; handout; penitent; madcap; infancy; idol (a person and doll); bagpipe (a bag
and a pipe); sausage (saw, sage); ladyship (lady, ship); Johnny-jump-up;
carpet (small car and cat).

The next two games require forfeits.

11. *Thimble.*—The leader takes a thimble and stands in the center of the room. All the guests are seated around the room and are
told to put the palms of their hands together. The leader then
passes around and makes a motion as if he leaves the thimble with
each one. When he has finished, he starts asking each one, "Who has
the thimble?" They all guess who has it. When all have guessed
(of course the one who has it has to guess someone else, and does
not have to pay a forfeit for so doing), the leader says, "Rise up,
thimbler." The one who has the thimble then rises, and all who
guessed wrongly pay a forfeit. The one who has the thimble then
passes it around again, and the game continues as before.

12. *Spin the Bottle.*—All the players are seated in a circle, and

the leader has them number all the way around and asks them to remember their number. The leader then spins a plate, or turns a milk bottle on its side and spins it around. As the leader does this, he calls a number, say 7 or 9. The one who has this number must catch the plate before it falls or the bottle before it stops moving. If he does not, he must pay a forfeit. Continue this until there are a sufficient number of forfeits.

13. *Redeeming Forfeits.*—When the forfeits have all been collected, there should be one person selected to sell the forfeits, and another over whose head the forfeits are sold. This latter person gives the sentence of penalty, or tells what the owner must do to redeem his property. The person giving the sentence or penalty should be seated in a chair with his back to the forefeits that have been collected. Standing back of him, the seller holds over his head each article collected as a forfeit.

The seller then says, "Heavy, heavy hangs over your head."

The person seated replies with "Fine or superfine?" This is asking whether the article belongs to a boy or a girl—"fine" meaning boy's article and "superfine," a girl's article.

After answering with "fine" or "superfine," the seller says, "What must the owner do to redeem it?"

The person over whose head the forfeits are sold should have a list of penalties written on a card in his hand to refer to from time to time. Of course he will want to think of some penalties impromptu. Some suggested penalties, or forfeits, are given below. The selling and redeeming continue until all the property taken from the guests has been redeemed.

14. *Forfeits*

(1) Ask a question that cannot be answered in the negative. (What does "yes" spell?)

(2) Put four legs against the wall. (Use a chair.)

(3) Kiss a book inside and out without opening it. (Inside and outside the room.)

(4) Put one hand where the other cannot touch it. (On his elbow.)

(5) Bite an inch off the poker. (An inch away from the end of it.)

(6) Imitate a donkey or some other animal.

(7) Sing a lullaby to a pillow and lay it down carefully.

(8) Keep on yawning until you make somebody else yawn.

(9) Imitate a small boy stung by a bee.

(10) Call your sweetheart's name up the chimney.

(11) Pat your stomach with one hand and rub your head with the other. Reverse.

(12) Say the alphabet backward. (Turn your back when you say it.)

(13) Show how a dude walks when passing a lady.

(14) Stand in the middle of the room in any position three people put you in.

(15) Say "Give me liberty or give me death" four times, emphasizing a different word each time.

(16) Stand on a chair and make a speech on any subject the hostess proposes.

(17) Imitate a book salesman trying to make a sale.

(18) Impersonate a traffic cop at a busy corner.

(19) Tell three people, designated by the leader, what you think of them.

(20) Sentence two people to be blindfolded and feed each other broken crackers with spoons.

(21) Say three nice things about yourself.

(22) Confess your worst fault.

(23) Tell the truth for two minutes and answer all questions asked you.

(24) Pose for your photograph.

(25) Poke your head through a ring. (Hold a ring near your head and poke your head with your finger through the ring.)

(26) Two players are told to stand on a newspaper so that they cannot touch each other. (Have a door between them.)

(27) Two players are blindfolded and told to start from opposite sides of the room and meet and shake hands.

(28) A couple are sentenced to feed each other a dish of ice cream with the spoons tied together with a six-inch string.

(29) Imitate a recent groom proposing.

(30) Imitate a recent bride accepting the proposal.

(31) Smile five ways.

(32) Find a person who is not ticklish.

(33) Laugh five ways.

(34) Make love to yourself.

(35) Make five ugly faces.

(36) Propose to the girl on your right.

(37) Snore five different ways.

(38) Bow to the wittiest, flirt with the prettiest, and kneel to the one you love the best.

(39) Leave the room with two legs and come back with six. (Bring back a chair.)

(40) Place three chairs in a row, take off your shoes, and jump over them. (Over the shoes.)

(41) Spell Constantinople, pronouncing each syllable as you go. (When the person comes to the syllable "ti" the leader should say "no." He will think he is wrong, but the leader is merely pronouncing the next syllable.)

(42) Wade the swamps. (A boy represents an Indian, a girl a squaw. They meet in the center of the room, the girl says, "My old Indian," without laughing; the boy says, "My old squaw," without laughing.)

(43) Telephone your sweetheart.

(44) Recite "Mary Had a Little Lamb."

(45) Sing one verse of "America," omitting every third word.

(46) Go to the table, crawl under it, and bark like a dog.

(47) Say "Mixed biscuits" ten times.

(48) Go to each person on one side of the room and bestow a smile on each.

(49) Grasp the left ear with the right hand and the nose with the left. Change hands, grasping the nose with the right and the right ear with the left hand.

(50) Shake hands with five persons in as many different ways.

15. *Old Sayings.*—Give each guest paper and pencil and ask him to write as many old sayings as he can think of. Give two or three examples out of the following list of old sayings. Also the leader may read the first part of the old saying and see who can give the last part quickest.

As busy as a (bee).

As dark as (pitch).

As green as (grass).

As bitter as (gall).

As fine as a (fiddle).

As clear as a (bell).

As dry as a (bone).

As light as a (feather).

As hard as a (rock).

As stiff as a (poker).

As calm as a (clock).

As quick as (lightning).

As ugly as (sin).

As dead as a (door nail).

As white as a (sheet).

As flat as a (pancake).

As red as a (beet).

As bright as a (dollar).

As proud as a (peacock).	As black as the (ace of spades).
As sly as a (fox).	As brown as a (nut).
As poor as a (church mouse).	As blind as a (bat).
As thin as a (rail).	As mean as a (miser).
As fat as a (pig).	As full as a (tick).
As cross as a (bear).	As sharp as a (razor).
As neat as a (pin).	As strong as an (ox).
As crazy as a (loon).	

10. *Memories.*—Provide guests with small booklets made from folding three sheets of 8½x11 paper and sewing it together. On the front write *"Memories."* Have a large stack of old magazines available so that the guests may look through them and select the pictures desired. Also provide scissors and paste for each guest. There should be a topic for each page, as the following or something similar: (1) Scenes from my childhood; (2) My first sweetheart; (3) My wife or husband; (4) His or her folks; (5) My folks; (6) Our home and car; (7) Our children; (8) My favorite pastime; (9) My work; (10) My next wife or husband; (11) My hopes for the future.

Guests are to cut out and paste in the pictures. Allow about fifteen minutes. Have judges to judge the booklets, giving a prize to the one who produces the best one.

17. *Refreshments.*—If sorghum can be obtained, have an old-fashioned candy pulling and use some of the candy for refreshments. Another suggestion would be hot biscuits and honey. Pop popcorn by the fire. Apple or berry pie.

18. *Properties*

(1) A number of proverbs written out with typewriter and cut into four parts for Jumbled Proverbs.

(2) Photographs of each guest taken twenty years ago, or more.

(3) A thimble.

(4) A plate or quart milk bottle.

(5) A list of forfeits for the one over whose head the pawns are being sold.

(6) Pencils and papers for old sayings.

(7) Small booklets, magazines, and paste for Memories.

chapter 32

Bean Party

THE BEAN, IN TIMES PAST, WAS QUITE IMPORTANT AND PLAYED A prominent part in the affairs of men. The Greeks and Romans used beans in gathering the votes in the election of magistrates. A white bean signified absolution and a black one condemnation. They were also used in a sort of ceremony in which the master of the family, after washing his hands three times, threw a black bean over his head nine times, saying, "I redeem myself and my family by these beans." In Germany and England, on the feast of the Twelfth Night, a cake was cut with a bean buried in it, and the one who had the good fortune to get the bean was to be crowned bean king. So why not build a party around the bean?

1. *Invitation.*—Send out the following invitation, and also state the time and place of the party:

> Bean porridge hot, bean porridge cold,
> Bean porridge in the pot nine days old.
> Some like 'em hot, some like 'em cold.
> Some like 'em in the pot nine days old.
> So we're having a Bean Party and want you sold
> On the idea of coming. Like 'em hot or cold?

2. *Decorations.*—Use green and yellow crepe paper streamers for decorating. Green bean vines, if they are available at the time of the party, may also be used.

3. *Cinderella Partners.*—Have each girl place one of her shoes in the middle of the room. The shoes are mixed up and piled in a heap. The boys stand in a circle or in two lines on either side of the room. When the leader's whistle is blown, they all grab a shoe.

The boy must then find the girl with the mate to his shoe, who becomes his partner during the party.

4. *Bean Trading.*—Give each guest ten beans. Throughout the evening whenever any guest succeeds in getting another guest to answer any question asked him with "yes" or "no," that one must give him a bean. At the conclusion of the party give a prize to the one having the largest number of beans. It would be well to have different kinds of beans for each bean stunt so that the beans will not get mixed. Bags of jelly beans make good prizes.

5. *Bean Guessing.*—Fill a small jar with beans. These should be counted as they are placed in the jar. Have the guests guess the number of beans. Have them write their guess on a slip of paper with their name. Award a bag of jelly beans to the one guessing closest.

6. *Beanbag Golf.*—This is a game that will easily consume twenty minutes and keep the guests interested. The partners play together. See Index.

7. *Beanbag Baseball.*—The group should be divided into two parts for this game, and a team of nine may be selected, or all may play. See Index.

8. *Beanbag Scramble.*—Look in Index under "Beanbag Scramble" for this game.

9. *Circle Throw Relay.*—The groups that have been divided for the baseball game may now have a relay. Have five beanbags for each side. Draw a circle about eighteen inches in diameter on the floor in front of each line and about twelve feet away. The first player, when the signal is given, must throw the beanbags, one at a time, attempting to throw them into the circle. They must be all the way in to count. Then this player must run up to the circle and pick up the bags and run back with them to the next man in line, taking his place at the rear of the line. There should be a scorekeeper for this game, and he is to give one point each time the bag is thrown into the ring to the side whose player gets it in. Give a bag of jelly beans to the side that gets most points and another bag to the side that finishes first.

10. *Jack and the Bean Stalk.*—Lest the leader may have some difficulty in securing a copy of the children's story "Jack and the Beanstalk," we are giving below the story. Name the guests after the objects mentioned in "Jack and the Beanstalk," as: Jack, Mother, house, cow, food, beans, beanstalk, window, bed, sky, road, woman, kitchen, giant, Englishman, supper, moneybags, gold, magic hen, table, golden egg, money, magic harp, boy, hatchet, vine. As the story is told, and of course elaborated on by the teller as he calls the names of the different things mentioned above, each guest who has the word called must get up and turn around. When the leader uses the words "Beanstalk," all must change places. The leader then tries to get a place, and if he succeeds, the one left out must continue the story.

The following is the story in full:

Once there was a boy named *Jack.* He lived with his *mother* in a small *house,* at the end of a long *road.* They were very, very poor; all they had in the world was a red *cow.*

One day *Jack's mother* said: *"Jack,* we must sell the *cow.* There is no *money* in the *house,* and we must have *food.* So drive the cow to town and sell her.

Jack tied a rope to the *cow's* neck, and started out to drive her to town. He had not gone very far when he met a man who had a bag of bright red *beans.*

The man said: "Whose *cow* is that, my *boy?"*

"It is our *cow,"* said *Jack.* "I am driving her to town to sell her."

"Oh," said the man. "How much will you take for your *cow?"*

"As much as I can get," said *Jack.*

"I will give you all these *beans* for her," said the man.

"Oh, such fine *beans!"* said *Jack.* *"Mother* will be pleased with the *beans.* We can eat them. Yes, I will give you the *cow* for the *beans."*

"Very well," said the man, and he gave *Jack* the *beans* and took the *cow. Jack* took the *beans* and ran home as fast as he could.

"Home again?" said his *mother.* "Did you sell the *cow?* How much did you get for her?"

"Oh, see, *Mother,* I got all these fine *beans* for her."

"Beans!" cried the *mother,* and she took the *beans* and threw them out the *window.* "Now, go to *bed,* you silly *boy."*

Jack went off to *bed,* crying and sobbing. In the morning he awoke early. Then he saw a strange *vine* with green leaves over his *window.* He ran to the *window* and looked at it. It was not a *vine;* it was a *beanstalk.*

"Oh, a *beanstalk,* a *beanstalk!*" cried *Jack.* The beans which his *mother* had thrown out had grown into a great *beanstalk* which went up and up and up, far into the *sky.*

Jack stepped out among its branches, and began to climb.

He climbed, and climbed, and climbed, and climbed, till at last he was up in the *sky.*

Here he saw a long, white *road.* He thought he would walk down the road and look about.

He had not gone very far before he came to a very big *house.* A big *woman* was standing at the door watching him.

"You had better go back," she said.

"Go back?" said *Jack.* "Why, I have come a long, long way, and I am very tired. Will you not give me something to eat and a place to rest in?"

"This is no place for *boys,*" said the big *woman.* "Do you not know that a *Giant* lives here? He will eat you up if he finds you here."

"Oh, dear, I am so tired and hungry," said *Jack.*

The *woman* was kind. She took *Jack* into the *kitchen* and gave him all the bread and cake he could eat.

He was still eating when he heard a great thump! thump! thump! on the stairs.

"Oh, there comes the *Giant,*" cried the *woman.* "Run, get in here, quickly, or he will eat you."

She opened the oven door, and *Jack* got inside.

Thump! thump! thump! and in came the *Giant,* crying: "Fee, fi, fo, fum, I smell the blood of an *Englishman!*"

"No, no," said the big *woman,* who was the *Giant's* wife. "No, no, you smell the meat on the table. Go wash yourself and get ready for *supper.*"

So off he went, and *Jack* looked out of the oven door.

"Keep still," said the *woman.* "After he eats, he will go to sleep, and then you can run away."

Soon the *Giant* had eaten his *supper.* He said to his wife: "Bring me my *moneybags!*"

His wife went to an oaken chest and took out three big bags of *gold* pieces. The *Giant* counted the *gold* pieces while his wife cleared away the *supper* dishes. By and by his head began to nod, and at last he began to snore so loudly that the whole *house* shook.

Then *Jack* slipped out of the oven, seized one of the *moneybags,* and ran. When he reached the *beanstalk,* he flung the bag down ahead of him because it was too heavy to carry. When he came to the bottom, he found his *mother* picking up the *gold* pieces out of the garden as fast as she could; for, of course, the bag had burst.

After that they lived happily on the *gold* pieces for a long time. When there was only one *gold* piece left, *Jack* climbed the *beanstalk* again. There was the same long, white *road,* the same big *house,* and the same *woman* at the door.

"Good evening," said *Jack*. "Can you give me some *supper?*"

"Go away, bad *boy!*" said the *Giant's* wife. "Last time I gave a *boy* supper, my man missed a whole bag of *gold*. I believe you're the same *boy*."

But *Jack* begged so hard that she gave him a bowl full of porridge. Before he had half finished, they heard the thump! thump! thump! of the *Giant* on the stairs.

Jack just had time to jump into a big copper kettle beside the fireplace, when in came the *Giant,* crying: "Fee, fi, fo, fum, I smell the blood of an *Englishman!*"

"No, no," said the *Giant's* wife. "It is the crows who have brought raw meat and left it on top of the *house*. Go wash yourself and get ready for *supper*."

When the *Giant* had eaten his *supper,* he said to his wife, "Bring me my *magic hen!*"

The wife went out and came back with a big, black hen with a shiny red comb.

The *Giant* put the hen on the table, and roared, "Lay!" and the hen laid an egg, all of *gold*.

"Lay another!" he cried; and the hen laid another.

The *Giant* played with the hen until he became tired. Then he closed his eyes and went to sleep. Then *Jack* came out of the copper kettle, and crept up to the table. He took the hen and ran.

Just then the hen began to cackle, and the *Giant* awoke and started after *Jack* and the hen; but *Jack* was too quick for him. The *Giant* went back to his *house* discouraged.

Jack ran very fast and soon came to the *beanstalk*. He climbed down to his home again.

"See what I have, *Mother,*" cried *Jack*. "See, it lays *golden eggs*." And *Jack* said, "Lay!" and, sure enough, the hen laid a *golden egg*.

Jack's mother sold the *golden eggs,* and then they had plenty of *money* for food.

One fine day *Jack* thought he would climb the *beanstalk* again. So up he went, and soon he came to the long, white *road* and the big *house*.

Jack didn't ask for food this time, but crept quietly into the *kitchen* and hid in the breadbox. No sooner was he hidden than he heard the thump!

233

thump! thump! of the *Giant* on the stairs. In came the *Giant*, crying: "Fee fi, fo, fum, I smell the blood of an *Englishman*."

"No, no," said the wife, who had just come in from the scullery. "It must be the bones of the lambs you had for *supper*, that I'm boiling down for soup. Go wash yourself and get ready for *supper*." So off he went to wash.

Soon he had eaten his *supper*. Then he said to his wife: "Bring me my *magic harp*."

The *woman* brought out a little harp and put it on the table.

"Play!" cried the *Giant*, and the harp began to play beautiful music.

Soon the sweet music sang the *Giant* and his wife to sleep.

Then *Jack* came out of the breadbox, and crept on his hands and knees to the table, and laid hold of the harp. Just as he began to run, the harp cried out, "Master! master!"

This noise awoke the *Giant*, and he started after *Jack* and the harp. *Jack* was soon halfway down the *beanstalk*, and the *Giant* was still coming after him.

As he came near the ground he cried: *"Mother, Mother,* bring me the *hatchet!"*

His *mother* came running with the *hatchet. Jack* took it and chopped down the *beanstalk*.

The *Giant* fell to the ground with a great thump, and never got up again. And that was the end of the *Giant*.

When *Jack's mother* saw the *Giant*, she said: "Oh, that is the wicked *giant* who stole all your father's *money*. Now we have our own again."

And *Jack* and his *mother* lived happily ever after, with the harp to keep them merry and the *magic hen* to lay *golden eggs* for them whenever they needed *money*.

11. *Beanbag Jump.*—A string about eight feet long is tied to a beanbag. The leader stands in the center of the circle of the players who are standing. He swings the beanbag slowly around, and the players must jump over it. The bag should not be above the knees, and anyone hit above the knees shall not be out. As the bag swings, each player must jump over it, and those failing to jump it are out. The object is to see who can remain in the circle the longest.

12. *Pass the Beans.*—Players line up facing each other. Each player has a paper cup. The leader starts the relay by dropping five beans, one at a time, into the cup of the first player at the

head of the line. There should be someone to help the leader to start the beans at the head of the other line. Each player has a straw like the ones used at soda fountains. The beans must be lifted and passed from cup to cup by putting the end of the straw against them and holding them on the end of the straw by suction. The five beans pass down the line, and the leader by this time will have time to be at the other end of the line, so the last player is to drop them one at a time into the leader's cup. The leader and her helper then start them back up the line. The line to get all of the beans back first wins.

13. *Beanbag Shuffleboard.*—Look in the Index for "Shuffleboard." Draw a court on the floor and play with beanbags instead of sticks.

14. *Bean Bottle Fill.*—Let one couple from each group compete in this contest. Use a small-necked bottle and a bowlful of dried beans for each couple. Give each a large kitchen spoon and let them fill the bottle with beans, using the spoons. It would be well to set the bottles in bowls also, so that the beans that spill can be easily picked up and poured back into the bowl when the bottle is most full. There is no reason why other couples might not try this also. In this case time the couples and give a prize to the couple that gets all the beans in in the quickest time.

15. *Beanbag Tag.*—Use a light beanbag for this. In fact, it might be stuffed with cotton with only a few beans in it. "It" stands in the center and counts five. He may count this five any way he chooses. He may count to four and then hesitate before he says "Five." As he says "Five" he throws the beanbag at one of the players, who dodges it. If the player is hit, he becomes "It" and the game continues.

16. *Beanbag Boards.*—Beanbag boards may be constructed by nailing two wide boards together and setting them up so that the edges will be like a V upside down. Make the board about two feet high and a foot wide. Cut holes in the front board about four, five, and six inches in diameter, the larger hole being near the bottom, the middle-sized hole in the center, and the small hole near

the top. These holes should be marked three, five, and ten. Players stand about ten feet from the board and toss their bags. If the bag passes through a hole, it counts. If it passes through the small hole at the top it counts ten; it counts five if it passes through the middle-sized hole in the center; and three if it passes through the large hole at the bottom. This may be played with partners and the score of both added together, the couple making the highest score winning. Each person may have five throws. This also may be played by sides, giving a prize to the side scoring the highest number of points. This board may be made from Beaverboard.

17. *Jumping Beans: Relay.*—The two groups line up as for relay race, facing a goal marked off on the floor about fifteen feet from the head of each line. The first player is given a handful of beans. He must run to the goal, take the beans, and place them on the floor, making letters with them, so that they spell the word "BEAN." He then must jump over them, pick them up, and carry them back to the next player in line, taking his place at the back of the line. The side that finishes first wins.

18. *Refreshments.*—Baked beans would make good refreshments. This may be Boston baked beans with brown bread, butter, and coffee. If this is not desirable, serve ice cream and cake. Bury a bean in the cake. The boy who gets the bean is to be crowned the bean king and may choose a queen, or vice versa.

19. *Properties*

(1) Ten beans for each guest for Bean Trading.
(2) Small jar filled with beans and slip of paper for each guest for Bean Guessing.
(3) Beanbags for Circle Throw Relay.
(4) Paper cups, beans, and straws for Pass the Beans.
(5) Small-necked bottles, bowls of beans, and spoons for Bean Bottle Fill.
(6) Beanbag fixed specially for Beanbag Tag.
(7) Beanbag boards.
(8) Eight-foot string tied to beanbag for Beanbag Jump.

chapter 33

Hobo Party

EVERY NOW AND THEN, WHEN OUR DUTIES SEEM A LITTLE IRKSOME, we are inclined to envy the freedom of the vagabond of the road and field. So for one evening let's pretend that we are hobos and revel in the freedom of clothes and manners that they seem to enjoy. A hobo party would fit well into the fall social program, because it is then that the southward migration of the hobo begins, or it would fit equally well into the spring program, when the return to the north is made.

1. *Advertising and Invitation.*—Posters are a very effective way of advertising a social. Several of these with pictures of tramps on the road and attractive wording should be put up in places where they will attract the attention of the people whom you wish to come to the party. Several members of the group might have themselves photographed as tramps and these pictures used on the posters. This would give quite a personal appeal to the poster.

Invitations should also be sent to everyone, and a form that might be used is suggested below:

> A Hobo Party we're having
>   Next Friday at eight;
> Come dressed like a vagabond
>   And bring along your "date."

Place ———.   Name of organization giving party.

2. *Decorations.*—The social room or recreation room might be arranged to resemble the interior of a freight car. Sacks of straw or sand, old boxes and barrels, broken-down chairs and planks could be substituted for regular seats. Placards reading "No Loaf-

ing," "No Tramps Allowed," and "No Smoking" would also create the desired effect. If desired, an outdoor setting could be arranged for the party. Plants or green foliage brought in from the woods could be used profusely about the rooms. A campfire, simulated by colored lights, with a battered pot or so, and from which place the refreshments might later be served, would add effective scenery.

The hobos should all be forced to gain admittance by a rear door.

3. *Costumes.*—Of course all guests must wear the clothes of a tramp. Faded, patched, and much worn clothing, shoes, and hats are certainly easily secured by all, and so everyone should make the most of the occasion to wear them.

Give a prize for the best tramp costume for both the boys and girls. The costumes should be judged by a group selected by the hostess or leader of the party, or may be voted upon by the guests as suggested elsewhere in this book.

4. *Mixing Games.*—Ask the girls to form a circle and then ask the boys to form a circle around the circle formed by the girls. The girls face out and the boys face toward the center of the circle, thus forming partners. Music is played and partners march around together. If partners are unacquainted, they must introduce themselves and proceed to become acquainted as they march. When the music stops, the girls step forward and the boys step back, thus forming new partners. They introduce themselves, and march around together as the music continues. This changing of partners should continue until the leader feels that all are fairly well acquainted.

5. *Matching Partners.*—The leader should cut out a sufficient number of silhouettes in advance so that there will be one for each guest present. Give each girl a silhouette of a girl and a pencil. On the back of this, ask her to write her weight, height, whether she is blonde or brunette, color of eyes and hair, size of shoe, age, and any other descriptive term the leader chooses. The silhouettes are then collected, mixed together, and passed out to the boys who must find the girl represented by the silhouette for his

partner for the next game, which is the hobo dance. No other clues should be given except the information on the silhouette.

6. *Marathon Hobo Dance.*—The partners formed by the above game arrange themselves in a circle. On the floor draw a number of fairly large circles. (The circles should be numerous enough and large enough so that it is necessary to walk through them as the music plays.) As the piano plays a march, all start marching around. The music suddenly stops, and all must stand right where they are. Those who are in a circle must drop out of the game. If either a boy or his partner are in a circle, both must drop out. The music is continued, and the marching begins again. Whenever it stops, those on circles must drop out. The couple remaining in the game the longest wins. A hamburger or hot dog sandwich might be awarded as a prize.

7. *Marble Market.*—This game, as well as the next two, will require a large table. Marble market is modeled after the old card game "Pit." Purchase as many different kinds of marbles as possible, taking care to have ten or multiples of ten of each kind. If it is possible to do so, buy as many kinds of marbles as there will be guests present. The guests are seated around the table, and each one is given ten marbles of different kinds. The object of the game is for each player to trade his marbles with the other players until he has succeeded in getting ten just alike. He then has a "corner on the market" and is the winner. At the beginning of the game, the leader announces that the "market is open." At the discretion of the leader, players may be allowed to trade only with the person on the right, then with the person on the left, the person directly across the table, and finally open trading may begin and the players may trade with anyone. Any number of marbles may be traded at a time, just so the players trade an equal number with each other. The game is over as soon as one person gets ten marbles just alike, or the leader may require several to complete their ten before the game is stopped. A bag of peanuts may be given the winner.

8. *What Goes There?*—The guests remain seated at the table for this game. The leader has collected a basket containing forty or

fifty small miscellaneous objects, consisting of a spool of thread, thimble, ball, potato, banana, comb, brush, spoon, pencil, powder puff, and so forth. The leader starts passing these around underneath the table. The players are allowed to feel the objects carefully, but must not look at them. The leader should caution the players not to call out the names of the objects. When all of the objects have been all the way around under the table and are back in the basket, the leader gives each a paper and pencil on which each player is to write the name of as many objects as he can remember. The player with the longest correct list wins. A box of Cracker Jack would be a good prize for this game.

9. *Jenkins Up.*—This is the third game to be played around the table. This time the players sit on either side of the table in even numbers, each side choosing a captain. Give a coin (a quarter is a good-sized coin to use) to one group. This coin is passed from hand to hand under the table. The captain of the opposite side suddenly calls out "Jenkins up." The group having the coin must all immediately raise their hands above their heads with fists closed. The same captain then says "Jenkins down," and all the players of the side holding the coin must at once bring hands down flat upon the table, with palms down. The captain of the side doing the guessing then calls for the players to lift their hands, one at a time, choosing carefully the hand he wishes raised each time. The object is to leave the hand covering the coin until the very last. Should he discover the coin before all hands are lifted, the side holding the coin scores one point for each hand still down. Only the captain is allowed to specify the hands to be raised. The coin is then given to the other group and the game continues as before. The leader may terminate the game when he chooses or before the game may fix a definite score of points to be reached in order to win. Give each member of the winning team a lollipop or a stick of chewing gum.

10. *Matching Partners.*—Now give the boys the silhouettes prepared for them and ask them to write the same description of themselves on the silhouettes as the girls were asked to do in the first instance. Follow the same procedure and pass them out to the girls

who now must search for partners. The partners thus formed are to work together on the next game, which is a writing game.

11. *A Hobo Tour.*—Give each person a pencil and paper on which the following writing game has been typed. Each sentence indicates the name of a city. The names of the cities are to be supplied by the guests. The guest having the nearest correct list wins. A bag of popcorn would be a suitable prize for this.

(1) Named for the angels. Los Angeles.
(2) A small stone. Little Rock.
(3) A Christmas shrub and what we knock on. Hollywood.
(4) The discoverer of America. Columbus.
(5) A boy's name and two thousand pounds. Charleston.
(6) A vital organ and the manufacturer of "flivvers." Hartford.
(7) Two trees. Palm Beach.
(8) Something fresh and Noah's boat. Newark.
(9) Named after an apostle. St. Paul.
(10) Named after a large prairie animal. Buffalo.
(11) A boy calling his mother and laughing. Omaha.
(12) Divine favor. Providence.
(13) The second note of the scale and the negative adverb. Reno.
(14) Its name means "body of Christ." Corpus Christi.
(15) Twenty-four hours and two thousand pounds. Dayton.

12. *Hobos Seek a Handout.*—Divide the guests into groups by counting off after the old army style, one, two, three, four, and so on. Have about six players in each group. Give each group a name, such as rooster, cow, dog, or cat. Have each group choose a leader. Then tell the groups that they are to search for their food. The food might consist of animal crackers, small candy hearts, peanuts, or jelly beans, hidden about the room. At a given signal all start hunting. No one is allowed to touch the hidden food except the leader of the group. When a member of the rooster team finds the food, he must stand and crow like a rooster until his leader comes to pick it up. This rule, of course, must be observed by all the groups—the "cats" must "meow," the "dogs" must "bow-wow," and

241

so forth. The group finding the largest number should be rewarded by being allowed to eat all that the others have found also.

13. *Packing Time for the Hobos.*—Have everyone seated in a circle. The leader begins the game by saying, "I am going on a trip, and I am taking an umbrella." Those in the circle do likewise, each one naming some article he is taking with him. The leader then tells what he is going to do with what he is taking, as "I am going on a trip and take my umbrella with me to keep off the rain." Each of the players in turn must then repeat the leader's sentence, substituting his article for the word "umbrella." Anyone who laughs while he is repeating the sentence must take the leader's place in the center. This might go around the circle several times before it becomes tiresome. When the second round is started, the one who is leader then tells why he is taking his special article, and the others must repeat the words, with the exception that they always substitute the name of their article for the one the leader has mentioned.

14. *Refreshments.*—For refreshments serve sandwiches and coffee. The sandwiches should be of various sizes and shapes, and not the dainty, well cut ones that we usually associate with party refreshments. Serve coffee in tin cups. Hamburgers or hot dogs could be served on buns, and hot chocolate could be substituted for the coffee, if so desired. One group we know served potato salad in milk cans with cracker sandwiches at a Hobo Party. Later "Green River," which was green punch, was served in the same can.

15. *Properties*

(1) Silhouettes of girls and boys, one for each guest. Pencils.
(2) Marbles in sufficient quantity to give ten to each guest.
(3) A large table.
(4) Basket containing miscellaneous articles. Paper and pencils for list of articles.
(5) A coin.
(6) Typed lists and pencils for Hobo Tour.
(7) Crackers, candy, or peanuts hidden about the room.

chapter 34

School Days Party

(COSTUME)

SEPTEMBER IS THE MONTH OF THE BEGINNING OF SCHOOL. EACH ONE
has fond memories of school days, so plan for an evening to be spent
in the schoolroom. Invite the guests to come in costumes reminiscent
of their school days.

1. *Costumes.*—The following are suggested for costumes. For the
girls, play dresses with bloomers, sunbonnets, middies, and skirts.
Some may care to go back to their grandmother's day and wear
the typical dresses of that day. The boys should wear overalls, knick-
ers, short pants with old-fashioned waists, with round collars, and
perhaps some come barefooted. A toe tied up with a rag would add
to the effect.

2. *Invitations.*—The following is suggested for an invitation:

SCHOOL DAYS PARTY   COSTUME

School days, school days,
Dear old Golden Rule days;
Readin' and writin' and 'rithmetic,
But without the hickory stick.
We will live all over again,
So don't come like women and men;
But come like kids you used to be,
And we'll have an evening of fun and glee.

TIME   PLACE

3. *Decorations.*—If it is possible to use a room that can be trans-
formed into one with the appearance of a classroom, this would be
ideal. At any rate, try to create this atmosphere by the use of blackboards, globe, maps, and so on. In a home, remove the lighter fur-

niture and bring in a desk for the teacher. Borrow blackboards from a school or church to put around the walls.

4. *Name and Characteristic Mixer.*—As the guests arrive, they should be greeted by the teacher, who may be the hostess, or whoever is in charge of the affair, and they may be assigned seats in the classroom. The teacher might tap the bell and state that as school has not been going on very long, some of the children might not be well acquainted with the others. The teacher might then suggest that one of the pupils suggest and lead a game that will enable them to get better acquainted. Of course this leader has been prearranged. Have this leader give each guest a large blank sheet of paper, a pencil, and a book on which to write. The guest goes to each other guest and learns his name, which he writes down on his paper, leaving room to write under his name one of the outstanding characteristics of this person. This he is to learn from someone else. This he writes on his paper under the name. It would be better to make these characteristics as humorous as possible. There might be a prize given to the one who has the longest list, and this list should be read.

5. *Opening of School.*—School should be opened in the regular customary manner by the salute to the flag and the singing of "America." Perhaps there might also be a good morning song.

6. *Arithmetic.*—The first class should be a class in arithmetic with the students reciting orally. Call on someone to recite the nines of the multiplication table and another to recite them backward. If one pupil makes a mistake, call on another to finish. Ask another pupil to count with Roman numerals to ten, and give the Roman characters to one thousand, as follows: I, I, III, IV, V, VI, VII, VIII, IX, X, L (fifty), C (one hundred), M (one thousand). Ask others to give some of the tables, such as the table for liquid measure, dry measure, and weights and measures. Those making mistakes should be put on the dunce stool and made to wear the dunce cap. Successful pupils should be given lollipops. The following tables might be used:

LIQUID MEASURE	DRY MEASURE
4 gills = 1 pint	2 pints = 1 quart
2 pints = 1 quart	4 quarts = 1 gallon
4 quarts = 1 gallon	2 gallons = 1 peck
63 gallons = 1 hogshead	4 pecks = 1 bushel

LINEAR MEASURE	LAND MEASURE (SQUARE)
12 inches = 1 foot	144 square inches = 1 square foot
3 feet = 1 yard	9 square feet = 1 square yard
5½ yards = 1 rod	30¼ square yards = 1 square rod
320 rods = 1 mile	160 square rods = 1 acre
5,280 feet = 1 mile	640 acres = 1 square mile

7. *Blackboard Relay.*—Divide the guests into two groups of equal number. Place a large blackboard at one end of the room, dividing it into two equal parts by a chalk line down the center. The groups line up standing one behind the other, facing the blackboard, the player at the front of the line being about fifteen feet from the blackboard. The object of the game is to see which group can write the most intelligent and the neatest sentence on the blackboard in the shortest time.

The players run to the board and write one word at a time. When a player has run to the blackboard, written his work, and run back to the line he must give the chalk to the one who is now at the front of the line and take his place at the back. The groups should not be allowed to get together and plan a sentence to write before the relay starts. The sentence should be entirely impromptu.

When the last player in the group has written his word, it should finish the sentence. The group that finishes its sentence first is the winner. The composition should then be judged from the standpoint of neatness and intelligence. This will make it possible for the group who failed to win the speed contest to get a consolation prize for intelligence and neatness. A small box of candy that can be divided among the players makes a good prize for a relay race.

8. *Geography.*—The next is to be a lesson in geography. Give each pupil a paper on which the following questions have been typed, making carbon copies, or mimeographed. Give each one a

245

pencil. A definite time may be set for the completion of the lesson. The teacher should then collect the papers, grade them, and perhaps reward the pupils with lollipops:

 (1) What state is an Army officer? Col.
 (2) What is Noah's state? Ark.
 (3) What state is a girl's name? Minn.
 (4) What state is a Catholic church service? Mass.
 (5) What state is a physician? Md.
 (6) What state is Coolidge's state Cal.
 (7) What state is a letter of the alphabet? O.
 (8) What state is a mineral substance containing metal? Ore.
 (9) What state is a personal pronoun? Me.
(10) What state suggests Monday? Wash.
(11) What is the bride's favorite? Kan. (Can) .

9. *Recess.*—The teacher should then ring the bell and announce that it is time for recess, and that the children can play. Have someone lead London Bridge or Looby Loo, described elsewhere in this book. (See Index.) Another game that might be played is The Prince of Wales Has Lost His Hat. The players are seated in a row or in a circle. Some place should be designated as the head. The players are numbered. The leader says, "The Prince of Wales has lost his hat. Some say that number four has it, and some say that number five has it, but I say that the one who has it is number nine." Then the leader starts counting and counts to ten. If number nine does not respond before the leader counts ten, he must go to the foot. If he does respond, he should respond in the following manner, "Who, sir, I, sir?" to which the leader says, "Yes sir, you sir," and they continue as follows, "No sir, not I sir," the leader then says, "Who then, sir?" The player says, "Number eleven, sir." The leader then tries to count to ten before number eleven can respond. The game continues in this way. A variation of this would be to have the player take the place of the leader if he fails to respond.

10. *Backward Spelling Match.*—Make this a spell-down match— in other words, all the players start, and when a player misses a word, he has to take his seat. The teacher has a spelling book, from which

he pronounces, at first using short words and gradually making them longer. The pupils are required to spell backward. This will create a lot of good fun.

11. *History.*—The history class could be arranged in the following way: Collect pictures of famous historical characters, such as Julius Caesar, Napoleon, George Washington, Abraham Lincoln, Theodore Roosevelt, and others. These are pinned around the room and numbered. The students identify these characters by number. Give a picture of one of these characters as a prize to the most proficient.

12. *Declamation Contest.*—The teacher or leader of the party should ask several older folks to come visit the school. While they enter, they should be introduced to the pupils as County Superintendent, Chairman of the Board, Supervising Principal, or President of the Parent-Teachers' Association. It might be amusing to have some of the guests impersonate the officers who perhaps will be well known to many of the guests. The teacher should then say that a declamation contest will be held in honor of the visitors. Mother Goose rhymes could be recited, and the pupils should use as much rhetorical display as possible. The visitors will serve as judges of this contest and award the winner with a medal made of cardboard and suitably inscribed. Some of the following Mother Goose rhymes might be used. "Mary Had a Little Lamb," "Mary, Mary, Quite Contrary," "Jack Sprat," "Tom, Tom, the Piper's Son," "Little Boy Blue," "Old King Cole," and others.

13. *Physiology Class.*—The class in physiology should next recite. The following is a set of questions and answers:

What part of the human body:
  (1) Is part of a wagon? The tongue.
  (2) Is a fraction of a yard? Foot.
  (3) Is a measure of the height of horses? Hand.
  (4) Is a band instrument? Drum.
  (5) Is a church musical instrument? Organ.
  (6) Is used with an anvil? Hammer.
  (7) Is a sailor's reply? Eye; Eye.
  (8) Is used to fasten boards? Nails.

(9) Is used by artists? Palate.

(10) Is a church? Temple.

(11) Is a tropical tree? Palm.

(12) Is a baby animal? Calf.

(13) Is a strong box? Chest.

(14) Is a male deer? Heart.

(15) Is a flower? Two lips, iris.

(16) Is a slang expression for nerve? Cheek.

(17) Is a small, timid, fast-running animal? Hair.

(18) Goes to school? Pupil.

14. *Noon Recess.*—The teacher announces that luncheon time has arrived. The visitors should be the judges of the costumes, giving a prize to the boy and girl who have costumes most typical of school days.

15. *Refreshments.*—While the costumes are being judged, the hostess should arrange the refreshments. The refreshments should be served in boxes typical of school days. These boxes can be procured from almost any bakery. The refreshments should consist of sandwiches, cake, and fruit. Punch could be served from a water cooler. It would be better to arrange it so that the boxes could contain different kinds of lunches. These students could trade around after the manner of school children.

16. *Dismissal.*—After the luncheon hour, the class in music could be conducted. This should consist of the singing of "School Days" and other familiar songs. School should then be dismissed.

17. *Properties*

(1) Pencil, paper, and book, for Name and Characteristic Mixer.

(2) Blackboards and chalk.

(3) Bell and desk for teacher.

(4) Flag, dunce cap.

(5) Lollipops for prizes.

(6) Paper and pencils for geography class.

(7) Pictures of famous people and pencils and paper for same.

(8) Cardboard medal.

(9) Papers for physiology class.

248

chapter 35

Indian Party[1]

(COSTUME)

IN THE AUTUMN, WHEN THE LEAVES BEGIN TO TURN FROM GREEN TO gold and the sun appears to be in a sort of hazy mist, and the weather is calm and serene and peaceful, we say that Indian Summer has come. Why not have a party built around the customs and characteristics of the first Americans? The Indians were a picturesque people, and some of their manners and customs are well known to all.

1. *Invitations.*—The following is a suggested invitation taken partly from and patterned after Longfellow's *Hiawatha:*

> By the side of Tenth and Olive
> Stands the wigwam of the princess,
> And she sends to all the village
> Messengers with wands of willow
> As a sign of invitation,
> As a token of the feasting,
> And she bids us all assemble
> For an Indian Party, Friday,
> And at eight we are to gather.

These invitations may be written on yellow paper and sent to the guests to be invited.

2. *Costumes.*—Request should be made that everyone come in Indian costume as far as possible. If costumes are not available, each guest should be provided with a feather headdress made of paper. Sometimes it is possible to purchase Indian headgear with feathers at a novelty or toy store. Boys may imitate Indian dress by wearing

[1] Prepared with the assistance of Miss Cynthia Pearl Maus.

swimming trunks or walking shorts and painting their bodies with rouge or lipstick. Girls may wear a blanket over their dresses and some sort of improvised headgear. Costumes vary widely among different Indian tribes, so no set pattern can be given.

3. *Decorations.*—If the party is held in a home or church recreation room, the room should be decorated with foliage, cornstalks, and everything to give the outdoor appearance. There should be a tepee in one corner of the room, and this tent should be in designs of scarlet. There should be a circle of mats and rugs on the floor on which the braves and squaws are to sit.

4. *Bead Stringing Relay.*—As the guests entered, they were informed to what tribe they belong. There should be two, three, or four tribes, depending upon the size of the group. About ten or twelve to a group would be enough. Call them the Cherokees, Seminoles, Blackfeet, and Navaho. The first game will be a bead stringing relay. Get enough small jars of wooden beads at the five-and-ten-cent store to have one for each tribe. These are placed in chairs in front of each line and about twenty feet away. When the signal is given, the front one in each line is to run to the chair and string a bead and then run back and touch off the next one on the end, taking his place at the back of the line. And so they run until the beads are all strung. The beads may be counted, and if desirable each one may string one or more beads so that the beads will all be used by the time they have all tried it one time. The group that finishes first wins.

5. *Things Associated with Indians Jumbled.*

(1)	Mumpaw. Wampum.	(10)	Sevabr. Braves.
(2)	Lapsc. Scalp.	(11)	Wasqus. Squaws.
(3)	Caresmas. Massacre.	(12)	Oseoapp. Papoose.
(4)	Maotkawh. Tomahawk.	(13)	Otm-mto. Tom-tom.
(5)	Owb. Bow.	(14)	Ebitr. Tribe.
(6)	Raw hapt. War path.	(15)	Rwa ecnad. War dance.
(7)	Arw tainp. War paint.	(16)	Sinacomc. Moccasin.
(8)	Roraw. Arrow.	(17)	Ecaep iepp. Peace pipe.
(9)	Fiech. Chief.	(18)	Secsnipr. Princess.

6. *Big Game Hunt.*—Before the guests arrived, the hostess has hidden around the room animal crackers with numbers on them or animals cut out of cardboard with numbers on them. The guests are told to find them, and the tribe that finds the largest number will get a prize. Prizes for the evening may be feathers to put in the headdress. In this case each one in the tribe that finds the largest number or whose total score, taking the numbers from the animals, makes the largest total wins.

7. *Indian Tribes.*—The guests are supplied with sheets of paper, typewritten, using carbons, or mimeographed:

What Indian tribe is:
    (1) A girl's name? Sioux.
    (2) Flowing streams? Creeks.
    (3) Known by its caws? Crow.
    (4) The name for a South Atlantic state? Delaware.
    (5) Slang for "You're wise to it." Huron (You're on).
    (6) A vowel and an herb? Osage.
    (7) Muddy lower extremities? Blackfeet.
    (8) To cut grass and bird of prey? Mohawk.
    (9) The name for a North Central state? Iowa.
    (10) The names for two other North Central states? North and South Dakota.

8. *Braves' Relay.*—Choose an equal number of braves from each tribe. They are to stand, one behind the other, in parallel columns facing a goal line about 20 feet away, or at the far end of the room. The front man in each line is given a basket with twelve potatoes in it. There is an empty basket at the goal line. When the signal from the leader is given, the first player in each line runs to the goal line, and transfers the twelve potatoes one at a time into the empty basket. He then runs back, giving his empty basket to the next player in line and takes his place at the back of the line. The player who now has the empty basket must run to the goal line and put the potatoes one at a time into his basket and carry the full basket back with him. The game continues this way until one line has finished. This line is declared the winner. The game may continue however with

the remaining tribes competing for second place (provided that there are three or more tribes competing).

9. *Squaws' Relay.*—An equal number of squaws are chosen from each tribe. They stand in parallel line facing a goal. This goal is about twenty feet from the head of each line and is made by a circle drawn on the floor about eighteen inches in diameter. In this are placed five Indian clubs or soft drink bottles. Each squaw runs to the circle, the first taking the clubs out of the circle, the next placing the clubs back in the circle. The tribe that finishes first wins.

10. *Archery Contest.*—Secure from the five-and-ten-cent store a bow and arrows. The target may be the usual target with circles on it, numbered so that the center circle about four inches in diameter counts twenty-five, the second circle, twenty, the third fifteen, the fourth ten, and the fifth five. The score of each one is kept and the score by tribes. A prize should be given the best individual archer and the prizes to the best tribe.

Another way to do this would be to cut from cardboard the shapes of animals, mounting these on bases so that they will stand up. Have some larger and others smaller. Graduate them so that to hit the small one will count twenty-five, the next largest twenty, the next largest fifteen, and so on. Give prizes in the same manner as described above.

11. *Medicine Dance.*—Squares or circles are marked off on the floor in such a way that couples marching around will not be able to avoid them. Someone plays a lively tune, such as "Turkey in the Straw" and all march. When the music suddenly stops, whoever is inside a ring must take a seat. This is done by couples, and if one of the two is in the ring, both must be seated. The object is to see which couple can remain on the floor the longest. This may be done twice if it goes over well the first time and there is plenty of time.

12. *Corn Toss.*—Members of each tribe will now assemble in their own group, standing in a circle. On the floor in the center of the circle a small bucket should be placed. Each person is given five grains of corn which they try to throw into the bucket. The tribe

which places most grains in its bucket is winner.

13. *Hopping Relay.*—Six contestants are selected to represent each group and are arranged in lines at one side of the room. At the opposite side of the room a large blackboard should be provided. The first contestant in each group should be given a piece of chalk and at the signal will hop on one foot to the blackboard, write the letter "I," hop back, and hand the chalk to the second man in his line, who hops to the board and writes "N," and continuing until the word "Indian" has been written.

14. *Refreshments.*—Some of the following are suggested for refreshments: Apples, nuts, popcorn, laughing water (lemonade), wolf meat (hot dogs).

15. *Properties*

(1) Small jars of wooden beads and bead thread for Bead Stringing Relay.
(2) Papers prepared for Things Associated with Indians Jumbled.
(3) Animal crackers with numbers for Big Game Hunt.
(4) Papers prepared for Indian Tribes.
(5) Small basket of potatoes for Braves' Relay.
(6) Indian clubs or soft drink bottles for Squaws' Relay.
(7) Bow and arrows for Archery Contest.
(8) Someone to play Medicine Dance.
(9) Corn for Corn Toss.
(10) Blackboard and chalk.

chapter 36

Measuring Party

THE FOLLOWING PARTY IS SUGGESTED AS A MONEY-RAISING PARTY FOR some organization in the church. It would not be profitable unless a large number attend, as the idea is for each one to give a penny for every inch he or she measures around the waist. A hundred people averaging thirty inches waist measure would bring in thirty dollars. However, this is more money than the average group will make in one night on a dinner or other feature.

Send out to all the members of your church and all friends who attend your church the following or a similar invitation:

> This little apron is sent to you,
> And this is what we wish you'd do:
> A little pocket in front you'll see,
> And for a special purpose it's meant to be.
> Measure your waistline, inch by inch;
> Don't draw in your breath, don't pull, don't pinch.
> Then for each inch you measure round
> In the apron pocket put a penny sound.
> This game is fair, you will admit;
> You "waist" your money, we pocket it.
> Now if the size of your waist you will not tell,
> Just slip in a dollar—'twill do quite as well.
> All "waist" money which the pocket pays
> The ——————[1] will use in the wisest ways.
> Bring your apron with you and don't be late;
> Place: ——————; ——————, the date.
> So dig up the cash and put on a smile,
> And we'll throw care away for a little while.

[1] Fill in the name of the organization giving this party.

Instead of the apron send overalls to the men. Use the same poem, substituting the word overall for apron—"This little overall is sent to you."

These aprons and overalls are very little trouble to make. They can be made from scraps of material. Just a piece of cloth cut in the shape of apron or overall with a bit of binding around it will suffice. Be sure to get the pocket on it, for that is the important part.

With such a large crowd and a group of such different ages, it would not be practical to try to play games. So a program will be necessary. It would be good to use all the talent in the organization on the program.

We would suggest the following as a program for such a gathering:

1. *Orchestra.* Use a Sunday-school orchestra or invite in an outside orchestra for this part of the program. Almost any orchestra will be glad to give their services for such a program. Two numbers.
2. *Vocal soloist.* If there is a good one in the organization, use that one; otherwise get one from outside.
3. *Recitation or monologue.* Humorous if possible.
4. *Comic skit.*
5. *Violin solo or saxophone solo.*
6. *Kitchen cabinet orchestra.* See Chapter 27, "Stunt Night."
7. Any other specialty number or good entertainer that can be secured for the occasion.

At a party of this kind refreshments should be served by the organization putting on the party. Some refreshments that are not too expensive should be served. Many times the syrup of bottled drinks can be purchased from bottling companies or supermarkets. One gallon will make four or five gallons of good drink when mixed with water and iced. Tea cakes or sandwiches can be served with this. Almost any bakery will donate paper plates to a church organization for a party of this kind as a means of advertising.

chapter 37

Fifty Party

ANY SOCIAL GROUP WILL WELCOME A CHANGE FROM THE USUAL PARTY
that is planned with mixing games, writing games, and quiet games.
In this volume we are suggesting three games that are to be played
around tables, and games, in which the whole group can participate.
No mixing games or get-acquainted games are needed, as the group
will be "mixed" before the party is over. The game of Fifty is the
first of three such games which we suggest. The others are Cootie
and Heart Dice. They are very similar, and yet there is enough difference in them to constitute a variety.

This game is played by any number of players in multiples of
four. About six to ten tables make a good party.

This party may be used as a money-making party by selling the
sides of the tables at from twenty-five cents to one dollar each, depending upon the financial ability of those who are to attend.

The equipment needed for this game is: Tables enough for the
guests who are to be invited, figuring four guests to the table. Also
two dice for each table. If it is not desirable to use dice, cubes can
be made at small expense from wood. Any mill could make them out
of wood. Gum wood cut into blocks three-quarters inch square could
be painted white with black figures on them. Get someone with a
small workshop at his home to saw these out. Anyone who is clever
with tools could make them with a plane, saw, and a piece of sand-
paper. It is not even necessary to have them painted, and the figures
could be printed on with ink. It will be found that in using a wood
block, made from gum wood, it is almost impossible to drop the
block even a distance of three inches without having it turn over.

256

Have figures printed on them corresponding to the numbers on a dice.

The game is scored as follows: Anything double except three and six counts five. Double three cancels all of your score for that game as well as that of your partner. Partners must begin again from zero, and mark only the score then made until the whistle blows. Double six counts twenty-five points. Fifty is a game, and the object is to see who gets fifty first. The leader blows a whistle and all start throwing. Each player gets only one throw and the cubes then pass to the left. They all play until some couple gets a score of fifty, at which time they yell, "Fifty." The game then stops, and all players add up their score for that game. If the game is too fast like this, and it is desirable to slow it up, have the whole group controlled by the head table. All must play until the head table scores fifty. This will eliminate some of the necessity for haste.

After each game the players progress and change partners. The tables are numbered, number one being the head table, and on down, depending upon the number of guests. The president and other officers of the society or class giving the party should be seated at table number one when the game starts. After that it will depend on who wins. The losers at every table do not change tables at the end of a game, but one of them should move to another side of the table so that he will have a different partner for the next game. The winners at each table progress to the next table, except the winners at the head table, who remain at this table, the losers going to the last or foot table.

The game is played with partners, the two across the table from each other being partners. Both keep separate score cards, although when one throws a winning number, it counts for his partner during that game, and if one throws a losing number, two number threes, it cancels his partner's score for that game. The keeping of separate scores is necessary as players progress and change partners, and the prize should go, not to any couple, but to the individual player getting the highest score.

Score cards should be prepared in advance by the hostess. Take a sheet of paper, size eight and a half by eleven inches, and draw lines one and a half inches apart across the paper. Then draw a line in the center of the paper the long way. This will make twelve squares on the sheet of paper, and these should be numbered from one to twelve. Each player is to mark his individual score in these squares for that game. It will be found that from twelve to fifteen games will fill an evening.

After the score cards have been filled, and twelve or fifteen games have been played, depending upon how many have been arranged for in advance, all players are asked to total their score. The player receiving the highest score and the one receiving the next highest may come in for prizes.

Refreshments of ice cream and cake or punch and cake may be served to the guests as they are seated around the tables after the conclusion of the game.

chapter 38

Alphabet Party

A NOVEL IDEA FOR A SOCIAL IS AN ALPHABET PARTY. IN SENDING THE invitations and preparing the posters announce that Mr. and Mrs. Alphabet will entertain. This may be made a pay social by charging each one one or two cents for every letter in his full name. Money earned in this way may be used to take care of the expense of the party or refreshments.

1. *Name Initial Mixer.*—Have a number of cards six inches square and colored crayons, and as each guest enters, the initial of his last name is printed on the card and hung around his neck with a string. Also write the full name on the card in smaller letters at the top, as an identification for those who may be strangers. When all the guests have arrived, tell them that they are to spell themselves into words. Each one is given a slip of paper and pencil and the game begins. The object is to see which one can have the largest list of words at the time the whistle blows. For example, Mr. A is standing near Miss T. They come together, and both of them can write At as their first word. They can go together until they find Mr. B and, using him, can spell Bat. If they stay together, they may find Miss H and be able to spell Bath. In these cases each one in the group can write down the word. Continue as long as the group is lively.

2. *What Letter Is?*—Each one is given a mimeographed or typewritten sheet of paper on which the following questions are written with the answer left blank:

What letter is—
  (1) An insect? B.
  (2) A large body of water? C.
  (3) Always with "you"? Q.

(4) A slangy letter? **G.**
(5) Our busiest letter? **I.**
(6) A bird? **J.**
(7) Part of a house? **L.**
(8) Familiar with Emma? **M.**
(9) A verb of debt? **O.**
(10) A vegetable that rolls off the knife? **P.**
(11) A clue? **Q.**
(12) A drink? **T.**
(13) The letter you love best? **U.**
(14) What green apples do to you? **W.**
(15) A sheep? **U.**
(16) Direction for a horse? **G.**
(17) The questioning letter? **Y.**

3. *Initial Letters.*—The leader holds an alphabet on cards six inches square, face down, and, taking off the letters one at a time, shows them to the group. For example, she starts with cities and says that the person first to name a city beginning with the letter on top of the pile gets the letter. Suppose the first letter is A. The first one to say Atlanta, Albany, or Atlantic City would get the card. After cities have been tried awhile, change to boys' names. Suppose the top card is B. The first one to say Ben or Billy would get the card. Change then to girls' names, and suppose the first card turned up to be C. The first one to say Carrie, Clara, or Christine will get the card. This is a lively game and full of interest and fun.

4. *What Matches Are Made Of.*—Give each one twelve wooden matches. Tell them that they are to arrange them into letters, or make letters with them that will spell the thing that matches are made of. The matches should be arranged so that they spell LOVE. L will require two matches; O will require four placed in the form of a square; V is made with two; and E with four. Love is the thing that matches should be made of.

5. *Dumb Spelling Match.*—A number is selected for this dumb spelling match, or if the group is small the whole group participates. When one spells a word incorrectly, speaks a letter when he should make a sign, or makes the wrong sign, he must sit down. The ob-

ject is to see who can stand up the longest. Words are pronounced by the leader, and should be selected in advance, those being chosen that have a large number of vowels in them. These are spelled by those participating by speaking the consonants and making the following signs for the vowels: For A the player holds up his right hand. For E holds up his left hand. For I he points to his eye. For O he points to his open mouth. For U he points to another player. If any of the vowels are spoken, if the wrong sign is given, or the word is spelled incorrectly, the player must be seated. Spell down.

6. *A "T" Quiz.*—This is a writing contest, and papers must be prepared in advance with the questions on them and blank spaces for the answers. The questions are to be answered with words ending in "ty."

(1) What T is something new? A novelty.
(2) What T makes us ill at ease? Formality.
(3) What T forms true friendship? Sincerity.
(4) What T is gained through the press and radio? Publicity.
(5) What T becomes a maiden? Modesty.
(6) What T is the best policy? Honesty.
(7) What T can be measured? Capacity.
(8) What T describes a want? Necessity.
(9) The political T? Party.
(10) What T is desirable in a menu? Variety.
(11) What T is the soul of wit? Brevity.
(12) The saint's T? Piety.
(13) The Socialist's T? Equality.
(14) The T of the silly girl? Vanity.
(15) The T of the thrifty man? Prosperity.
(16) The belle's T? Society.
(17) The skilled workman's T? Ability.
(18) What T do women desire? Beauty.
(19) The scientist's T? Electricity.

7. *Spelling Fun.*—Divide into two, three, or four groups. Each group is given an alphabet on cards six inches square with duplicate vowels. If the group is too small to give each one a letter, the leader should give some two letters. If this is not desirable, take out letters such as Q, Z, X, and J that are not so frequently used before

distributing the alphabet. It is not necessary to have a whole alphabet for this game. Each group selects a leader. The object is to see which group can spell the most words in a given time. There should be a scorer selected in advance; and if you have four groups, there should be two scorers. The scorer gives each group a mark for every word spelled. The words are spelled by the leader suggesting the word and the players who hold the letter arranging themselves in the proper order to spell them. Every word spelled counts one score or tally for the group spelling it. The winner has the largest number of tallies when the whistle bolws.

8. *The Game of D.*—Each player is given a piece of paper with prepared questions as below with the answer left blank:

    (1) D with one letter meaning to act. Do.
    (2) D with two letters, the name of a river. Dee.
    (3) D with two letters meaning a continual noise. Din.
    (4) D with two letters meaning a faithful friend. Dog.
    (5) D with three letters meaning an engagement. Date.
    (6) D with three letters producing gloom. Dark.
    (7) D with three letters, a silver coin. Dime.
    (8) D with four letters, a small napkin. Doily.
    (9) D with five letters, a stupid animal. Donkey.
  (10) D and five letters, two of a kind. Double.
  (11) D and eight letters, a camel. Dromedary.

9. *Word Tinkering.*—The leader gives the group two words, as the following, "Change man to hut." The players can only change one letter at a time, and the object is to see who can do it the quickest and with fewest changes. For example, in changing man to hut you could proceed as follows: man, mat, hat, hut. In changing dog to cat: dog, cog, cot, cat. Pig into sty: pig, big, bag, sag, say, sty. In changing head into tail: head, heal, teal, tell, tall, tail. Other words that the leader might suggest to be changed are: wheat to bread, tears to smile, wet to dry, comb to hair. Any two words can be changed, if they have the same number of letters in them, with a sufficient number of changes.

10. *Letters and Numbers*—See who can write his first, middle,

and last name, substituting for the letters the number of the letter as it appears in the alphabet. Thus Adam Bede would be written 1-4-1-13 2-5-4-5. After all have finished take up the slips of paper and pass them around again and see who can read the other person's name quickest.

11. *A B, C D Fish.*—Much amusement can be caused by the following display of letters which have been written on a cardboard in advance by the leader:

A B, C D Fish. (It is better to draw pictures of the fish.)
M N O Fish.
O, S A R Fish.

Ask the group to read what is written on the card. Perhaps someone will be clever enough to read it: Abie, see de fish. 'Em ain't no fish. Oh, 'es 'ey are fish.

12. *Bible Alphabet.*—Sheets of paper with the following alphabet to be answered with the names of Bible characters are distributed to the players:

A—The first man.   Adam.
B—Joseph's youngest brother.   Benjamin.
C—Where Jesus performed his first miracle.   Cana.
D—A woman judge of Israel.   Deborah.
E—Adam's wife.   Eve.
F—Who trembled before Paul.   Felix.
G—The Garden where Jesus prayed.   Gethsemane.
H—One of Noah's sons.   Ham.
I—Abraham's son.   Isaac.
J—His name was changed to Israel.   Jacob.
K—The father of Saul.   Kish.
L—Companion of Paul.   Luke.
M—The writer of the second Gospel.   Mark.
N—The builder of the ark.   Noah.
O—Ruth's sister.   Orpah.
P—The Apostle to the Gentiles.   Paul.
Q—A man that Paul called brother.   Quartus.
R—The wife of Isaac.   Rebecca.
S—The first king of Israel.   Saul.

T—A doubting disciple. Thomas.
U—Bathsheba's first husband. Uriah.
V—A beautiful queen. Vashti.
W—What is used in baptism. Water.
X—A short way to spell Christmas. Xmas.
Y—What the oxen of the Bible wore. Yoke.
Z—The father of James and John. Zebedee.

13. *A Was an Apple Pie.*—The players are seated in a circle, and the leader reads the following, and each player in turn must supply the missing verb beginning with the same letter of the alphabet. If a player fails, it passes on to the next. The words in parentheses are suggested verbs:

A was an apple pie, B (bit) it, C (cut) it, D (dived) at it, E (envied) it, F (fought) for it, G (grabbed) at it, H (handled) it, I (inspected) it, J (jumped) at it, K (kissed) it, L (longed) for it, M (mourned) for it, N (noticed) it, O (observed) it, P (pined) for it, Q (quibbled) about it, R (reached) for it, S (snatched) for it, T (took) it, U (upset) it, V (viewed) it, W (wanted) it, X (X-rayed) it, Y (yearned) for it, Z (zipped) at it, and I wish I had a piece in my hand.

14. *Writing Shorthand.*—Answer the following with letters of the alphabet which will make a word:

(1) Girl's name. MLE (Emily).
(2) Another girl's name. LC (Elsie).
(3) Another girl's name. KT (Katie).
(4) Pretty girl. QT (Cutie).
(5) To view. C (See).
(6) An insect. B (Bee).
(7) Part of the body. I (Eye).
(8) An explosive. TNT.
(9) State of joy. XTC (Ecstasy).
(10) A Tent. TP (Tepee).
(11) Kind of poem. LEG (Elegy).
(12) Number. AT (Eighty).
(13) A real substance. NTT (Entity).
(14) A slang expression. G (Gee).
(15) A foe. NME (Enemy).

(16) All right. **O. K.** (Okeh).
(17) Intemperance. **XS** (Excess).
(18) An image. **FEG** (Effigy).
(19) Poorly dressed. **CD** (Seedy).
(20) Not difficult. **EZ** (Easy).
(21) Jealousy. **NV** (Envy).
(22) A composition. **SA** (Essay).
(23) To surpass. **XL** (Excel).
(24) A creeping vine. **IV** (Ivy).

15. *Refreshments.*—Ask the guests what they want to eat. Tell them for an answer they must arrange themselves in formation so as to spell out what menu they want. There will be much fun as they try to get each other into formation. This can take place while the food is being prepared. Serve anything that is thought suitable. If they can be obtained, serve alphabet crackers with a drink such as punch or tea. Apple pie a la mode would be another suggestion.

16. *Properties*

(1) Lettered cards six inches square and crayons for each guest.
(2) Papers prepared for What Letter Is? A "T" Quiz, Game of D, Bible Alphabet, and Writing Shorthand.
(3) Alphabet on cards six inches square for each group.
(4) Blank paper and pencils for Word Tinkering and Letters and Numbers.

chapter 39

Athletic Party

AN ATHLETIC PARTY WOULD BE AN APPROPRIATE PARTY TO GIVE IN honor of a football team, basketball team, baseball team, or in fact any athletic team it is desired to honor. The games outlined in this chapter may be used in any home, although it is preferable to have a very large house or a large recreation room.

1. *Invitations.*—The following is suggested for an invitation:

ATHLETIC PARTY
HONORING HIGH SCHOOL BASEBALL TEAM
Y.W.C.A. RECREATION ROOM
DATE
There's a thrill in good old football.
What a thrill one feels
When a player makes a touchdown
With the whole gang at his heels!
Same is true of good old baseball
When a player makes a run;
But you'll get a thrill at our party
And have a lot of fun.

2. *Decorations.*—Use pennants and crepe paper streamers in the colors of the organization represented.

3. *Beanbag Golf.*—As the guests arrive, they are divided into couples by the leader and matched to play beanbag golf. The game is played in the following manner:

Different kinds of vessels and utensils are set around over the house or perhaps hung on the wall or placed on top of the piano, and these are numbered as the eighteen holes of a golf course. Have someone get from the country club in your city enough score cards for your guests and change these numbers to fit your course. For example, if the score card shows a 500-yard hole with five par, you might change this to five yards, three par. Each couple marks their own score, which score is the number of throws it takes each one to get their beanbag in the vessel. The rule of the game is that they must stand erect when they toss the beanbag; and if it falls in a place where they cannot stand when they throw it, the penalty for moving it will be one stroke. For example, if the beanbag should fall into the middle of a bed or into the window it would cost one stroke to move it.

Some suggestions for the holes, that is, vessels into which to toss the beanbag, are, for the long holes, dishpan, wastepaper basket, market basket, or large stew kettle. Another suggestion for these long holes is that they should be from five to seven yards from the place that is marked Tee. Have some dog legs, that is, have the vessel placed in such a way that they cannot toss the beanbag directly toward it but will have to pass around through a door either to the right or to the left. For the short holes, which would be two or three yards, use a vessel with a small neck into which the beanbag will just go. For example, a coffee pot or the bottom part of a small double boiler. A stone jar sitting on the mantel or piano would make a good hole. The arrangement of this golf course with dog legs and hazards, and so forth, will depend upon the ingenuity of the host. Get someone who plays golf to assist with laying out the course. Give a prize to the couple who makes the lowest score and the individual who makes the lowest score.

This game can be arranged and the course laid out so that as many as fourteen or fifteen couples can be playing at the same time. It enables the host to have those who come early to have something to do while the other guests are arriving. The game will create a lot of good, wholesome fun and will consume from twenty minutes to half an hour.

4. *Identifying Athletes.*—Cut out from the sporting page of the newspaper or from baseball and golf magazines the pictures of well-known athletes. Also there might be included pictures of those who

are prominent in their connection with athletics, such as owners of big league baseball teams, the High Commissioner of Baseball, or prominent radio and television sports announcers. Number these and pin them on the draperies and place them about the room. Give slips of paper to the guests and have them identify these athletes. Give a prize to the one getting the largest number correctly.

5. *Beanbag Baseball.*—Draw out on the floor or have drawn on a piece of Beaverboard or anything that can be spread on the floor the diagram below.

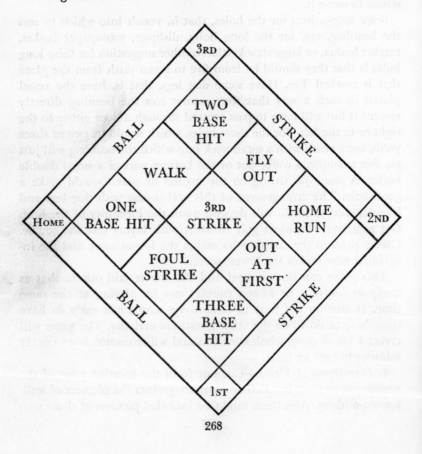

Divide the group into two equal parts by numbering one and two. Have someone from the even numbers choose eight other players from his group and someone from the odd numbers do likewise. The players stand about ten or twelve feet from the diamond laid out on the floor and toss the beanbags. There should be an umpire to decide into which square the beanbag falls, it being counted in the square where the most of it lies if it happens to be on the line. When a person tosses a beanbag and it falls on the "Fly, Out" or "Third strike," it means that there is one out for his side. Then the next player on his side tosses the beanbag; and if it falls on "Two-base hit," the umpire places something on second base to indicate that there is a runner on that base. Should the next player get a "Three base hit" or a "Home run," this will force the runner on second base home, and that side will have two runs. The game proceeds in the regular way—three strikes are out, two fouls and a third strike an out, four balls places the runner on first base, and three outs change the innings. Play only about five innings.

6. *Jumbled Baseball Terms.*—Provide players with a paper on which the following jumbled baseball terms are written. They are to unjumble them.

   (1) Ith. Hit.
   (2) Trikes. Strike.
   (3) Toshrpost. Shortstop.
   (4) Derilfe. Fielder.
   (5) Thacerc. Catcher.
   (6) Purime. Umpire.
   (7) Satex Aguerel. Texas Leaguer.
   (8) Nile diver. Line drive.
   (9) Cherpit. Pitcher.
  (10) Ricesacif yfl. Sacrifice fly.
  (11) Tubn. Bunt.
  (12) Revuc. Curve.
  (13) Od blue yapl. Double play.
  (14) Ginnni. Inning.
  (15) Orrre. Error.
  (16) Redflie's loveg. Fielder's glove.

269

(17) **Tab. Bat.**
(18) Athercc's tim. Catcher's mit.

7. *Blindfold Boxing Match.*—This is an excellent funmaker, but must be carefully handled by the leader. Get two pair of boxing gloves, put them on two boxers that have been chosen, draw a circle, put the boxers inside the circle, and carefully blindfold them. Turn each of the boxers around several times, so they will lose their sense of direction, and blow the whistle for the fight to start. They should be blindfolded so that their heads will be protected in case either of them should happen to get hit, but this is not the intention at all. The intention is to have them so widely separated that they cannot hit each other. Have two or three boys to act as teasers, and make them think that they have found each other. After the fun has gone long enough, give both a prize as the winner.

8. *Pop Bottle Football.*—This game is played with Indian clubs or pop bottles. See Calendar Party, page 21, under November.

9. *Football Guessing Contest.*[1]—Answers are to be made in musical terms:

    (1) What does the line need to do when hard pressed? Brace.
    (2) What decides the game? Score.
    (3) What kind of a football player does the coach call a man who on his first time out plays a fine game? Natural.
    (4) What does a football player who has been punched in the stomach need? Air.
    (5) With the score tied, for what does the better team pray? Time.
    (6) What does each team want to do? Beat.
    (7) What do players do on a muddy field when tackled? Slide.
    (8) What do players do between quarters? Rest.
    (9) What is the coaching squad sometimes called? Staff.
    (10) What is a game in which both sides make the same score? Tie.
    (11) What do they often do to determine whether or not a team has made first down? Measure.
    (12) Of what two terms would you be reminded by a backfield dressed in polka dot jerseys? Dotted quarter and dotted half.
    (13) What kind of head often spoils a good player? Swell.
    (14) For whom does she root at the game? Hymn (him).

[1] From *Phunology*, by Harbin. Abingdon Press. Used by permission.

10. *Balloon Volleyball.*—The group has already been divided into two parts, the even and the odd numbers, for the baseball game. Select eight or ten from each group, or if the whole group is not too large, let them all play balloon volleyball. Stretch a string across the room about six feet from the floor, or if the ceiling is high, it is better to have it even higher than this. Inflate a toy balloon to use for the volleyball. Each side tries to keep the balloon from touching the floor on their side. If the ball touches the floor on their side, the other side scores a point. Ten points will be sufficient for a game, the first side winning ten points being the winner of the game.

Another way to play this is to forbid the use of hands, allowing players to strike the ball only with their heads. This should not be played, however, with a mixed group.

11. *Athlete's Foot.*—Partners for refreshments are chosen by having the men sit behind the door which has been curtained off and stick a foot through the curtain. The girls are allowed to choose their partner by his foot, and will take the one selected.

12. *Refreshments.*—Serve the things that are generally found at athletic games—peanuts, popcorn, crackerjacks, bottled drinks, and ice-cream cones.

13. *Properties*

(1) A golf course, laid out in advance, and plenty of beanbags, so that each guest may have one.

(2) Pictures of well-known athletes cut out and pinned on the draperies and placed about the room.

(3) Baseball diamond drawn out on floor or on Beaverboard.

(4) Slips of paper on which are written Jumbled Baseball Terms.

(5) Boxing gloves and blindfolds.

(6) Pop bottles fixed for Football Game.

(7) Typed or mimeographed copies of Football Guessing Contest.

(8) Toy balloon and a cord long enough to reach across the room.

(9) Curtain to cover door.

chapter 40

Halloween Party

(*COSTUME*)

HALLOWEEN AFFORDS A SPLENDID OPPORTUNITY FOR A DELIGHTFUL
party. As unconventionality is the keynote, the occasion is conducive to a genuine good time. Witches, ghosts, devils, and elves
have their inning and wander about at will. On this occasion all
kinds of charms and spells are invoked for prying into the future
of each guest. Halloween should be a night when there is little
else but fun, laughter, and mystery. Invitations should state that
the affair will be a costume party and a masquerade. Everything
should be kept as secret as possible. The identity of each guest
should be a secret until all unmask.

1. *Invitations.*—The following are suggestions for invitations:

> If friendly ghosts you've never seen,
> Come to our house on Halloween,
> From seven to eleven the hours to stay,
> Dressed up in such an unfamiliar way
> That we won't know you from we don't know who.
> But over your costume don't worry and fuss,
> Just dress in a way that will puzzle us,
> Either spooky or fancy or all in a muss.
> Our home in the trees with fun we will fill.
> Reply, if you please. Yours, Mildred and Bill.

For the following invitation purchase at the bookstore or novelty
store some small owls and witches. One of these owls is placed at
the top of the page, and the following poem invitations follows,
with the witches placed at the bottom of the page:

On Friday evening, October twenty-third,
Our group will meet this wise old bird.
At the witch's den you'll meet your fate,
At eight o'clock. Now don't be late.
One hundred thirty-five Atlantic Avenue, Palm Beach,
Is where you'll have this Halloween treat.
Wear a mask to hide your pretty face,
And be on hand to take your place.
There'll be cats and ghosts both great and small,
And a jolly good time will be had by all.
Cordially yours, The two (pictures of witches).

2. *Initiation.*—Guests should be met at the door by a witch and conducted through a dark passage with a flashlight which is turned off most of the time. This passage should be infested with strange noises like grunts and groans and screams and the hooting of owls. A witch or ghost in the passage extends to the guest a hand which is a glove stuffed with ice-cold sawdust. An electric fan may be arranged in the passage so that it will blow strips of paper into the passing guests. Dress up someone as a dog, in crepe paper, with an improvised tail and false face. This dog should jump out and bark at the passing guests. Weird noises can be made by dragging chains over the floor. One of the ghosts may use a feather duster to tickle the faces of guests. A ghost on stilts has a terrifying effect. Another good stunt and one that produces a weird effect is to insert two small electric bulbs in eggshells so that they will work with a flasher button or can be turned on and off. These resemble two weird eyes in the dark. One of the ghost guides tells of the death of a friend and directs the hands of the guests to parts of the body. These are placed on plates, and the plates are on chairs or tables. The eyes are represented by two hulled grapes, the tongue by a raw oyster, the heart by a piece of liver, the lungs by a wet sponge, the brain by a dish of spaghetti.

3. *Meeting the Queen of Halloween.*—After the guests are brought into the room where the party is to be held, they should be directed to the Queen of Halloween. The Queen of Halloween is seated on a high chair and has an egg concealed in her hand. If

they shake hands too hard, the egg breaks. This will be very amusing to those who have preceded and will cause much merriment.

4. *Identification.*—Each guest is given a slip of paper on which to write the names of guests. A number has been pinned on each guest as he enters. These slips of paper have numbers corresponding to the number of guests. Guesses are by number. After about ten minutes or less declare the contest closed and bring up the guests, beginning at No. 1, and let them unmask. Give a prize to the one who guessed the largest number.

5. *Judging Costumes.*—Have a committee of three appointed to judge costumes. Give a prize for the most original costume, the funniest costume, and the prettiest costume. This may be handled as a sort of elimination contest, and let the guests decide by cheering which is the best in each class. Let the judges pick the three best in each class, and as the chief judge holds his hand over each, one of the three judges can decide by the cheering the best of the three.

6. *Bluebeard's Den.*—Have an adjoining room for Bluebeard's Den. Get some girls or women to pose as Bluebeard's seven murdered wives. They are arranged behind a sheet through which holes have been cut large enough for them to get their heads through. Red paint or red coloring of some kind should be sprinkled over the sheet. The faces of the girls should be powdered so that they will look ghastly. The light should be dim. Bluebeard is impersonated by a man who pantomimes the way he killed his wives. He may kill one with a hatchet, cut off one's head with a butcher knife, shoot one with a toy pistol so that it will make a report, choke one to death, stab one, and so forth. As he goes through this motion of killing each one in turn, they let out a scream. This screaming and the report of the pistol attracts the attention and excites the curiosity of the guests in the adjoining room. The guests should be brought in about four at a time. If the number of guests is not large, bring them in two at a time.

7. *Modeling.*—Give each guest a small quantity of modeling clay. Also give each one a cardboard about four inches square on which is written the name of something they are to model. Pass

around toothpicks which are to be used as tools with which to do the modeling. Some suggested models are: airplane, automobile, lamp, horse, cow, church, witch, jack-o'-lantern, turtle, cat, and so on.

8. *Jumbled Names of Halloween Objects.*—Give out a slip of paper on which the following jumbled words are written. Guests are supposed to write the word containing the jumbled letters:

   (1) Tsoshg. Ghosts.
   (2) Elesoksnt. Skeletons.
   (3) Arocdesnoit. Decorations.
   (4) Snilogb. Goblins.
   (5) Slow. Owls.
   (6) Skippumn. Pumpkins.
   (7) Kacj O'snretanl. Jack-o'-lanterns.
   (8) Kalcb stac. Black cats.
   (9) Tabs. Bats.
  (10) Chetisw. Witches.
  (11) Ppsale. Apples.
  (12) Osmetcus. Costumes.
  (13) Ksasm. Masks.
  (14) Shemerferstn. Refreshments.
  (15) Esagm. Games.
  (16) Shogt roitess. Ghost stories.

Give an appropriate prize to the one having the largest number correct.

9. *Dangling Doughnuts.*—Use a wire and let it remain loose enough to cause the doughnuts to dangle back and forth. Suspend doughnuts from the wire with strings tied around the doughnuts. Tie a wax paper bag over each doughnut. There are enough of them suspended from the wire so that each guest may have one. They stand after having selected a doughnut, and when the signal is given, without the use of the hands they are to take the paper bag off of the doughnut and eat the doughnut. The one first accomplishing this wins the prize.

10. *Ghost Story: Continuous.*—Someone is asked to start a ghost story, and each guest is to continue where the other leaves off. It

might be prearranged for one to start and another to conclude and have them sit side by side so that there could be a humorous ending to the story. Suppose, for instance, the first one should start a story in this manner: "One night a man was riding through a lonely country alone. It was raining. He passed a graveyard. He was not afraid of graveyards, but he happened to think that this was Halloween night. The owls were hooting nearby, and the wind was howling. Soon he saw the outline of a house. He went up to it and asked the man who answered his call if he could stay all night with the family. The man said: 'I have only one spare room in the house, and it is haunted. No one has ever been able to stay all night in it yet. I will let you have that room if you want to take a chance on it.' He went upstairs and went to bed. He placed his pistol under his pillow and tried to go to sleep." This would be a good place to leave off and let the story continue. After it has gone around the group, it might be concluded in the following manner: "After this experience, he got back into bed. As he was lying there, he looked down toward the foot of the bed, and in the moonlight, which had now begun to come in through the window, he saw a disembodied hand sticking up over the foot of the bed. He thought it was someone just trying to scare him, so he reached up to get his pistol. He said, 'If you don't take that hand down, I'll shoot.' The hand did not move. He said again, 'If you don't take that hand down, I'll shoot.' Still the hand did not move. He said, 'For the third and last time I say, If you do not take that hand down, I'll shoot,' and as the hand did not move, he pulled the trigger. He felt a sharp pain, and to his amazement he had shot his toe off. But he awoke to find that it was only a dream, and the sun was shining through the window."

11. *Jack-o'-Lantern Relay.*—Use four jack-o'-lanterns in which are lighted candles. The group is divided into four parts. These groups may be called Cats, Bats, Owls, and Ghosts. They stand in parallel lines and face a goal. At the signal the first one runs to the goal and back, holding the face of the lantern so that the draft will blow through. When the first one returns, he hands the lantern

to the one in front of the line and takes his place at the back. If the Jack-o'-lantern goes out, it must be relighted. The leader should provide matches for this purpose and be prepared to supply them as soon as the lantern is out. Use the largest room for this relay race, as the distance to be run will make it more interesting.

A good prize for this would be lollipops for everyone who took part on the side of the winning group.

12. *Apple Contest.*—Divide into groups of four each. This can be done by counting off 1, 2, 3, 4. Give each No. 1 an apple and a paring knife. No. 1 is to peel the apple and pass it on to No. 2. No. 2 must quarter it, No. 3 core it and drop it into a bowl of water. No. 4 must take it out of the water and eat it. The quartet that finishes first wins.

13. *Pumpkin Pie Contest.*—Choose about four or five boys and have a pumpkin pie eating contest. The one that can first satisfactorily consume a pie is the winner. A half pie would probably be better if the pies are large.

14. *Apple Relay.*—The players stand in line one in front of the other. An apple is started down the line, a player handing it to the next one without turning around—that is, he puts his hand behind his back as it goes down the line. As it comes back, he reaches behind his back to recover it without looking. If the apple is dropped, the one who dropped it is to recover it. This game will be a better race if the apple will take about four laps—that is, go down and up the line four times.

15. *Floating a Needle.*—Give each couple needles. Provide some lard to grease them with and bowls full of water. See which couple can first make their needles float. After the needles have floated, it is humorous to watch them. They will do strange things that will cause merriment. They may cling together or go to the opposite sides of the bowl.

16. *A List of Bad Omens.*—Give a prize to the one who can write the longest list of Halloween bad omens or superstitions. Have the one who has prepared the longest list in a given time to read his

list. Others may be asked to read other superstitions not read by the winner. The following is a list:

(1) Don't wipe on the same towel with anyone else. It means you will fight.

(2) Don't break a mirror. It signifies seven years of bad luck.

(3) If you sing before breakfast, you will cry before supper.

(4) Don't let black cat cross your path. You will have bad luck.

(5) Don't walk on the opposite sides of a tree or lamppost when walking with your escort. It means you will be separated.

(6) Don't walk under a ladder. Extreme bad luck is the penalty.

(7) Don't start anything on Friday. You will never finish it.

(8) If you turn over the salt shaker, throw salt over your shoulder to escape the bad luck.

(9) Don't view a new moon through the trees. It signifies bad luck.

(10) If you tell a dream before breakfast, it will come true.

(11) It is bad luck to return to the house after you have left it for a journey.

(12) When you get married, wear something old, something new, something borrowed, something blue.

(13) It is bad luck to hear a dog howl at night.

(14) Don't sleep in room No. 13 or have anything to do with this unlucky number, on peril of having bad luck.

(15) It is bad luck to raise an umbrella in the house.

(16) Don't kill hogs on the decrease of the moon; they will fry into grease when put into the pan.

(17) When you see a redbird make three wishes.

(18) Throw an old shoe after newlyweds.

(19) If you put on any garment wrong side outward, it is bad luck to change.

(20) If you marry in May, you'll rue the day.

(21) It is bad luck to sneeze before breakfast.

(22) Don't take the last biscuit; you will be an old maid or bachelor.

(23) It is bad luck for a bird to get in the house and circle over you.

(24) It is bad luck to rock an empty chair.

17. *Spinning Fortunes.*—Mark off a large piece of cardboard in squares three by three inches. There should be at least thirty-six of these squares. Paste in each of these squares the following fortunes, written out on a typewriter: Stick to him, he is worth it; You will take an ocean voyage; Your ship is coming in; Your dream will

come true; Don't be so catty; She is a beautiful blond; He tells you he loves you, while his fingers are crossed; Don't trust him; Twins for you; Beware of the Ideas of March; You are soon to enter politics; You will be married twice; Look for a juicy letter; Your fortune will be to marry a doctor; You will be happy though poor; You will be a great singer; You had better learn to cook; You will move to the farm and feed the pigs; The trouble with you is, you are too fickle; You will spend your honeymoon abroad; You will receive an unexpected legacy; He is handsome, so watch him; Blonds are your weakness; Roses for you; She will be beautiful but dumb; He will make money in oil; You will take a long motor trip; Single blessedness for you; You will still love him when he is bald; You will have many love affairs; You will be married in an airplane; She is fair but false; You will become a famous artist; He will marry you for your money; You will be twice married; Good night for you; Love in a cottage for you; Be brave, it may not be true; You had better say yes.

Place this cardboard with the fortune on a small table (a card table will do) and get some small tops. Let each one spin the top, and the square in which it stops is the fortune of the one who spins it.

18. *Fortunes in Flour.*—Use a large shallow vegetable dish filled with flour. The flour should be about one and one-half inches deep. Place the following articles in the flour: A ring with a set in it, wedding ring, small chain, thimble, candy or paper heart, button, coin, safety pin, straight pin, needle, pin point, pill, and tack.

Players are given a teaspoon and may scoop one time and take up a spoonful of flour. What they get, if anything, determines their fortune and is interpreted by the leader in the following manner:

Ring with set—First one to be engaged.
Wedding ring—First one to be married.
Small chain—Chained for life.
Thimble—Old maid.
Heart—A love affair.
Button—Bachelor.

Coin—Wealth.

Safety pin—Hello, daddy, or, You'll be a mamma.

Straight pin or needle—You're going to be married, and your troubles will soon begin.

Pen point—You'll be an author.

Pill—You need to take a pill.

Tack—Go sit on a tack.

19. *A "Cat" Guessing Game*.—Guests are supplied with papers with the following questions typed or mimeographed on them. They are supposed to answer with a word starting with "cat":

(1) What cat makes trouble? Catastrophe.

(2) What cat is a sauce? Catsup.

(3) What cat is a plant that grows in marshes? Cattail.

(4) What cat has horns? Cattle.

(5) What cat is a person used for a tool? Cat's-paw.

(6) What cat lived in Rome long ago? Cato.

(7) What cat is learned in church? Catechism.

(8) What cat is sent out by mail order houses? Catalogue.

(9) What cat is a waterfall? Cataract.

(10) What cat is wild? Catamount.

(11) What cat is a plant of the mint family? Catnip.

(12) What cat is a disease? Catarrh.

(13) What cat is an ancient burying place? Catacomb.

(14) What cat is an ancient instrument of torture? Cat-o'-nine-tails.

(15) What cat is a bird? Catbird.

(16) What cat is a church? Catholic.

(17) What cat is a fish? Catfish.

(18) What cat prepares food? Caterer.

(19) What cat is a flower? Catkin.

20. *Bobbing for Apples*.—Many people think that a Halloween party would not be complete without bobbing for apples. It is better to have the tubs filled with water on the porch or some place where they will not do any damage to polished floors. It is a good way to ruin clothing, so those who are particular about their dresses should not participate. Float the apples in tubs of water, and the one who gets the apple without the use of the hands gets

to eat it. Some of the boys will enjoy this sport better than the girls, and it would be best to have this event for the boys alone.

21. *Decorations.*—At this season of the year there are always decorations on sale at the bookstores and the novelty stores. You will want crêpe paper in orange and black with some red. Black cats, skeletons, and paper jack-o'-lanterns should be in evidence. The lights should be dimmed with crêpe paper or by the use of colored bulbs. In sections where they can be obtained, cornstalks and pumpkins will aid in decorating. In tropical sections use Spanish moss.

22. *Refreshments.*—Serve any convenient refreshments. Pumpkin or apple pie would be good. Use Halloween napkins. Paper plates of Halloween design may also be secured. Orange and black candy may be used as a part of the refreshments. Ice cream may be secured in Halloween colors. Cookies in shape of moon, cat, or witch may be used.

23. *Properties*

(1) Flashlight for witch who meets guests at door. Recorded noises of owls, groans, and so forth.

(2) Glove stuffed with ice-cold sawdust. Electric fan blowing strips of paper.

(3) Chains to drag over floor and make noise. Feather duster to tickle faces.

(4) Stilts for ghost. Costume for human dog.

(5) Small electric bulbs inserted in empty eggshells connected with flasher button.

(6) Hulled grapes, raw oyster, piece of liver, wet sponge, dish of spaghetti.

(7) Numbers to pin on each guest. Slips of paper for each guest.

(8) Room arranged for Bluebeard's den. Sheet with holes cut and smeared with red paint.

(9) Small quantity of modeling clay for each guest. Cards four inches square with name of something to model written on it. Toothpicks to use as tools.

(10) Slips of paper with jumbled Halloween objects written on them with typewriter if possible.

(11) Doughnuts covered with wax paper bags and suspended from wire with strings for each guest.

(12) Four jack-o'-lanterns with candles in them. Paper ones will do.

(13) Apples for Apple Contest. Four paring knives and four bowls of water. Apples for Apple Relay and Bobbing for Apples.

(14) Needles and lard and bowls of water for floating needles.

(15) Slips of paper and pencils for Bad Omens.

(16) Cardboard with fortunes for Spinning Fortunes. Two or three small tops.

(17) Vegetable dish of flour with objects for Fortunes in Flour.

(18) Typewritten sheets of "Cat" Questions Game.

chapter *41*

Television Party[1]

WHAT IS SO FULL OF IDEAS FOR A PLEASANT EVENING AS THE TELEVISION? Almost everyone has a television and almost everyone is a television fan. The things associated with television will furnish ample ideas for active and mental games, as well as impromptu and prearranged entertainment for almost any group.

1. *Invitation.*—The following is a suggested verse to send out as an invitation:

> At our Television Party we want you all,
> Young people short, and young people tall.
> The Social Committee has made a decision
> To entertain with games built around television.
> So come to the social room on next Friday night,
> For we promise you an evening of real delight.

2. *Decorations.*—Part of the program should be a television show put on by the guests themselves. Some of this program should be prearranged, but a large portion of it should be impromptu, or originate during the party. Arrange a "telecasting studio," which would really be the television screen to the guests who are not taking part but are spectators. This improvised television screen could be made like a large frame and covered with dark cloth or dark crêpe paper. It needs only to be high enough for a person to stand and wide enough for a small group. This might be arranged in an arch between two rooms in a home, such as between the dining room and living room. If the party is held in a recreation room at a church or at a social hall at the Y.M.C.A. or Y.W.C.A., a

[1] Prepared with the assistance of Mrs. Roy G. Ross, New York, N. Y.

stage will probably be available for use as a "telecasting studio" or screen. Those taking part in the entertainment program should stand in the improvised telecasting station so that it will carry the idea of a television show.

Some of the program may be acted behind a screen of white sheets, with the lights behind so arranged that the shadow of the characters will be cast on the screen. If it is too difficult to arrange the lights, simply have the characters act in the frame that represents a television or on the stage.

The stunts suggested below to be used on this type of program are those that require a reader to give the story while the players dramatize it with exaggerated actions. The following stunts from the *Cokesbury Stunt Book* (Revised) would be appropriate: "Bill Tell," "And the Lamp Went Out," "Roman Football Game," and "Victor Rings the Bell." Also, from the same book, "Humorous Dialogue," would be a good skit for two boys. These are only suggestions, and the leader should do some research and find other stunts to use for the program.

Additional decorations would be crêpe paper streamers. Another idea is to decorate the room to resemble an appliance store, with television and radio advertisements scattered about the room. These could be secured, in all probability, from a local appliance store.

The television program should take only a part of the evening, probably about forty-five minutes near the end of the party. So at the first part of the evening the party should proceed in the usual way.

3. *Opening Mixer: Television Stations.*—Hang around the neck of each guest a six by six inch card, lettered with colored crayons, giving the initial of the guest's last name. To make the cards, punch a hole in each of the top corners and tie a string in the holes in such a way that the string will slip over the head of the guest and hang around his neck. Guests should wear them all evening as they will be needed in the television program at the close. Each guest should

write his full name on the bottom of the card, in addition to having his initial on it.

Each guest is given a paper and pencil, and the leader explains that the guests are to try to form the call numbers, or call letters of television stations. For example, Tulsa, Oklahoma (Channel 2), is KVOO-TV. Those having these letters may get together, and will probably do so by someone who knows that call number, pulling them together. When they have arranged themselves so that the call number may be read, each one of the group may write the call number on his paper. When any player can get himself in as a part of any call number, he may write this number on his paper. The girl that has Springfield, Mo., will find the boy that has the greatest number of call numbers. The real television fans will probably know a lot of call numbers. If it should turn out that there are no guests or few guests with the key letters such as W or K, it may be necessary for some of the guests to use their first or middle initial in order to solve this problem. Whenever the leader feels that the game has continued long enough for the guests to be properly mixed and that the ice is sufficiently broken, she may stop the game. A prize should be given to the person who has been a part of the largest number of call numbers or call letters.

4. *Finding Partners: Stations and Call Numbers.*—Give a list of call numbers to the boys and the names of the corresponding cities to the girls. They are to match call numbers and cities. For example, the boy may have KYTV (Channel 2) or KTTS (Channel 10). These are call numbers of two stations at Springfield, Missouri. The girl who has Springfield, Mo. will find the boy who has one of the call numbers of the Springfield stations, or he will find her. Only a few of the larger cities, such as New York, Chicago, Cincinnati, should be used. Most of the well-known stations to the guests will be in the cities in the adjoining area.

5. *Television Static, or Snow.*—Give guests the following list of terms associated with television, with the letters jumbled. Let the couples, selected in the above game, work together in this game:

   (1) Ldai. Dial.
   (2) Bestu. Tubes.
   (3) Atscit. Static.
   (4) Etno ntroclo. Tone control.
   (5) Aornennuc. Announcer.
   (6) Tsnaoit. Station.
   (7) Halencn. Channel.
   (8) Locosen. Console.
   (9) Legsacttien. Telecasting.
 (10) Neersc. Screen.
 (11) Netaann. Antenna.
 (12) Cllyescoik. Kilocycles.
 (13) Cutirci. Circuit.
 (14) Teomre oronlct. Remote control.
 (15) Nctrreu. Current.
 (16) Mgrpaor. Program.

6. *Are You a Part of Television?*—Give each guest a sheet of paper and a pencil. They are to write the names of each person in the room that has in any part of his name a letter that occurrs in the word, "television." Give a prize to the one having the longest list of names.

7. *Television Spelling Relay.*—The guests should be divided into two or three groups of equal number for this relay. Have them stand in line, one in front of another, and all facing a large table on which have been placed stacks of cards with the letters of the alphabet printed on them with colored crayons. The leader should be sure that there are letters enough and duplicates enough to spell any word that is pronounced. But it would be better not to pronounce the words at all but to prepare a list to be written on a blackboard for all to see or on a cardboard pinned on the drapes, or typewritten on slips of paper and given to each group. There should be one judge for each group, and this person should be stationed behind the table from the group. When the game starts, the first player in line in each group runs to the stack of letters, picks from the stack the first letter of the first word and lays it on the table with the letters reading from the player's left to his right.

He then runs back and touches the next player in the front of his line and takes a place at the back of the line. As the words are completed, the judge for that group puts the letters back in the stack, and the next player starts the next word. The group that spells all the words first is declared the winner.

8. *Arranging an Impromptu Television Program.*—We assume that part of the television program, suggested at the beginning of this chapter, has already been arranged, such as recitations, readings, vocal or instrumental solos, orchestra, or humorous dialogue. Two of the television features, however, should be at least semi-impromptu—the news and the advertisements. Select two TV stations and ask the group of persons whose initials make up these call numbers to work together in a group. The first is to write advertisements and the second news. Such items as the following would be an advertisement: "Tom Smith, whose affections have been alienated from Betty Brown, now seeks a beautiful, but not too intelligent girl to take her place," or, "Wanted by Nettie White another Prince Charming to take the place of Hal who has been drafted into the army." For the news anything that has happened or is happening that is of interest to the group could be written and read for news. It should have a humorous turn. After the advertisements and the news have been assembled, one person in each group should be asked to read them on the television program.

9. *Television Program*

(1) The first thing on the program should be a *setting-up exercise.* Have a good leader who has been coached in advance to lead the following songs, asking the guests to go through with the exercises:

A GYMNASTIC RELIEF

(Tune, "Smile the While You Kiss Me Fond Adieu")

Smile awhile and give your face a rest, (All smile)
Stretch awhile and ease your manly chest. (Arms to side)
Reach your hands up toward the sky (Hands up)
While you watch them with your eye. (Heads up)
Jump awhile, and shake a leg, there sir, (Jump lively)

Now step forward, backward—as you were. (Step back and forth)
Now reach right out to someone near, (Shake hands with another guest)
Shake his hand and smile. (All smile)

Repeat the above song in double-quick time.

CHESTER

(Tune, "Yankee Doodle")

Oh, Chester, have you 'eared about 'Airry?
Chest got back from the arm-y,
I 'ear he knows how to wear a rose,
Hip, hip, hooray for the army.

In leading this song the leader moves about in the following manner, and the guests are supposed to make the same motions: When "Chester" is sung, both hands are placed on the chest; " 'eared" both hands on ears; " 'Airry" both hands on hair; "Chest" (in second line) both hands on chest; "back" hands to back; "Army" slap right arm with left hand, and left arm with right hand; "I" hands on eyes; "ear" hands on ears; "knows" hands on nose; "how to wear a rose" both hands folded on left breast; "Hip, hip" push fists into air as if giving a cheer, then bring them down and slap the hips with the palms; "hooray for the army" extend both arms into the air and shout.

Do this again one or two times in quicker time.

(2) *News.*—Have the news read that has been gathered by the group to whom it was assigned.

(3) *Reading the Advertisements.*—Call on the group to whom this was assigned.

(4) *Readings and Recitations.*—There are two or three good ones to be found in the "Gypsy Party," Chapter 28.

(5) *Vocal solo.*

(6) *Instrumental solo.*

(7) *Orchestra.*—If no orchestra is available, try the Gazoo orchestra elsewhere in this book. (See Index.)

Any entertainment features, such as a quartet, or a skit, may be added to this program, depending on the talents of the guests.

10. *Refreshments.*—Refreshments suggested for this party are Waldorf salad, sandwiches or wafers, and coffee, or iced or hot tea, depending upon the season in which the party is given.

11. *Properties*

(1) A large frame or stage for improvised telecasting station or television screen.

(2) Papers and pencils for each guest.

(3) A six by six inch card for each guest with a string arranged so that it may be put over the head and hung around the neck. This should be lettered, at the proper time, with colored crayons.

(4) List of familiar station call numbers with corresponding cities for the "Finding Partners" feature.

(5) Television static or "snow" prepared for each guest.

(6) Lettered cards for "Television Spelling Relay."

chapter 42

Progressive Hearts Party[1]

A CHANGE FROM THE USUAL PARTY OF GAMES AND STUNTS IS OFTEN welcomed by any group. We are suggesting in this chapter a game that is full of interest to all, the game of Heart Dice. Heart dice are manufactured by the Parker Brothers, Salem, Mass. Any number can play the game, and any number can play at a table. But as we are suggesting the game for a party in which from twelve to forty or more could play, we will speak of Progressive Heart Dice.

1. *The Game.*—Heart Dice is played with six cubes on which are written on the six sides of each the letters in the word "Hearts." These are thrown all at one throw by each player, and the player is only allowed to throw once, after which he must pass the dice to the player on his left. When four play at a table, the players across from each other are partners for that game, and when one of them scores, both can mark the score, and it counts for both. However, as one changes partners after each game, each must keep his score separately. So the game proceeds, each throwing the dice one time, until one couple gets a hundred, at which time they yell "Game," whereupon all stop and count up their score for that game. Then all winners at each table, that is, those who had the highest score, progress to the next table, except the winners at the head table, who keep their places while the losers go to the foot table.

2. *How to Score.*—One hundred is a game. Scores are made by the number of consecutive letters in the word "hearts" which appear when the dice are thrown, as follows:

H E, 5.
H E A, 10.

[1] Used by permission of the Manufacturers, Parker Brothers, Salem, Mass.

H E A R, 15.

H E A R T, 20.

H E A R T S, 25.

When anyone throws three H's, his entire score and that of his partner for that game is canceled. They must begin a new score and just mark off completely what they have already made.

3. *The Tables.*—In playing Progressive Hearts, play four at a table, those across from each other playing partners for that game. Partners change after each game, and each person gets a new partner. Even the winning players at a table should move, one of them taking another side of the table. Tables are numbered from the head table, which is number one, and on down, depending on the number of guests in multiples of four. Couples progress in the regular way, the winners at each of the tables, except the head table, progressing. The losers at the head table go to the foot table while the winners remain.

4. *Rules of the Game as Given by the Manufacturers.*—As we have made some changes in the rules, with the thought of speeding up the game, we think best to give the rules sent out by the manufacturers. We have made only one change and that is to suggest that all play until someone gets a game at which time they yell "Game," at which time all proceed to count up score and progress, while the manufacturers' rule is that as soon as six rounds are played at each table, the players progress. If it is not desired to make the game so hilarious, or to make the element of time a part of it, it would be better to use the rules sent out by the manufacturers.

(1) When arranging a game of Progressive Hearts, general rules and customs governing other progressive games may be applied. Four persons play at each table, those across the table from each other playing as partners. Any number of tables may be played, and six rounds are played at each table, after which the winners progress to the next table and there change partners, the losers remaining at the same table. When three H's appear at one throw at any table, the person who threw them and his partner must both cancel their total score for that game. In case of a tie score at any table, two opposing players roll all six cubes once each, the side then making the highest score progresses. (This score, however,

is not to be marked on the score card and does not change the players individual score.)

(2) The game of Hearts is played from right to left.

(3) Any number of players can play at one table. (Except in Progressive Hearts.)

(4) Each player has but one throw.

(5) All six cubes must be used at each play.

(6) The cubes may be thrown from the hand or from cups sold by the manufacturers.

(7) Players count separately for themselves, or jointly as one when playing partners.

(8) The reaching of one hundred points constitutes a game of Hearts; this, however, may be changed to any number by agreement before the game starts. [In playing Progressive Hearts, as suggested by the author of this chapter, if the game seems too slow, cut down the number of points required for a game.]

(9) In order to count, all cubes must lay flat and separately by themselves upon the table, otherwise the play would be called a dead throw and must be thrown over.

5. *Other Equipment Needed.*—Pencils and score cards should be provided. The manufacturers of this game sell a scoreboard with which the score may be kept. Score cards may be made by drawing twelve or fifteen squares on a sheet of paper and numbering these squares one, two, three, and so on. These numbers will represent the number of the game. Every time some couple in the group makes one hundred, that will constitute that game. About twelve or fifteen games would constitute a full evening of play, or about one and one-half hours.

6. *Prizes.*—Prizes should be given, a first and second, to the two players making highest scores. It is not possible to give prizes to couples as they change at the end of every game.

7. *Refreshments.*—Have a bonbon dish filled with heart-shaped candy at each place. Get ice cream in heart mold and serve with cake at conclusion of play.

8. *Using This Party as a Pay Social.*—This could easily be made a pay social by charging twenty-five cents a corner for the tables, or five cents a game, which for twelve games would be sixty cents each for the guests.

chapter 43

Birthday Party

ANNIVERSARIES ALWAYS MEAN A GREAT DEAL TO ALL OF US, AND SO IT is especially fitting to remember the day of a person's birth. The birthday party may be given for an individual or for an entire group and called "Everybody's Birthday Party." One group with which the author is familiar has a birthday party once every three months. At this time, all those having birthdays within that period of time are the honor guests and are given special attention and honor during the evening.

The suggestions here are for a birthday party for a large group, but may be adapted to a party honoring a single individual.

1. *Invitation.*—The following is a suggestion for an invitation:

> Solomon Grundy was born on Monday
> In the long, long ago.
> Someone else was born on Tuesday,
> Perhaps 'twas you, we do not know.
> But come to our Birthday Party
> Next Thursday night at eight,
> And we will celebrate your birthday,
> No matter what the day or date.

2. *Decorations.*—The decorations for this party may be varied according to the choice of the leader or hostess. The month or season of the year in which the party is held should motivate the choice in decorations. If a party is held in the Spring months (March, April, May), spring flowers should be used and streamers of crepe paper in pastel shades harmonizing with the flowers would make a lovely background for the party.

For the Summer months (June, July, August) continue the use of flowers, but choose those of more brilliant hue and use streamers of crepe paper of red and green or other bright harmonizing shades.

For the Autumn party (September, October, November) decorate the rooms with a profusion of autumn leaves and use cornstalks and pumpkins to suggest the season of the harvest.

The Winter party (December, January, February) should portray a snow scene. White streamers of crepe paper hung with icicles and tinsel, such as are used to decorate Christmas trees, would be quite effective. Cotton pinned to the curtains would also aid in suggesting the cold season.

If the party is to be given typifying birthdays of a certain month, the same scheme of decorating may be used with the symbols emblematic of the month added. For example, the decorations for February should also feature the Valentine or George Washington ideas.

If an individual is being honored on his birthday by a group of friends, interest is always added to the party if it is a "surprise." The group should assemble at some convenient or central point and go in a body to the home of the honor guest or to some other place where they have arranged by surreptitious means for the honoree to be. The guests should all enter together with shouts of "Happy birthday," "Many happy returns of the day," or sing the familiar song, "Happy Birthday to You," used by so many church and school groups.

If the group has decided to remember the honor guest with a gift from the entire group or with individual gifts, it would be well to make this presentation at this time. Someone of the group should be prepared to say a few words appropriate to the occasion as the gift is presented. If each guest is bringing a gift, decorate a market-basket or clothesbasket with crepe paper and place the gifts in it to be presented all together. If it is desirable, the gifts could be presented later in the evening, just before the refreshments are served. Whenever the gifts are presented, they should be unwrapped by the honoree and passed around among the guests, the gifts bearing the card of the donor.

3. *Opening Mixer: Birthday.*—Supply each guest with pencil and paper and ask them to shake hands with as many others as possible, writing down the name, the day, and the month of their birth. At the end of a time limit, the leader should collect the lists and give a prize to the person having the longest list. A small calendar would make a suitable prize. The leader should then read several of the longest lists, reading first the birth date and allowing others to guess whose birthday it is. If the group is not well acquainted, the leader should then call on the individual to rise and introduce him by name, so that all will feel properly acquainted.

4. *A Birthday Hunt.*—Write the names and birthdays of famous people on small slips of paper. Hide them about the room. At a given signal tell all the guests to start on a Birthday Hunt. At the end of ten minutes the guests must cease searching and count the slips they have found. The one finding the largest number should be asked to read them aloud. If a prize is given, a small birthday book would be very suitable. Some suggested birthdays of famous persons follow:

JANUARY

January 17, 1706, Benjamin Franklin.
January 18, 1782, Daniel Webster.
January 19, 1807, Robert E. Lee.
January 29, 1843, William McKinley.

FEBRUARY

February 4, 1902, Charles Lindbergh.
February 12, 1809, Abraham Lincoln.
February 22, 1732, George Washington.
February 27, 1807, Henry W. Longfellow.

MARCH

March 7, 1849, Luther Burbank.
March 16, 1820, Florence Nightingale.
March 19, 1813, David Livingstone.
March 24, 1820, Fanny Crosby.

APRIL

April 2, 1743, Thomas Jefferson.
April 3, 1783, Washington Irving.
April 17, 1837, John Pierpont Morgan.
April 23, 1564, William Shakespeare.

MAY

May 4, 1825, Thomas Henry Huxley.
May 25, 1803, Ralph Waldo Emerson.
May 27, 1819, Julia Ward Howe.

JUNE

June 17, 1703, John Wesley.
June 17, 1812, Harriet Beecher Stowe.

JULY

July 4, 1872, Calvin Coolidge.
July 8, 1839, John D. Rockefeller.
July 10, 1447, Christopher Columbus.
July 13, 1864, John Jacob Astor.
July 26, 1765, Robert Fulton.

AUGUST

August 6, 1809, Alfred Tennyson.
August 10, 1874, Herbert Hoover.
August 15, 1771, Sir Walter Scott.
August 29, 1809, Oliver W. Holmes.

SEPTEMBER

September 2, 1850, Eugene Field.
September 10, 1789, James Fenimore Cooper.
September 13, 1860, Gen. John J. Pershing.
September 15, 1857, William Howard Taft.

OCTOBER

October 22, 1811, Franz Liszt.
October 27, 1858, Theodore Roosevelt.

NOVEMBER

November 2, 1755, Marie Antoinette.
November 3, 1794, William Cullen Bryant.

November 6, 1860, Ignace Jan Paderewski.
November 10, 1483, Martin Luther.
November 22, 1819, George Eliot.
November 25, 1837, Andrew Carnegie.

DECEMBER

December 8, 1542, Mary, Queen of Scots.
December 9, 1608, John Milton.
December 25, 1642, Sir Isaac Newton.
December 28, 1856, Woodrow Wilson.
December 30, 1865, Rudyard Kipling.

5. *Making the Most of "Happy Birthday."*—Give the guests sheets of paper at the top of which have been written "Happy Birthday." Ask them to see who can make the longest list of words out of the letters in "Happy Birthday." The longest list should be read and a prize given to the one who wrote it.

6. *Obstacle Race.*—This game is very suitable for a large group, as only four or five men on each team are to take part while the others are spectators. The company should be divided into two or more groups and a team selected from each group. If the party is large, have four groups, Spring, Summer, Autumn, and Winter. A number of obstacles have been arranged on different sides of the room, and the teams line up on their side and wait for the blowing of the leader's whistle. When the whistle blows, they are to run to obstacle number one and do as directed by the sign on it. These may be arranged in any way, and the cleverness of the one who lays out the course is largely depended upon. The following obstacles are suggested:

(1) On a table have a paper and one pencil. Each one of the four must write his name, address, and the month of his birth. They may have this instruction in advance, or a sign may tell them what to do at each obstacle.

(2) Remove tie and replace it. Other suggestions are: Take off your coat, turn it wrong side outward, and put it back on.

(3) Get down on all fours and run like a rabbit to a goal. The second must not start until the first has reached the goal.

297

(4) Eat three crackers (one eating at a time) and whistle, at which time another begins.

(5) Hop to next goal on right foot, holding the left foot in right hand. One must reach the goal before the other starts.

(6) A folding chair is here. Each one is required to unfold it and sit in it and then fold it back up. Then the next one does it, until all have finished.

(7) Run to the next goal, taking three steps forward and two back. This is done one at a time and no mincing of back steps is allowed.

(8) Have a suitcase full of old clothes, and better and funnier, women's clothes. Each one must put on these clothes, run around the chair or table three times, and then take them off and give them to the next.

(9) Provide paper bags, about four for each player. They must inflate and pop these, one player doing this at a time.

(10) Walk to the goal, advancing only the length of the foot at each step. This is done by placing the heel against the toe at each step. This must be done one at a time, and when the last one gets in, his side is finished.

Of course there will be plenty of rooting by the guests while this is going on.

7. *Birth Stones and Flowers.*—Have typewritten copies of the birth stones and birth flowers to give to each guest. Leave blank the month that they represent and ask them to fill in the month. We do not have them in order, and they should not be, of course, arranged in order.

BIRTH FLOWERS	BIRTH STONES
Water lily. July.	Turquoise or ruby. December.
Snowdrop. January.	Agate or chalcedony. June.
Poppy. August.	Topaz. November.
Primrose. February.	Emerald or carnelian. May.
Morning-glory. September.	Opal or beryl. October.
Violet. March.	Diamond or sapphire. April.
Hops. October.	Chrysolite. September.
Daisy. April.	Bloodstone or jasper. March.
Chrysanthemum. November.	Sardonyx. August.
Hawthorn. May.	Amethyst. February.
Holly. December.	Ruby or onyx. July.
Honeysuckle. June.	Garnet. January.

8. *Happy Birthday to You.*—The leader stands in the center of a circle of the guests seated. He points his finger at a guest and says, "Happy birthday to you." The guest must respond with, "The same to you," before the leader finishes the phrase. If the leader points to a guest and does not say anything at all and the guest says, "The same to you," the penalty is just the same, and in either case the guest must take the leader's place and the game continues.

9. *Birthday Candle Race.*—The different groups line up for a relay race; and if there are four groups, they face four tables on which have been placed lighted candles. The players, one at a time, must run to the candles with a candle in their hand which has been given them. They are to light their candle from the lighted candle and race back to the head of the line. Then they must extinguish their candle and give it to the next one in line. If the candle goes out before they get back, they must go back to the table and relight it. When one has run, then he must take his place at the back of the line.

10. *Do a Stunt to Represent Your Month.*—Have the guests who are born in the different months of the year to get together and do something to represent the month in which they were born. If, for example, it was in February, something about Washington or Valentine Day should be given. If December, a Christmas stunt, and so on. Let the other guests guess what month each group is trying to represent.

11. *Making Famous Dates*—Get some cards about six by six inches square and print on them with colored crayons the nine digits and a zero. You will need one set for each group competing, plus extras for the dates which have two of the same digits, such as 1066 and 1781. For the list of dates given below each group will need two ones, two sixes, two sevens, two eights, and two nines. If there are four groups, let each group form in a corner of the room. There will be sixteen cards for each group. If there are fewer than sixteen players in a group, give some of the players two cards. When the leader gives a date, each group must try to get its players in formation with the proper numbers held in front of them, to form the date. The first group that gets the date correctly formed will be given a score of one point. The leader will need a couple of judges to help decide which group finished first.

If the group is a high school or college group, the leader may require that the year be known by the group when the historical event that occurred in it is given. For example, if he calls out "the discovery of America," the group must automatically form 1492. With younger groups it will probably be necessary to give the year with the historical event that took place in it.

In addition to the list of dates given below, the leader may use others that occur to him—such as the present year, the year the class will graduate, and so forth. The following gives a list of famous dates:

1066—Battle of Hastings.
1492—Discovery of America.
1517—Beginning of Reformation.
1620—Landing of Pilgrims.
1776—Declaration of Independence.
1781—Surrender of Cornwallis at Yorktown.
1812—War of United States with England.
1815—Battle of Waterloo.
1861—Civil War begins.
1865—Assassination of Lincoln.
1898—Sinking of the Maine. Spanish-American War begins.
1906—Earthquake in San Francisco.
1912—Sinking of the Titanic.
1918—World War I ends.
1927—Lindbergh's flight to Paris.
1939—Beginning of World War II.
1945—End of World War II.
1958—Alaska admitted to the union.

12. *Refreshments.*—For the observance of the birthdays of a large group, serve individual cakes with a candle on each cake. Ice cream should be served with the cake, or punch, chocolate, or coffee should be substituted.

If an individual birthday is being celebrated, by all means use the proverbial birthday cake, with candles for each year of age. The honoree should cut the cake for each guest present.

13. *Properties*

(1) Papers and pencils for Opening Mixer.
(2) Famous Persons' Birthdays on slips of paper hidden.
(3) Sheets of paper with "Happy Birthday" at top.
(4) Properties for Obstacle Race.
(5) Typewritten or mimeographed copies of stones and flowers for Birth Stones and Flowers.
(6) Eight candles for Birthday Candle Race.
(7) Four sets of six by six inch cards with the nine digits and a zero printed on them with colored crayons, plus duplicates in one, six, seven, eight, and nine.

chapter 44

Cootie Party

THIS PARTY IS NOT SUGGESTED FOR ANY PARTICULAR SEASON, FOR IT WILL be suitable for any time of the year. It is also suitable for any age group. It is particularly recommended for junior high and high school groups, although I have seen persons as old as seventy-five play it and get a great thrill out of it. It is, therefore, suitable for a group of mixed ages.

The game is played by any number of players in multiples of four. It would be of little interest unless there were twelve or sixteen players. The larger the group, the better and the merrier.

This party may be used as a money-making plan by selling the tables at twenty-five cents a corner or even a dollar a corner, if those who attend can afford to play. Another way of making money from it would be to charge five cents a cootie. Each time there is a change of tables, each player is to pay five cents. This would be for an average evening about sixty or seventy-five cents per person.

The equipment needed for a Cootie Party is as follows: Tables enough for the guests who are to be invited, seated four at a table. Score cards enough for each guest, as described later. Pencils and one of a pair of dice on each table. If it is not desirable to use dice, cubes may be made from wood, with letters painted on them. We wanted to use this game for a young people's conference group and felt that there might be some criticism for using dice, so we went to the mill and had blocks sawed from gum wood three-quarters of an inch square. We had these painted black and lettered in white. On the six sides of the dice, we placed the letters "B" for "Body"; "H" for "Head"; "T" for "Tail"; "E" for "Eye"; "F" for "Feeler"; "L" for "Leg." We found that these cubes worked quite as well if not better than the dice. It is almost impossible to drop one of them without having it roll over. They can be made at very little expense. Only one block is needed for each table of four persons, so one would need only ten for a group of forty.

When the leader's whistle blows, one person at each table takes one of a pair of dice or lettered cubes and throws. The person who is across the table is always one's partner. That is, they play partners during that cootie, and they work together on the cootie, one of them marking scores while the other one throws. As he throws, he does not take time to mark his score but merely calls out to his partner what he has made, and the partner marks it. Unless he throws a one, he must pass the dice or cube to the next person on the left, who throws, trying to get a one. One is a "body," and each player must have a one before anything else counts or before he can throw again. If a player gets a one, he may throw again, and as long as he gets anything he can "use" he can continue to throw. Prepare a score card as illustrated at the top of the next page.

The idea of the game is to make a high score. Each individual keeps his own score, and the one who gets the highest score should win a handsome prize. The game is a fast game, as one wants to try as many times as he can. Many times it would be found better to use card tables and not to pick up the die or cube at all, but merely to strike the table, if card tables are used, and in this way turn the die or cube. This will work better than one would imagine. So the game proceeds, each person trying to throw as many times as he can, and as soon as one person throws out or gets something he cannot "use," the next one throws.

As soon as someone completes his "cootie," he yells "Cootie," and the game stops. The game will be so exciting that it will be necessary for the leader to blow the whistle to stop the game. As soon as a "cootie" is completed, all count up their score for that number and write it in the number. For example, if a "cootie" was completed when another player only had a "body" that player would get "one." If he had a "body" and a "head" and "one eye" and "one leg," his

Cootie Score Card

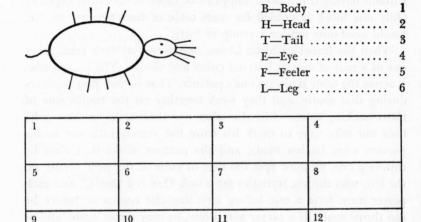

B—Body 1
H—Head 2
T—Tail 3
E—Eye 4
F—Feeler 5
L—Leg 6

1	2	3	4
5	6	7	8
9	10	11	12

score would be four. See the score card and study the marked card until this point is clear.

Marked Cootie Score Card

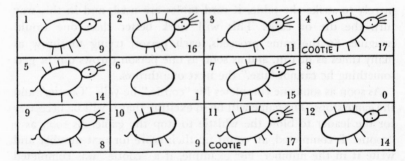

As soon as a "cootie" is made, there is an intermission to enable players to count their score, and then all should change tables. They progress in the regular way, the winners moving up a table toward the head table. One of the losers at each table moves to another side of the table, so that all will have a new partner each "cootie." The winners remain at the head table as long as they win, while the losers at the head table go to the last table, or the one considered the "foot" table.

After a "cootie" has been completed and the winners have progressed to the next table, a moment should be allowed to get acquainted before the next game starts. At this point each player should tell his name to his new partner, become acquainted with the two new opponents, and have a moment to converse. After this brief period the leader again blows a whistle, and the game is resumed.

At the conclusion of the twelfth or fourteenth "cootie," each player counts his score, and the one receiving the highest score is the prize winner. There might be another prize for the one having the largest number of "cooties," as this will be the same person in but few cases.

There is another thing that perhaps should be made clear, and that is that while those seated opposite at a table are partners for that "cootie," they keep individual scores. In other words, they each have a similar score at the end of the "cootie," and when they change tables, both the player and his partner should have the same score. Playing partners does not prevent each individual from keeping a separate score card, which he carries with him from one partner to the next.

Serve refreshments of doughnuts and coffee.

I do not know the origin of the game "cootie," but it was given to me by the Rev. Bruce Gannaway, a prominent Methodist minister. He states that he learned the game in Atlanta while a student at Emory.

chapter 45

Tacky Party

(*COSTUME*)

OCCASIONALLY WE ENJOY MAKING OURSELVES LUDICROUS; SO LET'S ALL come to the party in the queerest garb we can find and see who is the tackiest one present.

1. *Invitation.*—The following is suggested as a verse to be used for an invitation:

> A Tacky Party we're having on Friday night,
> And we want you to be there.
> Dress up so tacky that you'll be a sight,
> And an evening of fun with us share.

2. *Costumes.*—The guests should be told in advance that a prize will be given to the "tackiest" person present. It would be well to give one for the girls and one for the boys. If desired, the prize list could be extended, and, in addition to giving prizes for the whole tacky ensemble, separate prizes could be awarded for the tackiest hat, dress, or suit. Any sort of clothing may be worn, just so it is not the present mode of dress. Most any clothing ten years old or older will seem tacky for the girls. They could use all sorts of color combinations, with mismated shoes and hose. The old-fashioned clothes of our mothers' day, some of which nearly every family has stored away, would furnish ideal costumes for the affair. The boys could carry out the same ideas in choosing their costumes. Coats, trousers, ties, shirts, and vests of former grandeur would again come into their own. A tacky effect may be created by a clash of colors in shoes and socks, trousers and coat, shirt and tie. The boys may mix these colors in any crazy way.

3. *Judging the Costumes.*—The leader of the group should select several judges who will award the prizes to the proper persons. The judges may give their decision early in the evening or later, if they desire time to make a careful study of the merits of each. Another way of deciding the winners would be by ballot of the guests present. Arrange a ballot showing the different classifications to be voted upon, distribute these among the guests, and ask each one to vote for their own choice. These votes should then be collected and tabulated and the winners announced. If the latter method is used, it would be well for the leaders to conduct the opening mixer before the ballots are passed out. In this way the guests who are unacquainted will have an opportunity to meet the others, and also it will give each one a chance to "look the other fellow over."

4. *Merry Mix-Up.*—Girls and boys form two circles, the boys on the outside and the girls on the inside. The leader stands in the center. Someone who plays the piano well should be at the piano. The boys march clockwise and the girls march counter-clockwise. The leader calls out, "Sing 'Smiles.'" All sing and march around. When the song is over, all stop, and they are supposed to get acquainted with the one opposite. The music starts again and the pianist may play "Turkey in the Straw," stopping at intervals. Each time the music stops, the boys must introduce themselves to the girls opposite them. The leader may call different things for the group to do, such, as "Sing 'Let Me Call You Sweetheart' or 'Jingle Bells' or 'Farmer in the Dell.'" Each time a song is completed, they are to get acquainted with those opposite them. This may continue by the leader telling them all to laugh until the music stops, or to step high, or to hop. Continue this game until everyone has had an opportunity to meet everyone else. Do not make the stops very long. In any case, the game should not continue more than ten or fifteen minutes.

5. *Finding Partners.*—Have each of the boys take off one shoe. Pile them all in the middle of the floor. The girls stand around in a circle, and when the leader's whistle is blown, they have a scramble

to get the shoes. The girl is then ready to find the owner of the shoe. In this case, this may indeed be a merry mix-up as some of the boys may wear the same kinds of shoes.

6. *Golf for the Beginner.*—The object of the game, unlike regular golf, is to make a high score. Partners work together on this game, and each couple tries to think of and write on their card all the words they can during the time allowed for that hole. Any word will do as long as it begins with the letter for that hole. The leader has given each couple or guest an eight and one-half by eleven inch

GOLF FOR THE BEGINNER

PAR	PAR
G 10	E 15
O 14	B 16
L 11	E 18
F 13	G 17
F 8	I 9
O 17	N 12
R 20	N 11
T 11	E 14
H 8	R 13

sheet of paper on which is drawn the "course," as illustrated on the preceding page. One minute is allowed for each hole or letter, and each player is required to play only one hole at a time. In other words, the player is not allowed to write in the space marked for "O" while he is still writing on the space marked for "G." Par is indicated, which means approximately how many words the average person would write in one minute of time. Players are not allowed to repeat words. While there are two holes with the letter "O," different words beginning with "O" must be written in these. The same is true of the "F's" and the "N's." The leader holds the watch and allows one minute to write in the space marked "G." She then blows her whistle and players move on to "O." They are not allowed then to write any more words in "G" during the game. In this way it will require eighteen minutes to play the game, and at least five minutes more will be required to arrange for it and explain it. Give a prize to the couple making the highest score.

7. *Buzz.*—The players are all seated in a circle for this game. The leader explains that they are going to count off and each time a guest has a number in it that has a seven or multiple of seven, he must say "Buzz" instead. Players who fail to do this are required to sit on the floor in the center of the circle. The counting should go just as fast as possible. As the count proceeds, it will be somewhat as follows: 1, 2, 3, 4, 5, 6, buzz, 8, 9, 10, 11, 12, 13, buzz, 15, 16, one buzz, 18, 19, 20, buzz, 22, 23, 24, 25, 26, two buzz, and so on.

8. *Cross Questions and Crooked Answers.*—The boys line up facing the girls. The leader has two assistants. One of these assistants gives a question to each of the girls by whispering it in her ear. These should be as crazy and foolish as possible. The other assistant whispers a foolish answer into the ear of the boys. These questions and answers should be prepared in advance, so that too much time will not be consumed when giving them out. When the game starts, the girl asks the boy a question, and he answers it. If they laugh, they must go to the foot of the line. Those who do not laugh while the first round is being played are then eliminated and each one of the other couples must try to ask and answer their questions three times

without laughing. The game concludes when all couples have been able to ask and answer their questions with a straight face. If this is too long delayed, the leader may declare the game closed.

9. *One Word Suggests Another.*—The players are seated in a circle. The leader explains the game and suggests a word. Each player must then think of a word and keep the word in mind which the last word suggested to him. They call out the words as they go. For example, suppose the leader says "post office." To the next player, this may suggest "letter." "Letter" to the next player may suggest "lover." "Lover" may suggest "girl," "girl" "powder puff," "powder puff" "powder," "powder" "gun," "gun" "war," "war" "soldier," "soldier" "battle," and so on. When these suggested words have gone around the circle, start back and unravel. The last player tells the word that suggested his, and so on around the circle.

10. *Addition.*—The party should be divided into two or three groups for this game. Give each group figures from one to ten written on six by six cards. The leader calls a number as fifteen, twenty-three, or any other small number. Different groups try to get players in formation with numbers that will add up and make the number called. For example, suppose the leader calls twenty-one. A nine and a seven and a five form the column of figures. The object is, of course, to see who can have them quickest. There should be an umpire. Give a score of one to the group that finishes first.

11. *Where Am I?*—Where Am I? is a game that might well be used in such a party as this. One person is asked to leave the room. In his absence, the group decides where he is and what he is doing. For instance, he might be "in the gymnasium taking setting-up exercises." He must guess on his return where he is and what he is doing by asking questions that can be answered by "yes" or "no."

12. *Acting Advertisements.*—Count off in groups of four. Give each one of these groups an advertising slogan to act out and let the other groups guess what product is being advertised by the slogan which the group acts out. Slogans with action in them should be used—such as "Old Dutch Cleanser chases dirt." The

leader should look through a number of current magazines and make a list of advertising slogans to be given to the groups.

13. *Refreshments.*—Serve apple cider and cake. Another suggestion would be hot chocolate with marshmallows and cake.

14. *Properties*

(1) Prizes for winners of costumes.
(2) Paper prepared for each couple for Golf for the Beginner.
(3) Cards for Addition.

chapter 46

Thanksgiving Party

THANKSGIVING SEASON IS A TIME WHEN WE WANT TO GET TOGETHER for a party. Have it either on Thanksgiving Eve, Thanksgiving Day, or Friday, or Saturday following. It might be advisable to plan it after Thanksgiving so that those who are away at college could have time to return and be present.

1. *Decorations.*—In planning decorations it would be well to remember that Thanksgiving typifies the harvest season. Corn, pumpkins, fruit, and vegetables could be used for decorations. Autumn leaves could also add greatly to the attractiveness of the setting. There are many kinds of crepe paper that are made especially for Thanksgiving decorations. Turkeys, pictures of the Pilgrim Fathers, or Indian pictures may be used for decorations.

2. *Invitation.*—The following is a suggestion for an invitation:

> To our Thanksgiving Party
> We want to invite you,
> The things that we've planned
> We're sure will delight you.
> Turkeys and Red Men,
> Pilgrim Fathers and football,
> Will help to amuse you,
> Making sport for us all.
> Time and Place

3. *Mixer: Football Teams.*—Pin on the back of each guest the name of a football team, such as Florida, Georgia, Vanderbilt, Tennessee, Alabama, U.C.L.A., Oklahoma, Princeton, Army, Navy, Notre Dame. They are told not to let anyone see what is pinned on their backs. The leader then tells the guests that they are to try to

see how many names they can get on their lists, at the same time trying to keep anyone else from seeing what is written on their own back. Require them also to get the name and the color of the eyes of the person whose word they get. Let this continue for five or six minutes, and then have them count the number they have, giving a prize to the one who has the largest number.

4. *Story of Thanksgiving.*—Thanksgiving to God for blessings received had its beginning with the ancient Jews. They left their homes and dwelt for a week in booths made from the branches of palm, olive, or myrtle trees. The Greeks had a Thanksgiving day called the Feast of Demeter. The Romans observed a day in honor of Ceres, the fabled goddess of cornfields and gardens. In Old England the Harvest Home festival was observed at the full of the September moon. It was as popular a celebration as Christmas in England, and Queen Elizabeth ordered that there should be no servile labor performed on this day.

In the autumn of 1621 in the Plymouth colony the Pilgrim Fathers, after they had gathered their meager harvests, set aside a time of thanksgiving. Governor Bradford sent out four men to shoot game, and they came in heavily laden with wild game, principally wild turkey.

The friendly Indians, under Massasoit their chief, were invited to participate in the celebration, which they did, ninety of them coming and joining in the festivities. As only one hundred and forty persons were present, there were more Indians than whites. The Indians sent out hunters and killed five deer. So with venison, turkey, duck, geese, and a variety of fish, it was a feast indeed.

While it was primarily set aside as a time to thank God for the blessings given, it was a time of festivity and entertainment as well. It was a whole week of festivities, feasting, target practice, and Indian sports. The Pilgrim Fathers, thought to be so stern and unattractive, entered into the feasting, games, and war play of the red men, and joined in the helpful recreations throughout the week.

Thanksgiving as a custom spread to the other colonies, but was not nationally observed until President Lincoln issued a proclamation, setting aside the last Thursday in November as Thanksgiving Day and calling upon the people of the nation to observe it as a day of Thanksgiving to Almighty God for blessings received.

5. *The Landing of the Pilgrims.*[1]—Have someone read or recite the poem by Felecia Dorothea Hemans, "The Landing of the Pilgrim Fathers":

> The breaking waves dashed high,
>   On a stern and rockbound coast,
> And the woods against a stormy sky
>   Their giant branches tossed.
>
> And the heavy night hung dark
>   The hills and waters o'er,
> When a band of exiles moored their bark
>   On a wild New England shore.
>
> Not as the conqueror comes
>   They, the true-hearted, came;
> Not with the roll of stirring drums,
>   And the trumpet that sings of fame.
>
> Not as the flying come,
>   In silence and in fear—
> They shook the depths of the desert gloom
>   With their hymns of lofty cheer.
>
> Amidst the storm they sang,
>   And the stars heard and the sea:
> And the sounding aisles of the dim woods rang
>   With the anthem of the free.
>
> The ocean eagle soared
>   From his nest by the white wave's foam:
> And the rocking pines in the forest roared—
>   This was their welcome home.
>
> There were men with hoary hair
>   Amidst that pilgrim band:

[1] From *The Children's Hour*, Vol. IX. Houghton Mifflin Co. Used by permission.

314

Why had they come to wither there,
Away from their childhood's land?

There was woman's fearless eye,
Lit by deep love's truth;
There was manhood's brow serenely high
And the fiery heart of youth.

What sought they thus afar?
Bright jewels of the mine?
The wealth of seas, the spoils of war?—
They sought a faith's pure shrine.

Ay, call it holy ground,
The soil where first they trod:
They have left unstained what there they found—
Freedom to worship God.

6. *Apple Race: Relay.*—Divide into two or more groups, depending upon the number of guests. Have an equal number on each group. If there are two groups, they line up in two lines facing each other. A chair is placed at each end of each line. On the chairs at the head of the line are placed six apples on each chair. Each player in the line grasps the right wrist of the player on his right with the left hand. The first player in the line picks up an apple from the chair with his free right hand and puts it into the right hand of the party to the right, whose wrist he holds. It must be passed down the line this way, and if it falls, it must be picked up without those in the line breaking their hold. In other words all must stoop to pick it up. When all the apples have been passed down and are on the chair at the other end of the line, the person on the other end of the line starts them back. The object is to see who can get them all back first. Divide the apples among the winning team, washing them first so that they can eat them.

7. *Follow the Leader.*—Each player is given a sheet of paper and a pencil and some colored crayons. The leader then asks them to prepare for a drawing lesson. The leader begins marking on his paper and tells the guests he is drawing a picture of the "Landing of the Pilgrims," and as he draws he describes the "Mayflower,"

which they are to try to draw from his description. The leader should give the students plenty of time to draw and not rush the scene. He should then describe the Plymouth Rock. Some description of the scenery along the coast, the shape of the harbor, and the Indians may be given. Give a prize to the one who draws the best picture.

8. *Eggshell Football.*—Cover a table with white paper and mark off a football field. Goals may be made by driving nails down on each end of the field. Prick a small hole in an egg and empty its contents. There should be two or three eggshells in reserve in case one or more are broken. These eggshells may be painted like a football if desired.

A referee is chosen, and he places the ball in the center of the field. There should be about three players from each side blowing at the same time. One of these could be at the end of the table and one on each side of the table from both teams. When the ball goes out of bounds, the referee picks it up and places it down near the place where it went off. Players do not start to blow until the whistle is blown, or they may be penalized for being off side. A goal will count six. Change every two minutes and put in six new players. There should be a lot of rooting at this game, and it will be found to be very interesting and lively.

9. *Thanksgiving Menu.*—The players should be asked to suggest a Thanksgiving menu, each item of which will begin with a letter in Thanksgiving. The following is a suggestion:

T—Turkey.	G—Grits.
H—Hominy.	I—Ice cream.
A—Applesauce.	V—Vinegar.
N—Noodles.	I—Iced tea.
K—Kraut.	N—Nuts.
S—Sugar.	G—Grapes.

A prize may be given for the quickest, another for the most balanced menu.

10. *Turkey Hunt.*—Before the party starts, hide small turkeys

over the room. These may be purchased at a bookstore or novelty store or cut out of brown paper or cardboard. Tell the guests that they are all going turkey hunting and then tell them about the hidden turkeys. There will be a mad scramble to find them. After about five minutes blow the whistle and give a prize to the one finding the largest number.

11. *Archery Contest.*—As the Pilgrim Fathers were entertained by Indian sports, an Archery Contest will not be out of place. Cut out turkeys, rabbits, ducks, and deer from cardboard. These can be made to stand on the floor or on a chair by using a spring clothespin and clamping the animal with the pin and laying the pin on its side. Set all four of these animals on the floor or on a chair and line up the guests as for a relay race. Have two bows and sets of arrows. Give each one two trials and allow four points for every deer, three for every turkey, two for every duck, and one for every rabbit hit. Have a score marker for each side.

12. *Indian Drum Race.*—Line up in two lines facing each other. Keep the same divisions as for the other competitive games. One side may be called the Indians and the other the Pilgrims. One person is blindfolded and beats a drum. A dishpan may be substituted, although a trap drum is better. One of the players is given a tin can like a baking powder can, with rocks in it so that it will rattle. As long as the drummer keeps beating, the rattle passes back and forth. The line caught with it when the drum stops loses, while the other side wins five points. When the drum starts again, the rattle moves on. Continue the game not longer than five or ten minutes. A piano may be substituted for the drum.

13. *Feeding the Turkey.*—Choose one couple from each group and have the boy and girl sit facing each other. The girl is given a paper bag with twelve peanuts in it. At a signal from the leader she is to open the bag, shell the peanuts, and feed them to her partner. The others look on and root for their side. The couple that finishes first wins for its side and should receive a prize.

14. *Day of Thanksgiving.*—Each guest is given a piece of paper on which is written, "Day of Thanksgiving." Each one is asked to write

from the letters in the words of "Day of Thanksgiving" a list of things for which he is thankful. The ones who have the largest list will be asked to read them. If there is any question about any word being a cause for thanksgiving, the reader must explain why he is thankful for that particular thing. This will cause a lot of merriment. The following are some words that may be made: day, tank, hay, hat, night, oats, goats, sinks, skin, gag, fats, dogs, kin, kith, faith, nags, fogs, dots, soda, sofa, things, Katy, fan, sand, vision, sight, gain, and many others.

15. *Refreshments.*—Serve pumpkin pie and coffee. Another suggestion would be plum pudding with hot chocolate. Apples and popcorn balls make a good combination.

16. *Properties*

(1) Names of well-known football teams, written out with a typewriter to pin on backs of all guests.

(2) Twelve apples for Apple Race: Relay.

(3) Pencils, crayons, and sheets of blank paper for Follow the Leader.

(4) Two or more emptied eggshells for footballs, paper-covered table, nail goals.

(5) Paper and pencils for Thanksgiving Menu.

(6) Turkeys cut out of brown paper or cardboard. These may be purchased at bookstore or novelty store. These are for Turkey Hunt.

(7) Two bows and at least four arrows for Archery Contest. Also two deer, two turkeys, two ducks, and two rabbits cut out of cardboard and stood up with spring clothespins for targets.

(8) Trap drum, baking power can with pebbles in it, and blindfold for Drum Race.

(9) Two paper bags with twelve peanuts in each for Feeding Turkey.

(10) Slips of paper with Day of Thanksgiving written at the top.

chapter 47

Kid Party

(COSTUME)

THIS PARTY IS SUITABLE FOR A LARGE GROUP, ESPECIALLY A YOUNG people's conference, and it has been used successfully with such a group. The costumes will in themselves make the evening enjoyable. The thought that each one is expected to be a child and act like a child will be conducive to having a good time.

1. *Invitation.*—An invitation similar to the following one may be sent out:

> Backward, turn backward
> O Time, in your flight,
> And let's be kids again
> Next Friday night.
> We'll all meet at Jones',
> On Twenty-first Street,
> Dressed up like kiddies
> From heads to feet.
> Backward, turn backward,
> O Time, in your flight,
> And meet me at Jones'
> Next Friday night.

2. *Decorations.*—Some suggestions for decorations would be balloons suspended from the ceiling or tied to the electric fan so that it will blow them around. Have lollipops hanging around so that guests can find them. Crepe paper in bright colors will also aid in decoration.

3. *Costumes.*—Any kind of children's clothes or imitation of them would be suitable. Short dresses or shorts would be suitable for

girls. Another suggestion for girls would be to dress like babies, with some kind of improvised baby dress. Also they might dress like a schoolgirl with ribbons in the hair. Suggestions for boys would be short trousers, overalls, and barefooted.

4. *Judging Costumes.*—Three judges should be selected to judge the costumes. Prizes should be given for the best girl costume and the best boy costume. This may be done by the judges by eliminating all but a few of the best and let the group decide from these which is the best by cheering each one separately. The costume that gets the biggest hand will be the winner.

5. *Mixer.*—The group forms a line, one behind the other. The game is something like Follow the Leader or the Foolish Grand March. The leader runs or walks for a moment in the ordinary way, then changes and hops, skips, and jumps. All the others must follow the leader's example.

As a conclusion to this all join hands, and the leader winds up the group. This is called the "Spiral." The leader may then turn and reverse and unwind the group and let them again form a line around the room.

6. *Beanbag Scramble.*—Beanbags are placed on the floor as the group stands in a circle. There should be one less beanbag than players. Lively music should be played, and all should march around in a circle until the music stops. When the music stops all scramble for the beanbags. The player who fails to get a bag is out. The bags are again placed in the center, but one is taken away. Again they scramble, and the one who fails to get one is dropped. If it is desirous to speed up this game, more than one bag may be removed at a time. Finally there will be only two with one bag. Give a prize to the one who gets the last bag.

7. *The Doll Shop.*—One guest is shopkeeper and another the customer. The purpose of the game is to divide the party into two groups and at the same time provide a lot of action and fun for all. All of the guests are dolls and may be brought out and displayed at the will of the shopkeeper. All must be displayed before the game ends. The customer tells the shopkeeper that he wants to buy some

dolls, but that he does not want silly dolls that grin all the time. He wants solemn dolls. The shopkeeper argues that it is the mark of good breeding for a doll to smile. The object is for the shopkeeper to make the person who is being displayed as a doll to smile. If he succeeds, that person will remain on his side. If he cannot be made to smile in about thirty seconds, the customer gets him. The shopkeeper may go through all kinds of antics to make the player smile, such as making him or her to say Mamma and Papa or tickling the doll under the chin or saying crazy things about them. If the shopkeeper has a strong imagination and a sense of humor, this can be made extremely funny. When all have been displayed and the groups divided, have a tug of war. This may be done by the shopkeeper and the customer joining hands and all the dolls catching each other around the waist or by the shoulders and trying to pull the other group across a line.

8. *Balloon Ball.*—Balloon Ball is played with balloons for the balls. A line is stretched across the room about eight feet from the floor. The party is divided into two groups or teams. Two or three balloons are given to the players, and when the signal is given they start tossing them in the air, trying to toss them across the line and make them fall on the floor on the other side of the line. If they succeed in doing this, they receive a score of five points. It does not count when the balloon strikes the floor and has not been thrown over the line. A player may pick up the balloon and put it in play again. If a balloon breaks, it will count five points against the team in whose territory it was broken. Divide into three- or five-minute halves or quarters.

9. *Children's Games*—As this is a children's party, some of the old-time children's games may be used.

Drop the Handkerchief.—A circle is formed, and one person is given a handkerchief. He drops this behind someone in the circle. If that one can catch the one who drops the handkerchief before he gets back around the circle and into the place vacated, the one caught must go inside the circle. Those inside the circle have the privilege of grabbing the handkerchief when it is dropped behind one in the circle and chasing the one who dropped it.

Farmer in the Dell. As the words are sung, the action described in them takes place. The players stand in a circle with one on the inside of the circle to represent the farmer. At the singing of the second verse the farmer chooses a wife, at the third verse the wife chooses someone for the child, and so on until the lines, "The rat takes a cheese" are sung, at which time the game breaks up by all clapping their hands and shouting. If there is plenty of room, as when the game is played on the lawn, another verse may be added, "The cheese stands alone," and when all start singing this verse, all chase the cheese, and the one who succeeds in catching the cheese becomes the farmer when the game is played again. The words to to the song are as follows:

> The farmer in the dell,
> The farmer in the dell;
> Heigh-o, the merry oh,
> The farmer in the dell.

> The farmer takes a wife,
> The farmer takes a wife;
> Heigh-o, the merry oh,
> The farmer takes a wife.

Other verses are:

> The wife takes a child.
> The child takes a nurse.
> The nurse takes a cat.
> The cat takes a rat.
> The rat takes a cheese.
> The cheese stands alone.

Going to Jerusalem. Two lines of chairs are placed back to back. There is one less chair than players. Music plays as all march around chairs. When the music stops, all try to get a chair. One is left out. Take away another chair and continue until all are left out one at a time, as the leader takes away a chair every time the music stops. If it takes too long to play the game in this way, take away more than one chair at a time.

Last Couple Out. Couples line up one behind the other. One is in front and calls out, "Last couple out." The couple in the rear runs toward the front and tries to join hands before the leader catches them. If the caller is a boy, he tries to catch the girl. If a girl, she tries to catch the boy. If he suceeds, the one caught becomes his partner, and they take their places at the front of the line, and the other one becomes the caller. This is better played on the lawn than in the house, but it could be used in a large recreation room.

The Cat and the Mouse. The players all form a circle with the exception of two. One of these is the cat and the other the rat. The rat is inside the circle and the cat outside. The cat meows and starts to chase the rat. The players are to aid the rat and try to prevent the cat from catching the rat. They raise their arms for the rat to go through and bar the passage of the cat with them. When the rat is caught, he chooses one from the circle to become the cat. He himself takes a place in the circle, while the one who was the cat becomes the rat.

10. *Kiddie Car Race.*—Get two or more kiddie cars and select some of the boys for a Kiddie Car Race. This will be very amusing, and there will be rooting for the different individuals in the race.

11. *Balloon Race.*—Get some barrel hoops for goals. Strings should be tied to the balloons and small sandbags fastened to the strings so that the balloons will not be entirely blown away. Each player is provided with a fan, and with the fan he must by fanning the balloon make it go through the goal. Of course this game may be played with a large number of players, and the more the better.

12. *Blind Man's Wand.*—All players join hands and form a circle. One player, provided with a long stick for a wand, is in the center blindfolded. This stick should be from seven to nine feet in length, depending upon the size of the circle. Someone plays lively music, and all march around until the music stops. Then the blind man drops his wand, and the person on whom it falls must make some

noise like the barking of a dog, or the meowing of a cat, or must say something in a changed voice. If the blind man guesses who it is, the player must become the blind man. And so the game continues.

13. *Mimic.*—Two persons who know the game go into an adjoining room, and the guests are sent in one at a time. The doorkeeper tells the guests that they are to guess the name of the game that is being played—the name of the game, of course, is "Mimic." As the guest enters the room, the two persons there imitate everything that he does and say everything that he says. They imitate the way he stands, what he does with his hands, and so on. If he fails to guess the name of the game, which he probably will, they tell him what the name is, and he joins them in mimicking the next one brought in. As the number increases, the game becomes more ludicrous. If the room is small, some of the first ones who came in may leave to make room for those who come in last.

14. *Hopscotch Relay.*—Choose two or three players for this relay. Lay on the floor or ground three rows of sticks about two feet apart. Have about ten of these sticks in a row. The players hop to one end of the row and start back. One stick is taken away. When they reach the other end, another stick is taken away. And so on until the first player to hop over the last stick wins.

15. *Candy Scramble.*—Place bags of candy, lollipops, and small boxes of candy in the center of the floor. The players stand around in a circle and at the signal scramble for the candy. They proceed to eat the candy they get.

16. *Song Partners.*—Have the names of familiar songs written out in duplicate. Give one to the boys and the duplicate to the girls. At the signal from the leader all start singing or whistling their song. They try to find their partner who is whistling or singing the same song. This will create a lot of noise and fun. When partners are found, they cease singing.

17. *Refreshments.*—Serve ice-cream cones, animal cookies, and popcorn balls. If there is a fire, provide poppers and corn and let the guests pop their own corn. Toasted marshmallows would be another suggestion if there is a fire.

18. *Properties*

(1) Balloons, lollipops, crepe paper in bright colors.

(2) Prizes for best costumes.

(3) Beanbags for all but one guest.

(4) Cord stretched across room about one and one-half feet from ceiling for Balloon Ball.

(5) Handkerchief, chairs, and music for Children's Games.

(6) Two or more kiddie cars for race.

(7) Balloons tied to small sandbags, barrel hoops, and a fan for each player for Balloon Race.

(8) Stick or wand from seven to nine feet long and blind fold.

(9) Thirty sticks for Hopscotch Relay.

(10) Candy for Candy Scramble.

(11) Song names in duplicate.

(12) Popcorn poppers and marshmallows, with stick to toast them.

chapter 48

Christmas Party

EVERY GROUP OF YOUNG PEOPLE, EVERY SUNDAY-SCHOOL CLASS, AND every society expects to have a party for Christmas. The following plan is suggested as an outline for an appropriate party for the occasion. While we should have a good time, we should not forget the real significance of the occasion. By all means there should be the singing of Christmas carols, which will bring some thought of the real significance of the occasion to the attention of the group.

1. *Invitations.*—The following is a suggestion for an invitation to the Christmas Party:

> Three nights before Christmas,
>   When all through the town,
> Wise men and wise women
>   Will be looking around
> For evenings of fun
>   And places of cheer,
> Don't look any further,
>   Come right over here.
> For Thursday at eight,
>   The time has been set;
> Bring a gift for another,
>   And see what you get.

Give the address of the place where the party is to be held.

2. *Decorations.*—Use red and green crêpe paper streamers. Have bells hanging from the light fixtures. Use holly and mistletoe. There should be a Christmas tree with artificial snow and icicles and lighted with small electric lights. Evergreen plants will add to the beauty of the setting.

3. *Opening Mixer: Christmas Toy.*—Pin on the back of each guest the name of a Christmas toy. These cards on which the name of the toy is written should be numbered, and when the person has learned what toy he represents, the card should be transferred and pinned in front, and each one will thus be numbered. This is important, as the Christmas gifts later will be given by number. The game proceeds in the following manner: On the cards have been written names of toys, such as top, toy airplane, woolly dog, electric train, jumping jack, horn, pop gun, mama doll, toy automobile, tin soldier, building blocks, scooter bike, erector set, tinker toys, toy boat, jack-in-the-box, football, basketball, baseball bat, and so on. When these have been pinned on each guest's back, he then tries to learn what toy he represents by asking questions. All questions must be answered "yes" or "no," and the answers are to be correctly given. A guest may ask, "Am I an active toy?" If that person is a top, the answer would be "Yes." But if that person is a woolly dog, the answer would be "No." The guest may ask, "Am I an automobile?" "Am I a jumping jack?" and so on. When a guest has learned what he represents, he may transfer his card from his back and take his seat. When all have learned what they represent or the game has lasted long enough, the leader blows the whistle and asks all to be seated, and has all names transferred to the front, together with the numbers, which are to be retained.

4. *The Doll Shop.*—All the even numbers are placed on one side and the odd numbers on the other. Two persons are selected from the even number group to be the shopkeepers, and two persons are selected from the odd number group to be the doll shoppers. After the game has been played for five or six minutes, depending on how much time the leader wishes to take up with it, a change is made, and the odd group become the shopkeepers and the even group the doll shoppers, and an equal amount of time should be allowed the odd group. The object of the game is to see who can have the largest number on their side when the time is up. The game proceeds in the following manner: The buyers come to the doll shop and say they are interested in buying some dolls. They do not want dolls that are too serious. All the dolls that they take must be laughing, giggling dolls. The shopkeeper then demonstrates his dolls, which are the persons on his side. They walk with stiff legs and try to imitate dolls. The purchaser asks questions about them such as, "Will this doll go to sleep?" "Does this doll say 'Mama'?" The shopkeeper must demonstrate by making the doll say "Mama." Any other crazy question may be asked by the shopper, and if the doll laughs, he gets it. If the doll remains serious, he goes back to his side and another is demonstrated. After sides have been changed and the odd side has had an equal amount of time, a prize may be given to the winning side, such as a small jar of candy, or a bag of peanuts, or something that can be divided among the players on the group.

5. *The Same to You.*—Players are seated in a circle, and one is in the center. The one in the center points to a player in the circle and says, "Merry Christmas to you." The person thus addressed must say "The same to you" before the one in the center has finished. If he fails to do so, he must take the place of the person in the center. Also, if the person in the circle says "The same to you" without the one in the center saying "Merry Christmas to you," he must also take his place. This will result many times if the leader will quickly point to someone in the circle without saying anything. That person, anticipating that the leader will say "Merry Christmas to you," will say "The same to you."

6. *Hang Up the Christmas Stocking.*—This is played like all similar games, such as pinning the tail on the donkey, putting the shamrock in Ireland, and so forth. A mantel has been drawn on a sheet with crayons or lamp black. A place is marked for the stocking. Each guest is blindfolded and turned around and must walk to the mantel and pin the stocking the first place he touches. Give a prize to the one who gets the stocking nearest to the right place.

7. *Christmas Charades.*—Divide the company in four groups. This may be done by using the numbers already pinned on the guests. Start with one and add four each time as, 1, 5, 9, 13, 17, 21, 25, would form one group, 2, 6, 10, 14, 18, 22 another, 3, 7, 11, 15, 19, 23 another, and 4, 8, 12, 16, 20, 24 another. Let numbers 1, 2, 3, 4 be

the leaders of their groups. This could be arranged by giving these numbers to individuals who are capable of leadership and have given some thought to what they are going to do. Each group is to give a charade that will represent some phase of the Christmas spirit. Some suggestions would be the following: The coming of the angels, the shepherds visit the manger and the child, the coming of the Wise Men, decorating a Christmas tree, Christmas shopping, wrapping Christmas packages, standing in line to mail Christmas packages, addressing Christmas cards, opening Christmas packages, singing Christmas carols, and so forth. Each group in turn presents its charade, and the others try to guess what it represents.

8. *Christmas Nuts to Crack.*—

(1) A nut made from cream? Butternut.
(2) A seashore nut? Beachnut.
(3) A vegetable nut? Peanut.
(4) A nut that is the side of a room? Walnut.
(5) What nut should be given to bad children? Hickory nut.
(6) What nut is uncooked bread? Doughnut.
(7) A nut imported from South America? Brazil nut.
(8) A nut named after a girl? Hazel nut.
(9) A nut popular in Ohio? Buckeye.
(10) What nut is a canned vegetable? Pecan.
(11) What nut is a box? Chestnut.
(12) What nut is a hot drink? Coconut.
(13) Your answer when the check says, "What are you going to do with me?" Cashew.
(14) What nut is on your foot? A corn.

9. *Snowball Relay.*—Make some snowballs out of cotton about the size of a potato or tennis ball. Draw circles on the floor and put six snowballs in each circle. Players line up facing the circles. There may be either two or four lines, depending upon the size of the group. If there are two, they may be divided by the even and odd numbers given, or if there are four, they may be divided as already suggested for dividing for charades. At the sound of the leader's whistle the first player runs to the circle, picks up the snowballs one at a time and puts them outside of the circle; the next one must put them back. Each player, as he completes moving the balls, runs back and touches the person in the front of the line and takes his place at the back. The line that finishes first wins.

11. *Exchanging Christmas Bells.*—Each guest is given five or ten small bells cut out of red cardboard. They are given five or ten minutes in which to trade, that is, in which to attempt to get a larger number of bells. This is done by asking questions, and any person who answers either "yes" or "no" to any question must give up a bell to the one asking the question. A prize may be given to the one having the largest number of bells. Another way to use this game is not to have any definite time for it, but to give out the bells to the guest and let it run throughout the evening. Do not give them out, however, until after the first game.

12. *Hidden Christmas Bells.*—Bells cut out of green cardboard may be hidden about the room, and upon announcement by the leader guests may hunt for the bells. The one finding the largest number of bells wins the prize.

13. *Christmas Stagecoach.*—This is played like the game of Stage-coach. One person reads the Christmas poem, " 'Twas the Night Before Christmas" as the other players sit in a circle with all chairs full. The players are given words in advance, for example, house, mouse, reindeer, stockings, toys, and so forth. As the poem is read, the one who has the word must get up and turn around. At any time the person who is reading may yell "Santa Claus," and when he does so, all must change seats. If the leader secures a seat, the one left over becomes the reader.

14. *Candle Relay.*—Divide the company into two or four groups, depending upon its size. Line up facing four chairs placed in front of each line and about twenty-five or thirty feet in front of each line. Each person in the front of the lines is given a candle and some matches. When the leader's whistle blows, this person must first light the candle, and then run with it around the chair. If the candle is extinguished, the player must stop until it is relighted. The

group first getting all their players around the chair carrying the lighted candle wins.

15. *Christmas Presents.*—These have been brought by each guest and placed on the tree and numbered. The number should be concealed, or perhaps it would be better to have the presents put in a basket and numbered by the leader and then have the basket brought in just before time to give out the presents. Of course there will be a lot of crazy presents. These should be inexpensive, with nothing costing more than a dollar. As the numbers are called, the one holding that number comes up and gets his package and opens it and plays with it. This will cause a lot of fun. These presents are given out by number, using the numbers that have been pinned on at the beginning of the party on the toy card.

16. *Singing Christmas Carols.*—Near the close of the party all guests should gather around the piano and sing Christmas carols. This may be done by a group of the best voices concealed behind a curtain or in an adjoining room. A solo, such as someone singing "Silent Night," would be appropriate.

17. *Choosing Partners for Refreshments.*—The boys and girls are separated and sent into different rooms. The boys remain in the larger room, and the girls are sent into an adjoining room. Two persons have a list of active toys, and this list is whispered one at a time into the ears of the girls, while the same list is whispered to the boys. In other words, each boy and each girl is given the name of an active toy, so that one boy and one girl will have the same toy. Such toys as jumping jack, top, toy engine, airplane, toy auto, jack-in-the-box, toy phonograph, hand organ, toy accordion, and so on. The girls are brought in either one, two, or three at a time, or the whole group is brought in at once. It is better, however, to bring them in in groups of about three or four. The boys then imitate the toys they represent, and the girls are supposed to find their partners from the imitation of the toy. In other words, the girl that has been named Jumping Jack must try to find the boy that is trying to imitate a jumping jack.

18. *Refreshments.*—The following are suggestions for refresh-

ments: Coffee and sandwiches, Christmas cookies cut in star shapes. Another suggestion would be coffee and fruit cake with red and green candies.

19. *Properties*

(1) Each guest should bring an inexpensive gift. (The hostess should have a few extra, in case someone forgets to bring his present, or unexpected guests appear.)

(2) Names of toys written on cards, and these numbered, to pin on the backs of guests at the beginning of the party.

(3) Sheet with mantel drawn on it, pins, and stockings for Christmas Stockings.

(4) Typewritten copies, or mimeographed copies, of Christmas Nuts to Crack.

(5) Twenty cotton snowballs for relay.

(6) Enough small bells cut from red cardboard to give five or ten to each guest.

(7) Bells cut from green cardboard and hidden about the room.

(8) Poem " 'Twas the Night Before Christmas."

(9) Four candles and matches for Candle Relay.

(10) Song sheets or books and someone to play Christmas carols.

(11) List of toys for choosing partners.

chapter *49*

Box Supper and Cakewalk

A GOOD WAY TO MAKE SOME MONEY AND AT THE SAME TIME HAVE A pleasant evening is to have a Box Supper and Cakewalk. Such an affair must be carefully planned and organized, as its success depends almost entirely on what is done in advance.

There are two things which are absolutely necessary to the success of such an affair: First, plenty of girls to pack boxes and make cakes; second, plenty of boys to buy the boxes and take part in the cakewalk.

The first thing that should be done by any organization that is planning a Box Supper and Cakewalk is to appoint a committee to solicit boxes. There should be at least five on this committee, and its duty should be not only to solicit plenty of boxes, but it should be charged with the responsibility of getting boys there. If the organization is small and it is thought possible to have as many as twenty-five boxes, give the committee all the available girls' names, say seven, to each member of the committee. If the organization is large, divide out the available names among the five members of the committee and have each one seen individually. It might be advisable to enlarge the committee if the number of available girls is large. The girls should not only be pledged to bring a box, but should be pledged to bring someone to buy a box. This might be a husband, father, brother, sweetheart, or uncle. But the important thing is to have someone there to buy every box. There are usually several young women in every organization who do not ordinarily have an escort, and should a large number of these prepare boxes and there be no one to buy them, it would be embarrassing.

A large room is needed for this party. If there is not a home with a room large enough available, use a recreation room in the church.

When the boxes are all in, get some clever person to auction them off. There are three ways that this may be done:

1. *Incognito.* The boxes may be auctioned off without those who bid knowing whose box they bid on. The only thing they have to judge by is the size and beauty of the boxes. It is taken for granted that every girl will try to decorate her box and make it look as nice as possible.

2. *Identifying the owner.* Sometimes it adds interest to know the name of the one who packed the box. For example, suppose John Jones is particularly crazy about Mary Brown. The auctioneer says that he is selling Mary Brown's box. Immediately John Jones bids on it. One boy says to another. "Let's make him pay three dollars for it." So they start bidding against him, for they know that the one who buys Mary Brown's box gets to eat the good things in it with Mary. This little bit of competition makes the auction more interesting.

3. *A combination.* Sell some of the boxes, telling whom they belong to—especially those belonging to regular couples, and others who give their consent—and sell the others incognito.

After the boxes have all been sold, all the couples eat together. No box should be sold for less than one dollar, as it probably will cost a girl almost this much to pack a real good dinner. The boxes should bring from one to three dollars. It would be well to provide card tables or other tables to eat from. Also provide coffee or other drink to go with the meal.

4. *Cakewalk.* Five or six girls have been asked to bake cakes for the cakewalk. Tickets are sold for the cakewalk for ten or fifteen cents. As many as twelve or fifteen tickets at least should be sold for each cake, as each cake should bring more than one dollar. Those who have bought tickets take part in the walk while the others look on. If forty persons are present and the tickets are

sold for fifteen cents, you might sell ten tickets for each of four walks, thus making four cakes bring six dollars.

Suppose you have ten for the cakewalk. Let them stand in a circle around the room. Music is played as they march around. A person, blindfolded, stands in the center of the circle with a long stick, like a bamboo. When the leader's whistle blows, all stop and the person blindfolded drops his stick. The person on whom it falls gets the cake. This performance is repeated until all cakes are gone.

The auction, the eating, and the cakewalks will consume the evening, and no other games will be necessary.

chapter 50

Street Carnival

A GOOD WAY TO MAKE MONEY FOR ANY WORTHY ENTERPRISE IS TO have a Street Carnival. The church basement or recreation room would be the proper place to have such an event. An ideal place would be a room that had small rooms cut off so that they could be used for the different events. There should be rooms for the side shows, food booths, fortune teller, animals, and so forth. The following suggestions will be helpful in planning such an evening.

1. *Advertising.*—The first thing that will be necessary is to thoroughly advertise the Carnival. Large posters should be prepared and placed in prominent places bearing some such as the following signs, with pictures if possible: "Street Carnival, Friday Evening, October 10. A lot of fun for all. Admission, 25 cents." "Big Street Carnival Tuesday night at eight o'clock. Come one, come all. Under the auspicies of the _____ Club. Admission, 15 cents." Any other similar advertising should be used. The newspapers should have two or three stories about it. It would be well to have a committee to handle the publicity alone.

2. *The Museum.*—Have one booth arranged as a museum. A charge of admission of 5 or 10 cents should be made. Some of the following may be placed in the museum: September Morn (a card bearing the date September 1, 5 A.M.; the light of the World (a box of matches) ; a collection of marble (just some marbles) ; some things out of King Tut's tomb (anything that has never been in King Tut's tomb) ; the Home of Burns (use a smoothing iron) ; Portrait of Penn (a picture of writing pen) ; the Watch on the Rhine (a watch on an orange peel) ; a twelve Carat Ring (make

this with a dozen carrots placed in a circle) ; the One-Eyed Monster (a sewing needle) .

3. *Fortune-Telling Booth.*—The person operating this booth should be dressed as a gypsy or Hindu and should be clever enough to put it over. There are several ways that this may be done. Printed fortunes may be gotten from some book on the subject, or some study of palmistry may be made in advance. The person who is running the booth must be clever at extemporizing.

Fortunes may be written on sheets of white paper with lemon juice, using a penholder and pen point. You will find that this makes an excellent invisible ink. When this slip of paper is held over a lighted candle, the writing will plainly appear. The fortunes suggested in another part of this book may be used.

4. *For Men Only.*—The booth for men only should be an attraction for the ladies. But it may be required that when women are admitted they have to go in in pairs or be accompained by a gentleman friend. The booth merely contains articles used exclusively by men. A razor, men's trousers, leather belt, socks, tie, and so on.

5. *For Women Only.*—The men should be admitted only in pairs or with a lady. The booth contains articles used exclusively by women such as a dress, hose, high-heeled shoes, lipstick, and so forth. A small admission should be charged.

6. *The Monkey Cage.*—This booth should have several large mirrors hung in it. There should be some signs in it, such as the following: "Monkey Cage. If you don't believe it, look and see."

7. *The Girl Who Eats and Sleeps under Water.*—You may give some high-sounding name to this lady, such as Madam Marvel. A bucket of water is suspended from the ceiling and the girl is seated under the bucket of water on a chair. For the amusement of the guests she eats a bite of some food, says a few words, and places her head on her hands and pretends to sleep.

8. *Wild Animals and Birds.*—Select people with names of animals and birds for this booth, such as Mr. Fox, Miss Lyon, Mrs. Wolf, and so on. Other names that are common are Hare, Bear,

Beaver, Crabb. Names of birds are Crow, Drake, Sparrow, Hawk, Martin. If it is not possible to get people with these names, pictures of people in the city with such names may be used and the names written under the picture.

It will add to the interest at this booth if there is someone on the inside, either with a musical instrument such as a trombone, or some apparatus contrived for that purpose, making noises to represent the roar of wild animals and the squawking of birds.

9. *Hawaiian Musicians.*—Have some musicians dress in Hawaiian manner. For the boys this would be only ordinary clothes with a necklace of paper cord about an inch in diameter around the neck. For the girls a grass skirt may be worn over a bathing suit. This may be improvised with crêpe paper. Have music and singing by this group. Usually it is possible to secure someone who will play Hawaiian music on a guitar.

10. *Freak Show.*—In this show you may find the Performing Dogs (links of wieners suspended from a string), the Tame Ground Hog (links of sausage); Swimming Match (match floating on water); the Milky Way (row of milk bottles); How Ford and Rockefeller made millions (tin, spark plug, and gasoline can). Also there may be the Wild Man, using burlap sacks for clothing; the Bearded Lady, using crêpe hair beard or Spanish moss for beard; and the Fat Man, using the largest person in the group and stuffing him with pillows.

11. *Food Booths.*—Quite a good deal may be realized from the sale of candy, ice-cream cones, sandwiches, coffee, and cake. If this is donated, all money received will be profit.

12. *The Grab Bag.*—A bag may be arranged in the entrance or some prominent place called the Grab Bag. Charge 10 cents a grab. You can say that some of the articles in the bag cost 50 cents or $2. Each person gets one grab and must take the first article he touches. Most of the articles must be of small value. Have only four or five articles that are valuable.

13. *Mystery Fish Pond.*—Use an ordinary fishing pole and attach for a hook a spring clothespin or other spring snap. Arrange a

curtain in such a way that the hook may be thrown over. This may be done over a partition. The customer snaps a dime for bait on to the hook and throws it over. The one in charge on the other side takes the dime and fastens a package on to the snap. Some of these articles may be of value as bait for other customers, but most of them must be valueless to assure a good profit.

14. *The Green Pig That Eats Human Food.*—Place a mirror in the bottom of a box about a foot square. Over this box have a large green light bulb and a yellow bulb on a double socket. Charge 5 cents admission to see this show. The person looks in the box and sees his reflection in the green mirror.

15. *Side Show.*—Have the horse with his tail where his head ought to be. This is done by placing a toy horse, or sawhorse, arranging it so that his tail is in the food trough or hay manger. Variations of this is the cat with his tail where his head ought to be, using a toy cat and placing its tail in a saucer of milk. Another variation is the man with his hands where his feet ought to be, and the man sits with his hands in a pair of shoes. In the side show you might have a trip around the world. Take customers around a globe that sits on a table. You might also have the snake charmer, in which act a girl plays with toy snakes.

16. *A Trip to Mars.*—The customers are blindfolded and led into the entrance of the road to Mars. Along the route they are rocked and turned in chairs, swung in swings, made to climb out of a narrow window, pass through a narrow passage, climb a ladder, and come down a slide. This slide may be arranged from a window. Care should be taken to arrange such a trip so that it will not be dangerous.

17. *The House of Horrors.*—A ghost should do the ballyhooing for this booth. The room should be numbered 13 and should be dark. Customers are required to walk over boxes, mattresses, platforms on small rollers, up steps that fall when one steps on them. They find their way by holding to a rope or cord and on this cord are tied various articles such as a chicken's foot, cotton, feather duster, pieces of fur, and so forth. The cord may pass through a

dish of macaroni which in the darkness will feel like worms. This will send the customer out screaming.

18. *The Ferris Wheel.*—At a church carnival, which I shall describe later, I saw the Ferris Wheel which I shall describe. It was strongly constructed with upright posts extending about ten feet from the ground. On either side two pieces of timber two by six inches were crossed and braced together. A hole was bored through the intersection of these timbers, and they were arranged so that they would revolve on the two-inch pipe placed on the upright posts. These two by sixes should be sixteen feet long. At each of the four ends of the timbers seats are hung on three-fourth-inch pipes so that they will revolve. The wheel must be strongly constructed. It is operated by three or four boys, and is particularly for the amusement of children. If strongly constructed, grown-ups may patronize it also.

19. *Free Show.*—In order to send those who attend away satisfied with the evening it will be necessary to have some free show acts that are good. Usually in every city there is someone who performs sleight-of-hand tricks, or someone who does acrobatic stunts, or tumbling stunts, or someone who performs on the horizontal bar, or trapeze, or plays a violin in some unusual way. Use any of such acts that can be secured for the free show.

20. *Whoopee Carnival.*—The following is the outline of the arrangements and program of a carnival that was held at one of our local churches. It was held in a vacant lot adjoining the church and booths were improvised mostly from boughs of trees.

An eight-page program was printed and paid for with advertising. The advertising more than paid for the printing, as the program occupied only a small part of each page. The following announcement and program was printed in the program book:

Fortieth and Spruce, Whoopee Carnival, Thursday and Friday, July 16 and 17. Opens at 7:30 P.M. Presented by the Young People's Division of the Northwood Church. Trapeze performance blindfolded fifteen feet in the air by a former instructor of flying gymnastics at DePauw University. Performance 8:25 and 10 free. Main Show: Bill Doherty and his Club

Atlantic Orchestra. Flors Percy, tap number. W. E. Dennis, negro spiritual. Will Rogers and King Arthur. Harry Brown, Xylophone Solo, Double Quartette, Song with banjo accompaniment by Billy McKendrick. Violin selections by Bill Doherty; song, Loren Denny; tap dance number. Side Shows: ten-year-old fat boy, weight 425 pounds, Fortune Telling, the Green Pig, Reducing Lady, Freak Man, Palm Reading, Fish Pond. Food Booths: All the watermelon you can eat for a dime, or five cents a slice. Hot Dogs, Pink Lemonade, Ice Cream, Cake, Pie, Candy, and Orangeade. A real Ferris Wheel, Balloons free. You can't afford to miss this. For young and old.

The following newspaper story was printed in a local paper the day following the Whoopee Carnival:

It was Whoopee Night last night in the vicinity of the Northwood Church, when the great Whoopee Carnival being staged by the young people of the church was open to the public for the first run. A huge crowd was there. Everybody was in gay spirits and took in everything that was offered, both in the way of entertainment and refreshments. The carnival runs again tonight. Besides the Main Show, which was a splendid program beginning at eight o'clock, there were two trapeze performances and side shows, including a ten-year-old fat boy weighing 450 pounds, fortune telling, a green pig, a reducing lady, a freak, palm reading, and fish pond. Then the Ferris Wheel attracted old folks and young alike, while the watermelon booth, where you could get a slice for a nickle and all you could eat for a dime, the ice-cream stand, the hot dog counter, and so on and so on, were busy places every minute of the evening.

The program was then given by the committees in charge. The young people of this church realized a great deal of profit from this carnival.

chapter 51

Vanishing Party

ONE OF THE MOST EFFECTIVE MONEY-RAISING PARTIES, OR RATHER series of parties, that we have ever seen tried is called a Vanishing Party. It means soliciting all the friends of an organization and securing a small donation from each, and at the same time giving them value received in social contacts.

Let us suppose that a group of women in a church, society, or club desires to raise $250. They decide to give a Vanishing Party. Five women meet for an afternoon tea, each of them bringing a donation of 25 cents. This will amount to $1.25. Each of these women decides to give a tea on each Wednesday for the next four Wednesdays to which they will each be willing to contribute 25 cents. The next Wednesday afternoon there would be five women, each entertaining four other women. This would be twenty-five women, each contributing 25 cents and would bring in $6.25. Each one of these twenty-five women then agrees to entertain on the following Wednesday afternoon three of her friends, asking each of them to bring 25 cents. This would be one hundred women and would bring in $25. Each of these one hundred women is asked on the following Wednesday afternoon to entertain two of her friends, asking each to bring 25 cents. This would be three hundred women and would bring in $75. Each one of these women is then asked to entertain on the following Wednesday afternoon one of her friends and each to bring 25 cents. This would be six hundred women and would bring in $150. This is a total of $275.50. The party then vanishes, having accomplished the desired results.

This can be set up on a larger scale by having six, seven, eight, nine or ten women start it off. It can be set up on a smaller scale, having a smaller number of women start it. It will put quite a burden on the hostess to serve and pay both, and so it might be decided that the hostess would not be required to pay when she served. This will reduce the amount of money to be realized.

Another form of giving these parties is to appoint two ladies to give the first tea. These ladies invite 5 each, and each brings 25 cents. These ladies then give a tea to five other ladies, and so continue until the amount has been raised. Each hostess must be responsible for looking after those whom she invited to see that they give their teas. In this manner you would obtain the following results:

If two invite five and the hostess pays as well, that would be 12x25 ...$ 3
These ten then invite five at 25 cents each; this would be 60x25 15
These 50 invite five at 25 each; this would be 300x25 75
These 250 invite five at 25 cents each; this would be 1,500x25 375
                                                                     ————
   Or a grand total of $468

If the hostesses do not pay, the above plan would bring in $390.

This plan has been used effectively by a number of organizations. A church in Miami, Florida, raised $3,500 by this method.

chapter 52

Surprise Party

AS WE COME TO THE LAST CHAPTER OF THIS VOLUME, WE FIND THAT we have arranged a party for almost every occasion of the year, but that we have not included a Surprise Party. In planning such a party, we have in mind such occasions as a surprise birthday party for a relative or friend, a party to welcome the return of friends, or a "Bon Voyage" party for friends who are going away or going on a journey. The atmosphere will probably be very informal and a "programme" party would not be strictly in order. Such an affair may take the form of a dinner, or at least a buffet supper. This might well be followed by a talkfest or informal stories told by each member of the group. One group leader asked members of the party to tell of their most embarrassing moment. Another leader asked members of the group to tell how they met their escort, wife, or husband.

1. *Invitations.*—There would be no formal invitations, and the guests would probably be informed of the gathering by telephone or at a meeting of the group when the guests to be surprised are not present. The honor guests should be invited to come over for the evening for some purpose and when they arrive, they will find the other guests assembled and will be in for a surprise. Or, an engagement could be made with the couple to be honored, to go to the movies, and when their hosts arrive to pick them up, they could be told that it would be necessary to return to the house for some fictitious reason. The house would be dark, but when they entered and turned on the lights, they would find the guests assembled. If, on the other hand, it is to be a dinner party or buffet supper, simply invite the honor guests and tell them that they will

344

be called for when dinner is ready. Wait until the other guests have arrived to go for the honor guests.

If there is more than one family participating in the surprise party, the dinner or refreshments could be arranged by different members of the group, one family bringing the meat dish, another salads, another the rolls and coffee, and another the dessert. The dinner could be served "pot luck" or "covered dish" style. If only refreshments are served, different members of the group may be assigned certain items on the refreshment menu.

The games or stunts that are suggested for this gathering have in them the element of surprise.

2. *Corks and Dice.*—Give each guest a cork on a string about one yard long. (Run the string through the cork with a darning needle, Tying the string at the end after it is run through, thus securing the cork.) Other properties needed for this game are a pair of dice and beans or matches to use as chips. When the game is played, the guests should be seated around a large table or if the guests do not object, the game could be played on the floor.

Each guest has his cork on a string and twelve beans or matches. The corks are all piled up in the center of the table, or in the center of the group on the floor, with each player holding the other end of the string. The person starting the game has a small saucepan and the dice. He rolls the dice in the saucepan and dumps them on the table or floor. If the leader throws either a seven or an eleven, all players must jerk their corks away. The leader tries to turn the saucepan over the pile of corks and hold them. If he catches a cork, that player must give up one of his chips. If the player jerks away his cork when no seven or eleven has been thrown, he must also give up a chip. After three throws the saucepan and dice are passed to the next person in the circle, the former leader taking his place with the other players. The game ends when any player has used up his chips. If it is desirable to continue, redistribute the chips and start again.

3. *Copycat.*—Each guest is given a saucer and told to hold it by the edge in front of him. He is told that he is to be a Copycat and

do whatever the leader does. The leader rubs underneath the center of her saucer, then goes through the following motions and says, "I touch my eyes, my nose, my cheeks, my chin." The guests are told to close their eyes and do the same. The bottom of all the saucers except the leader's have been blackened with candle flame, and it will cause some hilarity when all the guests open their eyes and see that the others are spotted with black. Allow a little time to remove the damage and go on with the next surprise.

4. *Feeding Time at the Zoo.*—This will be a real icebreaker. Ask all the guests to kneel in a circle. Place an apple, cupcake, or a candy bar in the center of the circle. Tell the guests that you are going to give out the names of animals and that two guests will have the same name, and that when the name of that animal is called, both of those with that name are to try to grab the prize. Then have two persons who are in on the game pass around the circle and give the names. The catch is that all are whispered the same name, as for example, "Tiger." When the leader calls "Tiger," there will be a mad scramble of the entire group to get the prize.

5. *Mary, Where Are You?*—Arrange the guests in couples and seat the ladies in chairs. It is best if the chairs are in a circle around the room. The men stand beside the chairs. The leader tells the men that they are to leave the room and upon their return will be blindfolded and must try to find their partners. After the men have left the room, the leader asks the ladies to change chairs. To add to the fun the leader may give each lady the name of an animal whose voice she is to try to imitate to help her escort locate her, for she is not allowed to talk at all. The men may be brought in one at a time, or they may be brought in in groups. The game may end when the first man finds his partner or the first group find their partners, or it may continue until every man has located his partner. The men are allowed to talk but the ladies may not!

6. *Alphabet Traveling.*—Seat the guests in a circle. The leader asks each one in turn, "Where are you going?" The player must answer, using the letters of the alphabet from A to Z. He must give the name of a city or place that begins with his letter. He must also

state what he is going to do there, using three words beginning with the same letter, as per the following examples:

I am going to Atlanta to allow Alice air.
I am going to Boston to bake beautiful beans.
I am going to Cleveland to catch cautious cats.
I am going to Denver to delve down deep.
I am going to Elmira to enjoy eating everything.
I am going to Fargo to flee from Florence.
I am going to Georgia to gather good grapes.

And so on through the alphabet. If there are more guests than letters in the alphabet, start with A again. If a guest is unable to supply words for his letter, he must sit on the floor until the game is finished.

7. *Omega.*—Choose a category such as the names of rivers, cities, countries, girls' names, boys' names, and so on. The first player gives the name (assuming that the category is girls' names) Alice. The next player says, Eleanor, as E is the last letter in Alice. The next player must choose a name beginning with the last letter in Eleanor, as for example, Rose. E comes up again, but a name must not be used that has previouly been used. The player may choose the name Edna. After this names may follow, as Amy, Yvonne, Elizabeth, Helen, and so on. If a player misses, he becomes a third of a goat, and when he misses three times, he is out, and may be made to pay a forfeit or sit on the floor.

8. *Surprise Problem.*—It is fun, on occasions, to present a problem or brain twister and let the group try to figure it out. Give a token prize to the first one who comes up with the proper answer:

A man had a fine stable of race horses. To his first son he gave half the horses and one more. To his second son he gave half of the remaining horse and one more. To his youngest son he gave half of the remaining horses and one more. There were no horses left. How many horses did the father have in his stable? The answer is 14. (There are 8 horses for the first son, 4, for the second son, and 2 for the youngest son.)

9. *Acting Out Adjectives.*—Divide the guests into two groups. Each group chooses the name of some object in the room. When a group has chosen a word, as many players are selected as there are letters in the word. Each player takes a letter in turn and makes an adjective beginning with it and acts out the adjective. Suppose one side chooses the word television. When the players have selected adjectives to match their letters, they begin their acts. The following is an example of adjectives that may be chosen:

T—Tired.	I—Insolent.
E—Eager.	S—Saucy.
L—Lame.	I—Industrious.
E—Elegant.	O—Obstinate.
V—Violent.	N—Naughty.

As each player acts out his adjective, the other side tries to guess what it is. After three or four letters have been acted out, the other side will have a pretty good idea of what the word is. When the complete word is guessed, the other side takes its turn.

It would be well to select shorter words than the one suggested, such as phone, chair, table, picture, radio, and so on. Each side should be allowed only two or three words before the game concludes.

10. *Guessing Hands.*—Make a curtain out of old sheets, wrapping paper, or whatever is available. The ladies stand behind it and put their hands through holes which have been cut so that they may be identified by the men on the opposite side. All rings that might automatically identify the hands should be removed. This game may be used as a method of choosing partners for another game or for the dinner which may follow. It may also be a contest. The holes for the hands may be numbered and the men asked to write their identification of each set of hands by number. The prize may be given to the one having the longest list of correct answers, or this man may be penalized for knowing too much!

11. *Guessing Words.*—This is a group of words beginning with

348

T, which when the T is removed, leaves another word with a different meaning. The original meaning of the word is given, and the meaning of the word after the T is removed is given. The object is to guess the word. The leader has mimeographed the game so that each guest may have a copy, while she has the key on her list.

(1) To reproach with insulting words, a female relative. Taunt, aunt.

(2) Three persons together, the metropolis of Brazil. Trio, Rio.

(3) To decorate, the edge. Trim, rim.

(4) Labor, makes machines run smoothly. Toil, oil.

(5) Eye water, the hearing organ. Tear, ear.

(6) To impart knowledge, a number of persons or things considered individually. Teach, each.

(7) A story, a drink with small alcoholic content. Tale, ale.

(8) To catch a foot and stumble, to tear. Trip, rip.

(9) A correct statement, a girl's name. Truth, Ruth.

(10) A small city, to have possession. Town, own.

(11) A beaten path, a set of bars to hold things. Track, rack.

(12) A conveyance for passengers and freight, water dropping from the clouds. Train, rain.

(13) To ensnare, a gentle knock. Trap, rap.

(14) A change in direction, for making coffee. Turn, urn.

(15) A quick jerk, one who rides a broom. Twitch, witch.

(16) To twist together, an intoxicating beverage. Twine, wine.

(17) To reproach, a clever person. Twit, wit.

(18) A game fish, to put to flight. Trout, rout.

(19) The cost, a staple Oriental food. Price, rice.

(20) A mendicant beggar, an inclined walkway. Tramp, ramp.

12. *Show Your Ignorance.*—This is a game in which the men and the ladies may tease each other by asking the opposite sex questions on subjects of which they are supposed to know little or nothing. Have each guest write a question on some subject with which he is familiar and the opposite sex supposedly ignorant. Give each question to a person of the opposite sex, being sure that husbands or wives do not get the question of their spouse, or couples of their date. Given below are some sample questions:

Men May Ask the Following Questions:
(1) Explain the difference between stocks and bonds.
(2) What is the difference between compound interest and simple interest?
(3) Explain the principle of a jet engine.
(4) What does one mean by a double entry?

The Women May Ask:
(1) How many yards of cloth would you buy to make a size fourteen sheath dress?
(2) Tell how to make a cake.
(3) Make a list of food for a family of three for a week to be paid for with $15.00, giving approximate cost of each item.

After the questions have been written and distributed, ask one woman and one man in turn to give the answers. This will create a lot of talk and many humorous situations.

13. *Contraries.*—The guests are seated in a circle and one person is selected to be the leader of this game. He stands before one of the guests and goes through certain motions and makes some statements. The idea is for the other person to do the contrary thing or answer with a contrary statement. For example, if the leader of the game raises his right hand, the other guest must raise his left hand. If he makes a motion as if he were sitting, the opposite must stand, if he opens his mouth, the opposite must close his mouth, if he frowns, the opposite must smile, and so forth. If the leader makes a statement, the opposite must make a contrary statement, as for example, "Milk is white." The opposite must say, "Milk is black." The leader says, "Snow is cold," and the opposite says, "Snow is hot." Their dialogue continues until the person opposite the leader makes a bobble, and when this occurs, the opposite must take the leader's place.

14. *The Game of Cities.*—The object is to write the word ending in "city" as an answer to each of the clues, as follows:

(1) A very plain city. Simplicity.
(2) A well-advertised city. Publicity.
(3) The speedy city. Velocity.

(4) The peculiar city.   Eccentricity.
(5) The wise city.   Sagacity.
(6) A city that measures content.   Capacity.
(7) A rural city.   Rusticity.
(8) A city of need.   Scarcity.
(9) A lively city.   Vivacity.
(10) A city of power and brightness.   Electricity.
(11) A happy city.   Felicity.
(12) A savage city.   Ferocity.
(13) A city of doubleness.   Duplicity.
(14) The outrageous city.   Atrocity.

15. *Balloon Guard.*—Inflate a number of balloons and attach them with a string to the ankle or wrist of each girl. A partner has been selected for each of the ladies, and it is his duty to try to guard her balloon while at the same time he tries to destroy the balloons of the other ladies. The lady whose balloon is the last one to be destroyed is the winner, or rather the couple is the winning couple, and should be given a prize or some additional recognition.

16. *Ping-pong Putt.*—Give each player a ping-pong ball and a straightened out coat hanger for a putter. Indicate the "hole" by a chalk ring on the floor. It will be more interesting if the "tee off" takes place in another room than the living room, as for example a bedroom, hall, or dining room. If the course can be laid out so that one must putt the ball around doors and perhaps get under furniture, it will be more interesting. The player who gets the ball in the hole with the fewest number of strokes is the winner. It may be well to start the players one minute apart so that they will not get in one another's way. This is a good icebreaker as it starts the guests moving about and conversing informally.

17. *Human Tenpins.*—Select ten men and place them at one end of the room in the position of the pins in a bowling alley. Select two teams of four ladies each and let them roll rubber balls, a water-game ball would be about the right size, at the men. Whenever a man is touched by the ball, he is taken out and is counted as a point for the side that hit him. Let each side take turns at

rolling the ball. When all the men have been hit, the game is over and the side whose players have taken out the most men is declared the winner.

18. *Coin Trick.*—Before the party starts, the leader should prepare for this stunt by putting a dime in the hem of a man's handkerchief. Then, taking the handkerchief in his hand, he asks to borrow a dime from one of the guests for the stunt. In case no guest has a dime the leader should have one in reserve. When he has the dime, he places the handkerchief on the table and pretends to put the dime into it. He does not really put it in but keeps it concealed in his right hand as he folds the handkerchief. When it has been folded, he asks the person who gave him the dime to feel it in the handkerchief, and this is, of course, the one that was placed in the hem. He now places the folded handkerchief on a table and takes a glass of water and holds it under the table. He raps on the table with his left hand while holding the glass of water with his right hand in such a way that he can drop the dime into it at the same time he raps on the table with his left hand. He shakes the handkerchief to show that there is no dime in it and puts it in his pocket. He then displays the dime at the bottom of the glass of water to his astonished friends.

19. *Vanishing Coin.*—Hold a coin, preferably a half dollar, between the thumb and forefinger of your left hand. Make a motion with the thumb and finger of your right hand as if you were taking the coin from between the thumb and finger of your left hand, but instead of taking it, as you appear to do, you let the coin fall into the palm of your left hand. Then put your hand behind you and tell your friends that you are going to pass the coin through your body. Make a face as if in pain as the coin is passing through and then display your empty right hand and the coin in your left hand, where it has been all the time. Another way to do this trick is to open your right hand and show that the coin is not in it as it appears to be after you go through the motion of taking it from your left hand. Then squeeze the coin out of your ear with your right hand into the left, where it has really been all the time.

20. *Magic with Watches.*—Put a glove on your hand and have concealed in one of the fingers or the thumb a small but powerful magnet. Tell your friends that you can stop watches by touching them. This will work with most watches unless they are especially demagnetized. Tell the guests that you cannot make the sun stand still like Joshua, but you can make the hands of a watch stand still. Many will be surprised at your power to do this. As soon as the magnet is removed, the watch will start again. Be sure that the watch is running before you try the trick.

21. *Statues.*—There are two ways that the game of Statues may be played. One way is to take two players, preferably a man and a lady, into an adjoining room. Tell them that you want to arrange them as a double statue and when you have finished, they must remain perfectly motionless until they have been displayed to the others. Then invite in another guest, lady or man. Tell this person that you have arranged this couple as a double statue and you want suggestions as to how the statue may be improved. If the guest is a lady, she is to arrange the lady. She will probably place her in some grotesque shape. When she is finished, tell her that she is to take the place and position of the one she has arranged and keep perfectly motionless. A man is then brought in and asked to arrange the man so that the statue may be more effective. When this is done, he takes the man's place, and other guests are brought in one by one. It will become very amusing to those who have been through the ordeal and very hilarious as the game proceeds.

Another way to play this game and make it more active is to form a circle of guests and have them march to music around the room. When the music stops, everyone must keep the position he was in when it stopped. To move or to laugh disqualifies a player. The one who remains when all others have been eliminated is declared the winner.

22. *Something to Guess.*—Provide the players with paper and pencils and have a number of things arranged which they are to guess. Of course the leader must prepare this in advance and have

the correct answers so that there will be no delay. Some of the following are suggested:

   (1) The value of a jar full of coins.
   (2) The number of pages in a book.
   (3) The number of cards that the leader holds in her hand.
   (4) The number of beans in a jar.
   (5) The number of folds in a fan.
   (6) The length of the room in which the party is held.
   (7) The height of the ceiling.
   (8) The length of a coil of string.
   (9) The weight of an article held in the hand.
  (10) The number of stitches in a row of knitting.

23. *Dumb Crambo.*—The guests are divided into two groups of equal number. One group retires to an adjoining room and out of earshot. The other group decides on the name of some activity, one which has several other activities rhyming with it. The side that has retired then sends in one of its players, and he is told a word that rhymes with the chosen activity. Let us suppose that the activity chosen is "lend." The other side, which has retired, is given a word that rhymes with "lend," as for example, "send." The other side then begins to think of all the activities rhyming with "send." They may think of bend, tend, mend, fend, rend, spend. They come into the room where the other side is waiting and begin to act out their guesses one by one. As they do their act or mimic, they will soon know if they are right or wrong. If they are right, they will be applauded, and if they are wrong, they will be jeered and booed. They must continue until they hit on the right word. When the first group to leave the room has acted out the right word, the other group must retire and have its turn. The following is a list of words that convey the thought of activity:

> Cling, fling, sling, ring, wring, sing.
> Wink, drink, sink, think, slink.
> Buy, spy, shy, fry, dye, die, lie, cry, sigh.
> Treat, cheat, meet, pleat, eat, compete.

Write, fight, sight, delight, indite.
Play, pray, lay, pay, delay, say, gay.

24. *A Bomb.*—This game should be conducted in an atmosphere of grim tragedy, while the actions must be comic. Yet any player who grins, smiles, or "shows his teeth" must be excluded from the game. A circle is formed and the leader passes some small article to the second player in the circle, who asks, "What is it?" The leader replies, "An A Bomb." The second player passes it to the third who asks again, "What is it?" Instead of answering, this player turns to the leader and asks, "What is it?" When he receives the answer, "An A Bomb," he passes this word on. And so it goes around the circle, with each player having his questions referred back to the leader. After the first complete playing of the game, a second round may start. At the beginning of the second series the second player asks the leader, "Did it hurt somebody?" The leader nods and shudders. After this the question passes down the line, back to the leader, each one asking the question and each one finally passing on the nod and the shudder. The third question might be, "Was he badly hurt?" To which the leader answers, "Blown to a thousand fragments (sob)." The last question may be, "Have the other bombs been detonated?" The answer may be, "No, one may explode any minute." The last round should be conducted in double-quick time.

25. *Balloon Joust.*—The guests are divided into two equal sides. This may be done by standing in a circle around the room and counting off by 1 and 2. The "Ones" take one side and the "Twos" the other. These are stationed on opposite ends of the room, and one side is given balloons of one color, and the other side is given balloons of a different color. These balloons may or may not be on strings. When the leader gives the signal, which may be the blowing up of a balloon until it bursts, the contest starts. The object of the game is for one group to cross the room and try to keep their balloons intact while destroying the balloons of the opposite side. At a signal from the leader all play must cease, and the players go

to the opposite side of the room from that which they started. The balloons are then counted and the side which has the largest number intact is declared the winner. A good prize would be a box or package of candy that may be divided among the group.

26. *Well-known Nicknames.*—This is a group of assorted nicknames that most everyone should know, but it is unlikely that anyone will be able to give them all. Have the list mimeographed and give each guest a printed sheet, with the leader having the answers on her list.

PERSONS:

    (1) Honest Abe.   Abraham Lincoln.
    (2) The Bard of Avon.   William Shakespeare.
    (3) Old Hickory.   Andrew Jackson.
    (4) Old Rough and Ready.   Zachary Taylor.
    (5) The Lone Eagle.   Charles Lindbergh.
    (6) Buffalo Bill.   Col. Wm. F. Cody.
    (7) Mark Twain.   Samuel Clemens.
    (8) Mr. Republican.   Senator Robert Taft of Ohio.

STATES:

    (1) The Empire State.   New York.
    (2) The Old Dominion.   Virginia.
    (3) The Lone Star State.   Texas.
    (4) The Volunteer State.   Tennessee.
    (5) The Keystone State.   Pennsylvania.
    (6) The Sunflower State.   Kansas.
    (7) The Hoosier State.   Indiana.
    (8) The Granite State.   New Hampshire.

CITIES:

    (1) The Windy City.   Chicago.
    (2) Gotham.   New York.
    (3) The City of Brotherly Love.   Philadelphia.
    (4) The Magic City.   Miami, Florida.
    (5) The Eternal City.   Rome, Italy.
    (6) The Holy City.   Jerusalem.
    (7) The City of David.   Bethlehem.
    (8) The Crescent City.   New Orleans.

27. *Guess Who.*—The guests stand in a circle. One of the guests is chosen to be "It," and is blindfolded and placed in the center of the circle. As the guests promenade around the room or march to music, "It" catches one of the guests, which stops the music. "It" may feel the face, hands, and clothing of the guest caught in making the identification. If "It" succeeds, the person identified becomes "It" and takes his place in the center of the circle, and the game continues. If "It" fails to identify the player caught, he must continue until he is correct.

28. *Refreshments.*—Suggestions have been made at the beginning of the Surprise Party as to refreshments. A dinner is suggested, or at least a "covered dish," or "pot luck" dinner. It was suggested, also, that if only refreshments were served, members of the group should be asked to bring the items on the refreshment menu. Another suggestion is that the group make *Granny's Bible Cake* (From sunshine Magazine, not copyrighted because this magazine is glad to have its material used again. This recipe comes from Miss Janet Preston of Edinburgh, Scotland. The writer, with the assistance of his wife and the cook, has tried this recipe and finds that it is delicious.) This would be a good stunt for a ladies' class, a ladies' group, a group of Intermediate girls, or a Girl Scout troop to try. The leader must secure the ingredients in advance and have proper cooking utensils at hand. If it is used at the Surprise Party, the members of the group giving the party may divide the ingredients among themselves. The leader telephones Mrs. Jones and says, "At the surprise party for the Smiths we are all going to bake Granny's Bible Cake. You are asked to bring ¼ pound of Jeremiah 24:1, chopped." This will create a great deal of interest and curiosity in advance.

THE RECIPE:
    (1) ½ cup Judg. 5:25 (last clause).
    (2) ½ cup Jer. 6:20 (second clause).
    (3) 1 tablespoonful I Sam. 14:25.
    (4) 2 large Jer. 17:11.
    (5) 1 cup I Sam. 30:12 (second clause).

(6) 1 cup Jer. 24:1 (Chopped).
(7) ¼ cup Num. 17:8 (Blanched and chopped).
(8) 2 cups I Kings 4:22 (first clause).
(9) Season to taste with II Chr. 9:9.
(10) Pinch of Lev. 2:13.
(11) 3 teaspoonfuls Amos 4:5.
(12) 1½ tablespoonfuls of Judg. 4:19 (last clause).

METHODS:

(A) Mix ingredients 1, 2, 3, to a cream—Prov. 23:14.
(B) Add ingredient 4—Still Prov. 23:14.
(C) Add ingredients 5, 6, 7. Still Prov. 23:14.
(D) Add ingredients 8, 9, 10, 11, having previously mixed them.
(E) Lastly add ingredient 12.
(F) Lev. 26:26 in a slow oven for approximately 1 hour.

The following is a list of ingredients for the leader's use. The ingredients are numbered in the same way as the first list of ingredients given in the recipe:

(1) Judg. 5:22 (last clause). "She brought him butter."
    ½ cup of butter.
(2) Jer. 6:20 (second clause). "Sweet cane from a far country."
    ½ cup syrup or molasses.
(3) I Sam. 14:25. "There was honey on the ground."
    1 tablespoonful of honey.
(4) Jer. 17:11. "That sitteth on eggs."
    2 eggs.
(5) I Sam. 30:12 (second clause). "Two clusters of grapes."
    1 cup of raisins.
(6) Jer. 24:1. "Two baskets of figs."
    1 cup of figs (Chopped).
(7) Num. 17:8. "Bare ripe almonds."
    ¼ cup of almonds, blanched and chopped.
(8) I Kings 4:22 (first clause). "Fine flour."
    2 cups of flour, sifted fine.
(9) II Chr. 9:9. "There were no spices such as those."
    1 teaspoonful of cinnamon, ¼ tsp. nutmeg, ¼ tsp. cloves.
(10) Lev. 2:13. "Season . . . with salt."
    ¼ teaspoonful of salt.

(11) Amos 4:5. "Of that which is leavened."
2 teaspoonfuls baking power, 1 teaspoonful soda.
(12) Judg. 4:19 (last clause) . "A bottle of milk."
1½ tablespoonfuls of milk.

METHODS:

(A) Mix ingredients 1, 2, and 3. Prov. 23:14; "Thou shalt beat him."
Beat well.
(B) Add ingredient 4. Prov. 23:14.
Beat again.
(C) Add ingredients 5, 6, and 7. Prov. 23:14.
Beat together.
(D) Add ingredients 8, 9, 10, 11, having previously mixed them.
(E) Lastly add ingredient 12.
(F) Lev. 26:26. Bake in a slow oven for approximately 1 hour.

29. *Properties*

(1) Corks on strings, dice, saucepan, and beans or matches for chips.
(2) Saucers which have been blackened for Copycat.
(3) Apple, cupcake, or candy bar for Feeding Time at the Zoo.
(4) Blindfold for Mary Where Are You?
(5) Curtain or sheet or wrapping paper, pencils, paper, and prizes for Guessing Hands.
(6) Mimeographed sheets for Guessing Words.
(7) Pencils and paper for Show Your Ignorance.
(8) Mimeographed copies for Game of Cities.
(9) Balloons for Balloon Guard and Balloon Joust.
(10) Ping-pong balls and straightened out coat hangers for putters.
(11) Rubber ball for Human Tenpins.
(12) Coins for Coin Trick and Vanishing Coin.
(13) A small magnet and glove for Magic with Watches.
(14) Articles prepared for Something to Guess.
(15) Mimeographed sheets for Well-known Nicknames.
(16) Ingredients for Granny's Bible Cake.

Alphabetical Index

Classified Index

ACTIVE GAMES

QUIET GAMES